The Stories Economists Tell
Essays on the Art of Teaching Economics

David Colander
Middlebury College

The Stories Economists Tell
Essays on the Art of Teaching Economics

David Colander
Middlebury College

McGraw-Hill
Irwin

Boston   Burr Ridge, IL   Dubuque, IA   Madison, WI   New York   San Francisco   St. Louis
Bangkok   Bogotá   Caracas   Kuala Lumpur   Lisbon   London   Madrid   Mexico City
Milan   Montreal   New Delhi   Santiago   Seoul   Singapore   Sydney   Taipei   Toronto

McGraw-Hill
Irwin

The Stories Economists Tell
David Colander

Published by McGraw-Hill/Irwin, an imprint of The McGraw-Hill Companies, Inc., 1221 Avenue of the Americas, New York, NY 10020. Copyright © 2006 by The McGraw-Hill Companies, Inc. All rights reserved.

1 2 3 4 5 6 7 8 9 0 PTS/PTS 0 9 8 7 6 5

ISBN 0-07-322751-X

www.mhhe.com

Contents

Preface

Teaching is the most important thing that economists do. It's what we get paid for, and what has the largest long-run impact on society. It gets far too little attention from economists. Because I think teaching is so important, I have devoted my career to thinking and writing about how we translate the abstract ideas that economists discuss in theory into what we teach. The set of essays included in this volume are a selection of my writings on the subject that, I hope, will stimulate others to think about the issues of teaching. These selections are meant to be easy reading (There's far too much hard reading in economics.), and to be read in any order. A reasonable reading strategy is skimming the introductory section which surveys the ideas and articles, and then going to those that interest you.

The essays are written for faculty, but I often let my students read them. No, let me be honest; I often assign them to my students (I doubt that they would read them otherwise.) in order to get them thinking more deeply about what they are being taught. Too many texts teach economics as the truth. The texts don't provide the truth, but, kept in perspective, what they do provide is quite useful, and I want my students to learn that. Joan Robinson once said that the reason to learn economics is to avoid being fooled by economists. I don't go that far, but I would agree that students don't get enough warnings in the texts they study. If this book helps add a few warnings to a few classes, it will have served my purpose.

David Colander
July 2005

Dedicated to the memory of Ken Koford,
an economist through and through and a close friend.

May he always be finding wild and crazy ideas.

Acknowledgements

As with any book there are many people to thank: in general, there are my family, my students, and my friends, who contribute in many ways to everything I write. I would especially like to thank Jessica Holmes who wrote one of the essays with me, and Dave Horlacher who read the essays and challenged me on lots of points, as well as the reviewers and editors of the initial articles who improved the articles in many ways.

I would also like to thank Marty Quinn and Lucille Sutton of McGraw Hill for urging me to put this collection together; Pam Bordenhorn for work in organizing and compositing it; Aja Hamal, for looking up references, Helen Reiff for proofreading and doing the index, and the many economists who have written in to me with ideas about teaching. Finally I would like to give a special thanks to Jenifer Gamber for overseeing the production of the book and for giving me clear editorial advice on each article. I didn't follow my friends' advice on every point, so I retain sole responsibility for what's said.

Variations of these essays were previously published in a variety of places, and I would like to thank the various journals and publishers listed below for permission to reprint them. The articles originally appearing in the *Journal of Economic Education* were published by Heldref Publications and are reprinted with the permission of the Helen Dwight Reid Educational Foundation.

Articles are listed in order of their appearance in this book.

"What We Teach and What We Do" *Journal of Economic Education*, Vol. 36, 3. Summer 2005. pp. 249-260.

"Caveat Lector: Living with the 15% Rule" *Australasian Economic Journal*, March 2004. Vol. 1, 1. pp. 30-40.

"The Art of Teaching Economics" *International Review of Economics Education*, Vol. 2, 1. 2004. pp. 63-76.

"Thinking Like an Economist: A Consideration of the Economics Major in American Higher Education" *Journal of Economic Education*, Volume 22, 3. Summer 1991. pp. 227-234.

" 'Little Think' Economics: Is that All there Is?" *Eastern Economic Journal*, Vol. 30, 2. Spring 2004. pp. 333-335.

"Integrating Sex and Drugs into the Principles Course: Market Failures vs. Failures of Market Outcomes" *Journal of Economic Education*, Vol. 24, 1. Winter 2003. pp. 82-91.

"Complexity and the Principles Course" *Kentucky Journal of Economics and Business*, Vol 21. 2002. pp. 112-121.

"Complexity, Muddling Through, and Enviromentalism" (adapted from "Complexity, Muddling Through, and Sustainable Forest Management" in *Economics, Natural Resources, and Sustainability: Economics of Sustainable Forest Management* Sashi Kent and R. A Berry, (eds.). 2005

"On the Treatment of Fixed and Sunk Costs in Principles Texts" *Journal of Economic Education*, Summer 2004.

"Teaching Keynes in the 21st Century" *Journal of Economic Education*, Vol. 30, 4. Fall 1999. pp. 260-364.

"The Stories We Tell: A Reconsideration of AS/AD Analysis" *Journal of Economic Perspectives*, Vol. 9, 3. Summer, 1995. pp. 169-188.

"Telling Better Stories in Introductory Macro" *American Economic Review*, May 2000. pp. 305-322

The Strange Persistence of the IS/LM Model" *History of Political Economy*, Vol. 36. Supplement 2004.

"Reform of Undergraduate Economics Education" in *Educating Economists* David Colander and Reuven Brenner, eds, Ann Arbor, University of Michigan Press, 1992.

"Reform of Graduate Economics Education" in *Educating Economists*, David Colander and Reuven Brenner, eds., Ann Arbor, University of Michigan Press, 1992.

Introduction

I'm an economics teacher, and proud of it; it's what I do. I teach economics in the classroom and I teach economics with my textbooks. I'm also an economist (and proud of that too). In my role as an economist, I look at my role as a teacher and try to understand why we economists teach what we do, and why the economics we teach is often different than the economics we practice. Much of my own economic research consists of studying the economics teaching profession as a case study of how organizations operate. I ask such questions as: Why do economists spend so much time teaching simple graphs and models that don't capture what's going on in the economy? What ideological slant is hidden between the lines of the seemingly neutral models and arguments in textbooks? Why do the models presented in textbooks change so slowly? And, why are the textbooks so slow to reflect major changes in the way economists think and analyze the economy? These, and similar questions, fascinate me. The set of essays in this volume reflect some of my ponderings about such issues.

As you can probably gather from the opening paragraph, this is not a traditional book on economics education. It is a book that concentrates on the *economics* part of economics education, not the *education* part. In this book I have little to say about the structure of classes, what tests adequately cover the material, or many of the other topics that often are discussed in books about economics education. In this way, I'm like most economists. While most economists teach, their interest is not in how economics is taught; it's in studying how people and economies behave.

Where I suspect that I differ from most economists is that I look at the economics profession through the eyes of an economist, and subject what economists do and teach, and what they write in their textbooks, to the same critical analysis that economists use to analyze the rest of the world. Doing this does not reveal an especially pretty picture, as was made clear by my previous books of essays on the profession, *Why Aren't Economists as Important as Garbagemen?* and *The Lost Art of Economics*. This book differs from those previous books in that it focuses on economics teaching and textbooks, not on the broader economics

1

profession. Because I've written four textbooks on various aspects of economics, which have gone through numerous revisions, I've had to think hard about economic pedagogy, and have struggled to figure out what economists actually teach, and why we teach it. The essays in this volume reflect that struggle.

Why Do Economists Teach So Many Seemingly Irrelevant Models?

I became interested in studying the economics industry when I first started taking economics courses in college. I continually asked, why are they teaching me these formal, abstract, and often seemingly irrelevant models? Why don't they teach me more about the economy? My teachers' answer to these questions was that I needed to learn the models in order to understand the economy. Since I was an undergraduate, I accepted that answer—that's what undergraduates are supposed to do. But the answers were not satisfying to me. Then I went on to graduate school. In graduate school, the models got more complicated, but they still didn't teach me much about the economy. So I asked the same questions of my graduate professors. Their answers were the same, but again the answers didn't work for me—the models weren't teaching me much about the economy.

Given my doubt that what I was learning was relevant, it may be surprising that I didn't drop out. Despite my feelings that economic models weren't teaching me anything about the economy, I nonetheless felt that I was gaining an understanding of economic reality—an understanding that was different than what I had before. How this happened, I was not sure; it could have been some side effect of learning the models; it could have been the result of discussions with other students on economic issues, or it could have been self delusion. Whatever it was, the feeling that I was actually better understanding the way the economy worked was enough to keep me in economics.

Of course, I can't be sure of my motivations; it could also have been that subconsciously I knew that because I was building up specific human capital in the economics field, my opportunity cost of leaving was rising. But even if I was motivated by protecting my human capital, the very fact that I posed the questions within an opportunity cost framework suggested that I was hooked on economics, because that opportunity cost reasoning is precisely the reasoning that best characterizes what economists mean when they say "thinking like an economist." The point is that somehow, the years spent studying economics changed how I thought. I was more cynical, although it wasn't a mean-spirited cynicism; I simply approached the world by asking what's in it for the agents involved, and I assumed that the agents were asking that same question. Economists generally don't express that cynicism in pleasant conversations, even among colleagues. They keep it tucked away, papered over by a veneer of pleasantries and assumed virtuosness. Civil conversation supposes that other people are virtuous. But if the person is an economist, you can also assume that underneath that veneer of civility is a search for the self-interested strategy guiding the other, and himself.

Economic thinking involves stripping away the veneer of civility, and considering people's less-than-virtuous motivations. Some economists get carried away with that striptease, and believe all people are driven by selfishness and greed. They take models based on selfishness and greed as gospel. But that just doesn't fit my view of people or the world: individuals are motivated in varying degrees both by selfishness and selflessness. Economists base their models on pure selfishness because such models are more easily constructed; bringing in altruism complicates models enormously. By talking with economists, I now know that most economists agree that these models aren't gospel, and trying to integrate selfishness with selflessness is a major research area in economics. It's the reason for the enormous expansion in behavioral economics. But back when I was a student the difference between the models and economists' beliefs was not clear to me, because I was taught the models, not the underlying beliefs.

Central Themes in the Essays

As the economic way of thinking slowly took over my approach to problems and understanding of the world, I found that I was better able to communicate with economists, although I have to admit that I became less able to communicate with noneconomists. (I'm not very good at surface pleasantries.) Something in the economics educational process worked for me, and the models I had regarded as irrelevant seemed to have changed my intuition and abilities. This insight—that learning irrelevant models can actually change one's views and create abilities that can be relevant—is one of the central themes of the essays in this book: *The models we teach in economics are often irrelevant in understanding particular issues, but they are nonetheless useful in training one's intuition and in increasing one's ability to understand economic issues because they are calisthenics of the mind.*[1]

Of course, calisthenics on their own are not sufficient. That's a second central theme in these essays: *Economic pedagogy will be much more meaningful and relevant for students if we go beyond teaching the models, and talk about how the models are not the truth, and how they do not fit reality well.* I've spent my career calling for changes in economic pedagogy and economic education that I believe will better convey to students, and to the broader public, what economics reasoning is. Somehow, the reasonableness of economists in casual conversations is lost in the formality of their pedagogical models and the simplicity of the texts. I recognize that pedagogical choices have to be made. Many of the pedagogical choices reflected in the current presentations are defensible, but they would be far more defensible if they were presented as what they are—pedagogical simplifications, not the truth. Current textbooks need to supplement the models with much more discussion of the limitations of the models and how they can nevertheless be appropriately used in thinking about policy.

A third, related, theme that shows up in these essays is that once we tell students that the economics we teach is not the truth—whatever that might be—and that economics is much more than the models in the textbooks, then we can continue to teach pretty much the same models and material that we do now. Thus, paradoxically, I often end up supporting the current pedagogical simplifications as reasonable. Economics is, in my view, an important part of any undergraduate's education, and what we teach has to be seen in that context. Radical changes may well undermine the important role that economics plays, and thus must be considered carefully.

What Defines an Economist's Approach?

What I'm advocating in these essays is that economists supplement the models we currently teach not by teaching the economic way of thinking in a narrow sense of applying textbook economic reasoning to policy issues, but by teaching economic wisdom—*the economic approach to understanding reality*. For me, three elements define the economic approach to understanding reality and lead to economic wisdom. The *first* is to consider the incentives faced by the people involved in a real-world economic issue. The *second* is to figure out how the various incentives are likely to play out. This second element is usually called modeling, but it doesn't have to be, and indeed often should not be, formal modeling; it is simply combining the incentives of different people to arrive at <u>an aggregate outcome.</u> The *third* element is to bring the insights gained from the first and second steps <u>to the data.</u> This three-part approach, for me, defines the economic approach, and students should know that approach.

Many economists, including me, have criticized economics for focusing too much on the second element and have complained that teaching economics has become nothing but a technical modeling exercise. As the models have become more and more technical, requiring more and more formal definitions of what is meant by incentives, the intuitive, common-sense nature of economic reasoning, which is at the core of the economic approach, has been <u>replaced by mathematical logic,</u> which often borders on a pathological view of people. My earlier discussion of models should make it clear that I agree with much of that criticism.

However, while I agree with the criticisms of modeling, I often do not agree with the strongest of these critics, who want to replace a pedagogical emphasis on formal modeling with a focus on the economic way of thinking. I specifically do not define what I advocate with the phrase "economic way of thinking" because of that phrase's previous association with an approach that assumes people are perfectly rational and selfish, and that suggests that models that incorporate those assumptions explain everything. This approach was first presented to me as the "Chicago approach" to economics, but that descriptor is probably no longer appropriate. As Chicago economics has evolved, the "thinking like an economist" approach today is probably better called the "Rochester approach" to economics.[2]

Stephen Landsburg's highly entertaining book, *The Armchair Economist*, illustrates the Rochester approach. In this book, Landsburg delights in showing how economic thinking puts economists in direct conflict with many commonly-held notions. For example, we should not be worried about stealing; from society's viewpoint, stealing is simply a transfer of wealth. And, we should oppose nasty preschool teachers who teach pro-environmental views; they are brainwashing our children. According to Landsburg, efficiency should be the sole goal of society; any other goal is biased and value-laden.

While there is some reasonableness in what Landsburg has to say, much of it seems to be written for its shock value. Overall, the book makes a good, provocative read for students, but the nature of the argumentation is inconsistent with good economics and good pedagogy.

Good pedagogy challenges students to reexamine their views. It gets those who support the market to question that support, and those who oppose the market to question that opposition. The Landsburg approach does the opposite; it tends to reinforce the views of those students who support market solutions, but not make them think critically about their views, and to put off, and hence fail to engage, the thinking of those students who disagree.

The problem is that he makes selfishness a virtue. He seems to imply that not to be selfish is itself selfish and immoral, and if people act selflessly, this will undermine the workings of the economy. The problem with this approach is twofold. *First* it does not describe people. As I stated above, people are a complicated maze of selfishness and selflessness. And *second*, it is not good economic reasoning because it makes simple models more relevant than they actually are. It is like playing a Mozart symphony on a flutophone.

The economic approach that I advocate does not assume that people are only selfish. It does not make a fetish of selfishness. Selfishness is simply an assumption we rely on to make modeling easier. In short the Rochester approach to economics—to explain everything in terms of selfish economic incentives alone—is a great game, but it is not great economics.

My biggest problem with the Rochester approach is that it doesn't direct the student to the final element of economics—bringing the insights to the data. Simplifying models is only acceptable when their results can be empirically verified. The economic approach to understanding reality always asks: Does the model fit the data? Do other models also fit the data? How can we test the alternative models to see which better fits the data? Bringing the models to the data is central to economic thinking. Unfortunately, empirical data in economics is often limited, and is often insufficient to allow one to discern which model or explanation is best. In most cases a broader sensibility about people and the reasonableness of assumptions and models must govern our understanding and our choice of explanations. The Rochester approach seems to have no broader sensibility.

Ideally, we would teach such sensibility in our statistics courses. Unfortunately, the teaching of statistics often becomes as focused on technical statistical issues as micro and macro courses are focused on technical models. Too often, what students come away with from their statistics course is the belief that statistics tells us what's right and wrong.

They have a knowledge of some formal probability and statistics theory, but little sense of what the data are actually telling us. Many students actually believe that a 99 percent confidence interval means that we are 99 percent confident in the results. In my view, it is just as important to teach students about the limitations of statistical techniques as it is about its strengths. What's relevant to economics is more than just formal statistics; it's an educated common sense about the significant limitations of statistical testing. Statistics does not provide us with an infallible tool for finding the truth. At best it provides us with a guide to separate out some things that probably are not true. Students need to be taught that.

Good economic pedagogy directs students how to try to find the mix of the three elements of the economic approach that is appropriate to the problem at hand. Unfortunately, advocating this "appropriate mix" approach to teaching undergraduate economics often puts me in conflict with advocates of each of the elements, who generally advocate specializing in their particular element. This book, by pulling together some of my writings on the teaching of economics, is designed to make my broader approach to economics clear.

Some General Thoughts about the Essays in this Volume

One of the aspects of my generalist approach is a belief that institutions matter, because the relevant incentives are found in institutions, not in abstract models. Unless you understand the actual institutions, you can't understand what motivates people. That's one reason why I chose to study the economics teaching industry. Being a part of it, I have a good sense of academic institutions and the incentives that academics face.

As I stated above, my approach to the economics profession and to economics teaching is quite different than the approach of most researchers who study academics, teaching, or the economics profession. Much of the writing on teaching is done by educationalists, for want of a better word. Educationalists write in *educationalese*, just as I write in *economese*. There's a clash between these two cultures and languages, and the essays in the volume reflect that clash. Educationalists focus on the structure of, not the content of, education; I see structure as secondary and content as central.

Because so few economists write about teaching from an economics perspective, I've become a bit of an evangelist for the economics approach. I believe in it, and I put my arguments in strident form. When pushed, I generally waffle a bit, round off the sharp edges, and show how reasonable I actually am. But in essays designed to get people to think, rounded corners are too soothing; sharp edges keep readers awake and thinking. So the essays in this book have some sharp edges.

Economists are likely to have mixed feelings as they read these essays. Many will tend to like my pro-economics evangelist tendencies. Who wouldn't like someone going around saying that what you do is good? But many others will tend not to like my pointing out the foibles and dirty laundry—foibles that all professions have, and most hide rather discretely. But, in the past they have tolerated it. For me, that says something positive about the economics profession.

The essays are a selection from a large group of essays I've written on economic textbooks and economic pedagogy, and when they are critical of the profession they are also critical of me, since I am part of the profession. The papers have been edited and rewritten from their original form to better fit into the volume, and to update the arguments, but the general ideas of each of the papers have not been changed.

The papers are divided into four separate sections. The remainder of this introduction provides a brief overview of the papers.

The Economics Major: What We Teach and Why We Teach It

The first set of essays focuses broadly on what it is that we are teaching in economics, and how we came to teach what we teach. These essays should provide a good sense of the approach that I take to understanding the profession, and, more generally, to understanding the world.

The first essay, "What We Teach and What We Do," considers the content of economics, and reflects the first question I had when I took economics: Why are we teaching what we do? It argues that what economists teach in undergraduate economics is quite different than what we do in our research, but there are reasons for that. Specifically, we are not teaching future economists. We are teaching students who will be using the ideas of economics in their lives and business decisions. Our current courses are quite good at conveying economic ideas, even though they do not nicely capture what economists do. It is not clear that revising the courses to better convey what we do would succeed in achieving those ends, and thus the current structure of the courses may be preferable to any conceivable realistic reform.

The second essay, "Caveat Lector: Living with the 15% Rule," considers economics textbooks, and is a guide to students reading textbooks. It captures that same "living-with-institutions" theme of much of my work, but places the theme in the specific context of the textbook writer, explaining why what is in the texts is there, how it can be justified, and how change comes about. While the essay's specific focus is on economics textbooks, it is relevant for my view of how economic analysis is best applied. By that I mean that to be an effective critic one must have a strong sense and understanding of the institutions one is studying, and of the difficulties and costs of change.[3]

The third essay, "The Art of Teaching Economics," considers pedagogy in economics. It was written in reaction to some educationalists who argued for a new paradigm in teaching. This essay reflects my view of what might be called *the progressive educational establishment approach* to pedagogy and teaching. The essay argues that while the new paradigm in teaching has some reasonable aspects, ultimately content, not delivery, is what matters. Any consideration of teaching that does not put content first, and the new paradigm does not, has serious problems.

The fourth essay, "Thinking Like an Economist," was a response to a commission report on the economics major by a group of economists. That report was written by economists concerned with undergraduate economic education and with the teaching of undergraduate economics. As I state in the essay, had I been on the commission, I would have signed on. But looking at that report from the vantage point of an outside observer allows me the freedom to consider the commissioners' motivations and incentives. Commissions take off the sharp edges, and round off the corners, so that they tend to offend less than is useful. My essay was designed to offend economists. It looks hard at what we teach and points out an ongoing theme in this book—that many of the models we teach are not meant to be empirically estimated, nor applied to the real world. Instead, the models serve either a hurdle function, meant to exercise the student's mind, or an organizing function, meant to help students to structure their thinking about an issue. I argue that there's nothing wrong with models serving these functions, as long as they are taught as what they are, and not presented as models that will be empirically validated.

The fifth essay, "A Capstone: To What, and For Whom?" written jointly with Jessica Holmes, makes the same point as the previous essay in a different way. It argues that the current structure of the economics major should be seen as a pillar of a broader liberal arts education, not as a set of pillars preparing someone to be an economist. Because of its structure the economics major is not a good candidate for a capstone course. Trying to do too much can work against a strong educational foundation, and can undermine what the current economics major does so well.

The last essay, "'Little Think' Economics: Is That All There Is?" extends the argument about what we teach to graduate education. It was initially written in response to a request by the Hayek Society of the London School of Economics to contribute a piece to a journal they were starting that would explore suggestions for graduate students. They had seen my writing, and I expect that they thought I would write something that would be very compatible with their views. I sent in the article and never heard from them again.[4] I'm not sure whether it was the normal bureaucratic problems of fledgling student groups, or the fact that they didn't like what I had written. It could well be the latter since the point the essay makes, I suspect, is not the one the graduate students wanted to hear. The point is that, yes, much of the math we do may well be an irrelevant hurdle, but hurdles are part of the nature of all systems. If you want to play the game, jump the hurdles.

Teaching Micro

The second set of essays considers the teaching of microeconomics. The first of these, "Integrating Sex and Drugs into the Principles Course," argues that the structure of current principles texts misleads students about policy options. The essay argues for modifying the micro presentation to include not only market failure, but also failures of market outcomes—situations when the market is doing everything it is supposed to, but the result is socially undesirable—as reasons for government intervention. It further argues that doing so will make the principles course more exciting to students and provide them with a better foundation for thinking about policy.

The second essay, "Complexity and the Principles Course," argues that there are two story lines that economists tell—a complexity story and the efficiency story. The texts currently tell only the efficiency story, even though the complexity story may be the more relevant story for understanding the economy and real world economic problems. They do so for pedagogical reasons—the complexity story is a difficult story to tell, and is not easily reducible to simple graphs and models. The paper argues that in the short run, the efficiency story will remain the only story told, but that in the longer run, as the technology of teaching moves away from print books, and towards computer-based and on-line instruction, the complexity story will become the story that economists tell; the efficiency story will become a sidelight.

The third essay, "Complexity, Muddling Through, and Environmentalists," carries the above argument further, arguing that the appropriate framework within which we should be teaching economics is a complexity framework, more similar to what Classical economists used, rather than the control framework that we currently teach in the texts. I suggest that the control framework is actually just a pedagogical tool that is useful as part of a broader reasoning process that belongs in the art of economics. The essay argues that within that broader complexity framework, economics is not in enormous conflict with environmentalists' views although it sometimes seems so when considered in what I earlier called the Rochester approach to economic thinking.

The final essay, "On the Treatment of Fixed and Sunk Costs in Principles Texts," looks at a particular problematic treatment in texts—fixed and sunk costs. In this case, however, I come out not for change, but for maintaining the status quo, arguing that the gains from the proposed solution are not worth the costs. The paper is relevant to broader issues for two reasons. *First*, by looking at the costs and benefits with knowledge of the real institutional structure, it shows the economic reasoning process applied to economics pedagogy. *Second*, it shows the type of consideration that I believe should be given to each of the elements of our principles course, and the difficult decisions that must be made about them.

Teaching Macro

The third set of essays concerns what we teach in macro. Macro is separated from micro because macro is a different pedagogical animal than micro, both in structure and content (although from the way that macro is currently taught in graduate school, the difference is not so clear). In these essays I argue that although modern macro began with the writings of John Maynard Keynes, it has evolved enormously since then so that, at the research frontier, one can hardly recognize the relationship between macro taught in graduate school and the macro taught in principles and intermediate courses. These essays deal with why this separation has occurred and whether the structure of undergraduate macro should continue to reflect the structure of its historical beginnings, even as what is taught in graduate school does not.

The essays in this section are all connected by my view that while the foundations of macro lie in complex systems analysis, the structure of the current presentation of macro in both graduate and undergraduate courses makes it impossible to teach macro as a sub-branch of complex systems. The pedagogical issues in macro concern how we reconcile the difference between a presentation that would make the complex systems nature of the macro question clear, and the current presentation that presents macroeconomics as a dynamic stochastic general equilibrium problem. The four essays in this section convey the difficulties I see in reconciling these two approaches, and show what I consider to be acceptable and unacceptable pedagogical simplifications.

The first essay, "Teaching Keynes in the 21st Century," considers the Keynesian legacy. In it I argue that the Keynesian vision that the market economy left to its own devices might not gravitate to a desirable equilibrium is an important idea to convey to students. In the late 1990s when the essay was first written, some economists believed that we had a new economy, in which recessions were a thing of the past, and that this Keynesian view was obsolete. I ague that that view was wrong, and that we needed to incorporate models that warned people against that view. I argued that various simple Keynesian models can present this vision as long as they are not taught as the truth, but simply as models that capture possible tendencies in economies. I further argue that Classical economists knew that, and that their arguments against Keynesian policy were not so much against Keynes' theory, but against the practicality of Keynesian solutions, and the problems associated with them. To incorporate such arguments I argue that if we are teaching about macro market failure we must simultaneously teach about macro government failure.

The second essay, "The Stories We Tell: A Reconsideration of AS/AD Analysis," expresses my concern with the AS/AD model, which has become the central model taught in macro. This essay explains how I regard that model as pedagogically misleading, and I offer alternatives to deal with the problem. My favored solution was not adopted by the profession, in part because it was more complicated than most professors were willing to present, and in part because of the strong inertia of existing models. Fighting these losing battles for change helped shape my views about the 15 percent rule and how textbooks work.

The third essay, "Telling Better Stories in Introductory Macro," is also about the stories we tell in macro. This essay, however, focuses on how we teach <u>growth theory in macro.</u> It argues that we should separate the teaching of ideas from the teaching of models and emphasize that the models are calisthenics of the mind. I argue that we should present students with <u>an historical introduction to growth</u> and <u>focus on case studies</u> rather than on technical models to convey our ideas. It also advocates the use of simple <u>simulations, such as the Game of Life</u>, to convey to students the <u>complexity of the growth process</u>, and some possible patterns that might develop.

The final essay, "The Strange Persistence of the IS/LM Model," <u>relates to the intermediate</u>, rather than introductory, economics course. It discusses the evolution of the IS/LM model, and why that model has remained central to the intermediate presentations of macroeconomics. It argues that initially, the model was meant to convey to students economists' theory of the macro economy, but that it is no longer used that way. Instead, it is used as a handy tool to talk about policy almost independently of theory. The paper demonstrates the difference by comparing Gardiner Ackley's treatment of the IS/LM model in the 1960s with Greg Mankiw's treatment in the early 2000s, arguing that it is precisely because the IS/LM framework obscures the workings of the model that it has remained central to pedagogy.

Some Thoughts on Reform

The final two essays in the book consider issues of reform to educational institutions. They are revisions of papers that I wrote in 1992 when I was strongly advocating a change in graduate education. (I still advocate change; I have just given up much hope of actually changing the system much.) The first of these, "Reform of Undergraduate Economics Education," argues that teaching undergraduates is the most important role for economists, and that therefore graduate economics education should be designed to prepare them for that job. The paper argues that currently graduate schools do not do that, which means that their students, who will be the future teachers of undergraduates, are poorly prepared to teach economics the way I believe it would best be taught. It argues for doing better by doing less, and suggests a number of reforms that I believe would improve undergraduate economics education. Specifically, it argues that there needs to be a match between the research being done by undergraduate economics professors and the skills that they are teaching their students, and that if the two pull in different directions, the conflicting pulls will undermine the teaching function of the college.

The second essay is entitled "Reform of Graduate Economics Education." I include it because even though my interest is in undergraduate economics education, that interest means that I must also be interested in graduate education. People teach what they learn, and unless graduate economics education changes, undergraduate economics education will not change. In the essay I argue that training future teachers of undergraduate economics should be a central concern of graduate education. I argue that intermediate-tier programs are the most likely candidates for reform because while they cannot compete with the top schools in training students for graduate teaching and theoretical research, they can become very competitive in economics if they differentiate themselves, and focus on preparing students to teach undergraduate economics. I suggest that demanders of graduate economists organize and make their needs known, thereby encouraging product differentiation.

A Final Comment

The above introductory comments should give you a good sense of the papers and my approach to teaching and pedagogy. While all the papers are connected to my central themes, they are independent, and can be read in any order. I believe that most readers will find that the papers convey a quite different view of pedagogy, and of economics, than is often found in the literature, and thus are, I hope, worth taking a look at.

Notes

1. Having discovered that, I then discovered that Bob Solow had said it earlier and better (as he had with many of my insights). See the discussion in endnote 10 on page 31 of the essay, "What We Teach and What We Do."
2. Initially this approach was associated with the University of Chicago, and the University of Rochester was a satellite of the Chicago school of economics. Recently, as the influence of Milton Friedman and George Stigler wanes, Chicago has changed, and more people associated with this approach seem to have Rochester rather than Chicago connections.
3. Political scientists make a distinction between strategy and tactics. Strategy relates to theory; tactics relate to implementation. Economists do not have that distinction, because, for academic economists, all interactions are strategic. What I am arguing is that real change is all tactical, with strategy serving a background role, and only being applied with a full sense of the tactical problems.
4. About a year thereafter Ken Koford, the editor of the *Eastern Economic Journal*, asked if I would contribute a piece to the editor's corner, so the essay was originally published there.

Part 1: General

The Stories Economists Tell

1
What We Teach and What We Do

Fifty years ago what we taught in the principles of economics course reflected reasonably well what we did in our research. That, however, is no longer the case; today what we teach has a more nuanced relation to what we do. The reason is that the economics profession and the textbooks have evolved differently.

In my writings on the economics profession and on economic education I have discussed these differing evolutions and have argued that the way modern economists use theory and the way that they relate theory to the empirical evidence have evolved so significantly that modern economics needs to be given a new name to distinguish it from neoclassical economics. Those changes have been little remarked upon because they have occurred incrementally, not in sudden jumps, and the large cumulative movement can be seen only when one looks at the profession from a more distant perspective than most economists take.[1]

This chapter deals with the implications of the changes that have occurred in the profession for the way economics is taught and the way economics is presented in the micro principles textbooks. First, I summarize the changes I see happening in the profession. Second, I discuss the stories that the principles textbooks tell in micro. Third, I discuss how those stories might change to better reflect what economists currently do.[2]

What Economists Do

All fields of research evolve, and economics is no exception. With the developments in analytic methods and computing technology in the last 50 years, it would be surprising if it were otherwise. Fifty years ago computers were, practically speaking, nonexistent, and empirical work in economics consisted of running simple regressions calculated with mechanical calculating machines. Analytically, calculus was then seen as advanced mathematics, and deductive reasoning with two-dimensional graphs was still considered advanced theory. Macro was in its infancy; and while there was hope that in the future macro econometric models would be developed into viable models, work on the simplest of such models was considered cutting-edge research. Simple consumption function and demand for money equations were at the forefront of theoretical and empirical research.

Today's economics is fundamentally different from the economics of 50 years ago. The reason is simple: technology has changed. Economists' training today is statistically sophisticated, and in many ways the "metrics" has progressed faster than the "econo." Today, computers are integral to research, both in analytic methods and in empirical work; today, data and theory are constantly being related in ways that were never considered by economists 50 years ago. Analytically, serious consideration of dynamic issues, which 50 years ago was beyond the analytic purview of even the most sophisticated mathematical economist, has replaced comparative statics on the forefront of theoretical issues, and the idea that you could do graduate work in economics without extensive mathematical training has become almost unthinkable.[3] Two-dimensional graphs, the mainstay of theory through the 1950s, are today seen as simplifying pedagogical devices, not as engines of analysis.

The increase in the analytic and statistical sophistication of the profession has been accompanied by a growing acceptance that the economy must be analyzed as a "complex system" rather than as a highly complex "simple system."[4] Simple systems, no matter how complex, can, in principle, be analyzed analytically and controlled, at least in a stochastic sense. Complex systems cannot. Although we are still a long way from complete acceptance of this complexity vision of the economy, cutting-edge research is moving in that direction, and is, in my view, the future of economics.

Simple and complex systems differ in their micro foundations. Simple systems can be studied from micro foundations alone, by which I mean that one can build up from an understanding of the fundamental elements of the system to an understanding of the whole system. Complex systems involve emergent properties, and cannot, in their entirety, be understood from an analysis of the components of that system. There can still be micro foundations, but the micro foundations of complex systems are contextual, and can only be understood in reference to the existing system and its history. Such complex systems are built up in path dependent stages, making individual optimization within such systems history- and institution-specific. This means that institutional structure is central to understanding a complex system, and that any assumed rationality must involve some boundedness.[5] Parts of the system may be understandable using simple deductive analysis, but other parts will not be.

The acceptance of the economy as a complex system changes the focus of economists' analysis. In a simple system it makes sense to analyze idealized agents, and to see economics as the study of infinitely bright agents interacting in information-rich environments. The acceptance that the economy is complex makes such an analysis less relevant for understanding the economy and changes the focus of analysis to the study of reasonably bright individuals interacting in information-poor environments. It also changes the way in which economists think of their role in policy. Specifically, it moves them away from an economics of control framework—a framework within which infinitely bright economists with full knowledge of the system design policy—to an economics of muddling-through framework—a framework within which reasonably bright economists with limited knowledge of the system provide inputs into a larger policy process.

The acceptance that the economy is complex also suggests quite different research strategies than are appropriate for the study of simple systems; it requires less reliance on deductive theory, and more on pattern analysis and inductive analysis. It involves more emphasis on studying how real people behave rather than on studying how infinitely rational people behave. Thus it involves a movement away from the holy economic trinity of rationality, greed, and equilibrium, and toward a broader economic trinity of purposeful behavior, enlightened self-interest, and sustainability.[6]

We can see the acceptance of complexity in the economics profession in the changing nature of research being done, especially by younger professors. Today research is characterized by a blossoming of behavioral economics studies, which consider how people actually behave. This work does not assume full rationality, but instead attempts to study purposeful behavior. Similarly, the growing field of experimental economics provides a way of describing the behavior of agents in the economic model, rather than assuming "rational" behavior. Experiments are introducing alternative ways to specify the degree of rationality and greed to assume in models.

Another element in the change is the rise of evolutionary game theory, which embeds the maximization process in an evolutionary system in order to gain insight into how institutions and norms develop; it then defines rationality locally in terms of evolutionary stable institutions, rather than globally. Still another element of the change is the rise of New Institutional Economics, which is focused on integrating institutions into economic analysis. Finally, there is the rise of agent-based modeling, in which the researcher creates a virtual environment allowing various behaviors of agents to compete, and then sees which behaviors actually survive.

The acceptance of the complexity of the economy can also be seen in the empirical work that economists do. Most of this work has little to do with formal testing of economic theories consistent with general equilibrium, but instead involves informal testing of various ad hoc theories. This work focuses on pulling information and insight from data, not on issues such as proving demand curves slope downward. Modern empirical work is more often than not a search for patterns in data—a type of highly sophisticated data mining—not a test of theories.

Consider the recent work of Bertrand and Mullainathan on discrimination (2004). By conducting a field experiment in which they changed the name of a job applicant, they provided strong evidence that discrimination exists in the labor market. In their research little in the way of economic theory was used directly. Although they discussed the results in terms of asymmetric information, screening, and statistical models of discrimination, the results stood on their own. The work was simply a well-designed field experiment that added insight into our understanding of the operation of the economy and the degree and nature of discrimination that exists. Another example is the oft-cited work on abortion and crime by Donohue and Levitt (2001). Again, the work is primarily statistical in nature with only loose guidance from economic theory. These examples are not unique; most applied work in microeconomics today is highly empirical and has only the loosest connection to general equilibrium theory.

The search for patterns in data can also be seen in the new work on power law relationships, such as Zipf's Law (Gabaix 1999) which some dynamic systems exhibit. Once a system has been shown to exhibit a power law relationship, researchers can study the system replicator dynamics that might lead to such results, and thereby gain insight into the system. In this work researchers rely on computing power to find patterns in the data, rather than using statistical work to test theories. They then attempt to structure theories that are consistent with the data. Theories that are not consistent with those patterns must be modified or abandoned.

In summary, economics today is not the economics of our grandparents' generation, our parents' generation, or even the economics of the generation of economists currently in their mid-40s. It has evolved significantly; it is more technical in an applied mathematical sense, but often less technical in a pure mathematical sense than the economics associated with general equilibrium analysis.[7] It is loosely designed around models and modeling, but those models are less likely to be tied to general equilibrium foundations. It is more consciously empirical than the earlier work.

What Economists Teach

Ultimately, the teaching of economics boils down to the telling of stories. In the principles of economics textbooks we tell stories that are meant both to give students a sense of what economic analysis is (often expressed as teaching students the economic way of thinking) and to provide students with insight into how the economy operates. For most undergraduates the mathematics used in cutting-edge modern economics research is the equivalent of Greek, and thus, the textbooks have been, understandably, slow to incorporate the changes. The economic approach in the micro textbooks in large part still reflects the research approach to economics that economists followed in the 1930s to 1960s. In fact, the current structure of the textbooks still reflects the structure that was developed in the 1950s with Paul Samuelson's textbook. With the mathematical and statistical gulf between the research that economists do and the training in mathematics that undergraduates have growing ever wider, it becomes harder and harder to relate what we do to what we teach.

Were the majority of economics students planning to go on to become economists, the answer about what to do about this situation would be easy: increase the mathematical and statistical requirements of studying economics. But fewer than 1 percent of the students taking principles of economics courses will ever go on to become research economists; the overwhelming majority will go on to work in a variety of other careers in which the significant mathematical training necessary to read the current research of economists, although helpful, is unnecessary. The "increase the math requirements" solution will not meet their needs. This means that the stories economists tell must be embedded in highly simplified models, which have varying degrees of relationship to the more complex models that are actually being worked on by economists.

To say that the textbooks do not reflect the research being done does not mean that what we teach is irrelevant or wrong, nor does it mean that we should change what we teach. The deciding factor of what we teach in principles should not be what is most up-to-date, but what adds the most value to students' understanding of the economy. Given that decision factor, there are numerous pedagogical reasons why we might choose to teach something different from the latest research that economists do.

In my view, what we currently teach is extremely valuable to students, and we can continue to teach what we currently teach with only slight modifications, and feel good about doing so. So my argument is not that we should fundamentally change what we teach; my argument is just that there is an understandable tension between the simplicity and definitiveness of what we teach and the complexity and ambiguity of what we do in research. It is an open question how the textbooks should relate to students the actual process of what economists do, and of how researchers believe the economy operates.

In micro, the story we tell in the textbooks is probably best described as the "efficiency story." It is a two-part story—one part about how rational individuals approach problems, and a second part about how markets channel rational individuals' actions into results that are beneficial for the common good.

The story of the rational individual focuses on scarcity and constrained optimization; it directs students' attention to the TASNSTAFFL (There Ain't No Such Thing As A Free Lunch) law, opportunity cost, and how individuals economize to deal with scarcity. The focus of this story is on rational choice; students are taught a variety of models—the profit-maximizing model of the firm, the utility maximizing model of the individual, and simple game theoretic models such as the prisoner's dilemma—that either reinforce that efficiency theme or have meaning in relation to it. In order to arrive at definite results, the rationality used in these models is narrowly defined in relation to utility maximization, and the behavioral foundations of individuals' actions generally receive little attention. The presentation is generally deductive rather than inductive, and there is little discussion of empirical evidence that might support or contradict the presentation in the book.[8] Issues that cloud the efficiency story, which are on the cutting edge of modern theory, such as endogenous tastes, path dependency, and endogenous institutional structure, are avoided.

On the aggregate level, the story is a bit more complicated; it integrates the decisions of individuals into aggregate results through the market place. These integrative stories use perfect competition as a reference point, and provide students with a discussion of how markets channel individual interests into results that reflect the common good. As was the case with the story of the individual, these aggregation stories rely on a narrowly defined hyper-rationality that requires individuals to maximize well-defined intertermporal utility functions specified over all goods, meeting a number of axiomatic conditions such as transitivity of preferences, and on a careful specification of what is meant by the common good. Specifically, the story told is one of how a perfectly competitive system is driven by the invisible hand of the market to a Pareto-optimal result in which no one can be made better off without someone else being made worse off. This aggregate efficiency story relies heavily on the narrowly defined rationality assumption. If individuals are not rational, as rational is used in its formal sense, it is impossible to arrive at the aggregate efficiency conclusions of the second part of the efficiency story.

In terms of policy, the focus of the story told in the principles course is again centered on efficiency. It conveys to students a sense of how restrictions on voluntary actions limit the attainment of efficiency, how externalities and monopoly can create a gap between social and private costs, and how, through appropriate taxation policy, government can correct those market failures and work to equate marginal social costs with marginal private costs. It is a control story in which there is a knowable social optimum that government policy is designed to achieve.[9]

There is much to be said for teaching this efficiency story. It is excellent for shedding light on many issues about which students don't have a good understanding, and for shedding light on some important economic policy problems. But it has a number of well-known limitations. For example, it leaves out issues of dynamic efficiency, and does not convey to students how less-than-competitive markets are more conducive to technological change than are perfectly competitive markets. It also misses many of the broader issues of policy in which the policy problem is not market failure, but instead failure of market outcomes.

Students learn the lessons of this efficiency story in varying degrees. Higher-level courses expand on the efficiency story, but the central theme remains the same—the study of a system in which rational individuals optimize subject to constraints. What changes in the upper level courses is that the structure of the system being controlled, and the nature of the control, becomes more complicated—moving from a simple constrained static maximization story to a stochastic dynamic optimal control story, depending on how highbrow the upper level course is. But the textbook story, although more complicated, is the same. You have this system in which rational individuals are optimizing, and economists are the rational controllers who structure the rules and policies to optimize the social welfare of the system.

Bringing the Micro Story Up to Date

The current textbook micro story developed in the 1930s and became the textbook story beginning with Paul Samuelson's textbook. At the time it was developed, it was a reasonable description of how cutting-edge economists thought about the economy and of what they did. As I stated above, computers as we know them did not exist, and sophisticated empirical work was difficult and extremely costly. The profession was still digesting the analytics of the general equilibrium model, and Walrasian general equilibrium was still on the theoretical front lines.

Today, the textbook micro story we tell is still useful, but it is no longer on the forefront of theory, nor does it reflect how economists approach policy problems. I think it nonetheless can be justified as a useful fable that we teach to students to convey important lessons. These lessons carry over to a broader set of issues, and while the specific results of the model are not robust, there is a feeling that the broader stories told—TANSTAFFL, optimizing at the margin, and the positive effect of competition—are robust.

As I argued above, however, the specific stories we are telling in the models can no longer be supported as a description of how research economists at the cutting edge think about issues. Modern economists use an inductive empirical approach that is only loosely guided by the theory that incentives matter. They don't test theories; there is no disproof of the efficiency story that would cause them to give it up. As I stated above, in modern economics, incentives still matter, but the standard of perfect rationality, greed, and equilibrium is being replaced by a standard of purposeful behavior, enlightened self-interest, and sustainability.

Ultimately, I suspect, the textbooks will better reflect the changes that are occurring in economics. The profession replaces itself every 35 years or so, and as that happens, what is taught will change, because teachers generally teach what they have learned. But it will be a long time happening because of the built in user problem. Too much human capital is tied up in the current pedagogical approach for it to disappear quickly.

Given this institutional structure I expect that the change in the principles textbooks will take place in two ways. The first is an evolution of the current story as it is modified by the changes that are occurring. But there is no way that existing textbooks can ever fully capture the new approach because they are built on a foundation that was built in the 1950s. Thus the second path will be an entirely new type of text, built on induction, one that jettisons the supply/demand framework and much of the analytic foundations of the efficiency model. Given that the current approach to teaching is built into the current institutional structure, both in course offerings and in the structure of the textbook market, I suspect that this second path is a long time in the future, and will probably occur only as print textbooks give way to on-line presentation of material and alternative methods of instruction. Thus, my focus here is on the less dramatic evolution of current textbooks. Specifically, let me consider five ways in which I think the micro textbook could change to better reflect the new work.

Models as Calisthenics, not as Truth

The first change that would better integrate modern work with the models presented in the textbooks is a change in the way the models are presented. Instead of presenting them as blueprints of reality, embodying truth, we can present them as logical exercises that can be helpful in understanding the economy. This allows us to tell students about the more complicated approach that modern economists take while still teaching students the simpler models. Such an approach to models is consistent with a complexity vision because in that vision even the most sophisticated models we have today are far below the sophistication we need to understand the economy.

Let me explain what I mean by this. If the economy is a complex system, models are not used as a blueprint, but rather as a guide to stimulating thought about the economy and as a means of structuring analysis. In this "theory as a guide" approach, when there is a difference between practical experience and theory, pure theory is not the guiding factor—practical experience guided by theory is. Ultimately, induction, not deduction, underlies all reasoning about complex systems.

To justify my teaching models as calisthenics, I explain to students that their minds are like my body—a bit flabby—and that both could use a bit of exercise; the models they are learning are designed to provide precisely that, and although they do not prepare students to understand economic reality, they do provide the training that eventually will help them understand the issues better.[10]

A Decrease in the Emphasis Given to Efficiency

The current micro story is designed around efficiency, as if that were a goal of society. Actually, efficiency only becomes a goal in a highly rarified model, and achieving efficiency is a reasonably desirable goal only if one accepts all the assumptions of the model that underlie it—costless redistribution of income or homothetic tastes, no interdependent utility functions, and full rationality of individuals. Modern economics recognizes that, and treats efficiency as a useful shorthand for maximizing total output independent of distributional consequences. When those assumptions don't hold, economists' role is not to design policies that achieve efficiency, but instead to design as cheaply as possible the policies that achieve whatever goals society specifies. Economists are not specifying the goals, they are only specifying how best to achieve those goals. It was that recognition that led J. N. Keynes (1891) and Robbins (1953, 1981) to emphasize the importance of maintaining a separate branch of applied economics and not drawing policy implications from theory.

One method of incorporating this broader approach into the textbooks is to introduce into the presentation failures of market outcomes in addition to market failures. Failures of market outcomes occur when the market is doing everything it is supposed to, but society still doesn't like the result. These failures can occur, for example, because of psychological issues in which individuals' actions do not reflect their true desires. Discussion of such psychological issues would allow the incorporation of insights from behavioral economics. Another reason these failures can occur can be because of distributional issues. Raising distributional issues emphasizes to students that consumer surplus reflects demands at the current distribution of income, not welfare of society as most students think of it. A final reason these failures can occur is when moral considerations override efficiency considerations, such as the examples pointed out by Sen (1970).

A Change in How Equilibrium Is Presented

A third change that can better relate the economics in the current textbooks to modern research is in the presentation of equilibrium. Specifically, I would change three aspects of the way in which equilibrium is discussed in the textbook.

The first change is to present equilibrium as a state of the model, not as a state of the economy.[11] In this view of equilibrium, the existence of equilibrium does not mean that one believes that the economy is ever going to arrive at an equilibrium; it simply means that there are forces pushing the economy in that direction, and that, other things equal, which they never are, the economy would move there.

A second change I would propose that would make the textbooks more consistent with the modern approach is to present a multiple equilibria model. The standard models now used in principles textbooks are all unique equilibrium models. Complex systems generally have an infinity of, or a large number of, equilibria, which means that equilibrium selection mechanisms become very important; these equilibria selection mechanisms choose which of the many equilibria the economy will gravitate towards. Discussing such forces would involve a larger discussion of institutions than currently exists, and a greater emphasis on public choice and rent seeking.

A third change in the discussion of equilibrium that would make the books more consistent with modern research would be to present alternative ways in which individual agent equilibria are connected to aggregate equilibria. Currently, aggregate equilibria are equated with all agents within the model also being in equilibrium. The complexity vision of the economy offers an alternative aggregate equilibrium in which no individual agents are in equilibrium, but in which the aggregate is in a type of equilibrium in the sense that it will not have a tendency to move from where it is. It is a statistical equilibrium consistent with what one sees in statistical mechanics, not a static equilibrium. Statistical equilibria are much better suited to explain equilibrium in the aggregate economy, and offer a number of advantages in explaining observed phenomena to students. Consider profits, which in the current standard textbook exposition cannot exist above the opportunity cost of implicit factors of production. If the system is in statistical equilibrium in which fluctuations of system elements offset each other (Foley, 1994), that need not be the case, because profits are guiding agents in their decision making, and there is no reason why the profits being made in the economy could not exceed the losses; when that happens it means that the economy is growing because, on average, people are making decisions that are panning out.

Present Rationality as Reasonableness Rather than as Rationality

Another change we can make is to get the students thinking in terms of reasoning that involves higher levels of rationality, rather than the simple rationality that the textbooks currently focus on. One way I do this in class is with the following game, which is called the beauty contest game. (Nagel, 1995) In this game I pass out small sheets of paper on which each student is asked to write a number between 0 and 100 that they believe will be two-thirds of the average of all the numbers chosen by the group. For example, if the average number chosen turned out to be 30, the winning guess would be 20.

After playing the game I discuss with the class the nature of the decision process appropriate for this decision. The logic of the problem pushes toward an answer of zero, but it will only be an acceptable answer if everyone chooses it, in which case there is no single winner. It is much more reasonable to see it as a game of behavioral strategy, as are almost all of the decisions we make in real life. What's interesting about this game is that usually the results are relatively easily predictable for the group playing, and in the initial round, the winning guess is generally somewhere around 20 to 25 when played by students unfamiliar with the game.

Right after playing and discussing this game, we play another called the average game, in which students are asked to pick a number between 0 and 100 that is the average of all numbers picked by the students. Here, the expected answer is fifty, but since we play this game immediately after playing and discussing the previous game, again, the expected answer seldom occurs. Inevitably, because of a carryover from the last game, some students choose a lower number, and the winning number is generally closer to 35 or 40. Again behavioral considerations are integrated into the discussion.

More Focus on Increasing Returns, Path-Dependencies, and System Resilience

A final change that would better incorporate new work in advanced theory into the textbooks is a greater focus on increasing returns and path dependencies. Currently, such issues are presented only as addenda because they do not fit the efficiency story. However, once multiple equilibria models have been introduced, increasing returns and path dependencies become important elements of the equilibrium selection mechanism. This raises the question of equilibrium resilience as a goal of a system, and an important policy question becomes whether agents in a system want a shift from one equilibrium to another to occur. In ecological economics there are models in which there are sudden changes from one equilibrium to another, as the forces of change have built up beyond a certain level. Currently there are no models in the principles textbooks that introduce the importance of resilience in systems; all the models in those textbooks suggest to the students that change always occurs incrementally. By including a model that has a sudden change— and a shift point—one can convey to students the essence of the policy implications of nonlinear dynamic models.

New work being done in agent-based modeling such as the work of Leigh Tesfatsion and Blake LeBaron allows one to give visual demonstrations of sudden shifts. Eventually, agent-based modeling will be central to the teaching of principles of economics. Currently, it is unfamiliar to most professors. One way in which I present the idea of multiple equilibria to students is with John Conway's game of life (available online) that conveys to them how easy it is for a small change to occur, and encourages them to think in terms of dynamic processes rather than static models.

Concluding Comments

My discussion of what we do and what we teach may have made it seem that the textbooks are hopelessly out of date. Let me reiterate the point I made above: that is not my view; the textbooks do many things, and keeping up with the latest developments in what economists do is only one of them. The principles of economics course has, in my view, enormous strengths; the "no free lunch" lesson alone—one of the most important lessons that a student can learn—fully justifies the micro course. The macro principles course gives students a good sense of the aggregate forces that drive our economy, a sense of what inflation and unemployment are, along with a working knowledge of monetary and fiscal policy. Given the opportunity costs, both these courses are fully justified.

Because I believe that the current courses have enormous value, I am hesitant to change too much in the current presentation, even though I agree that what we teach does not reflect what we do. Maintaining compatibility between what we teach and what we do isn't a requirement of good teaching in economics. Before we make any changes in the principles course to better reflect what we do, we want to be sure that those changes do not dilute the strengths of the current presentation. I am not sure whether we are ready to do that, which is why I stick with the standard presentations in the textbooks, even though in my research, I spend time thinking about problems being considered by modern research. Teaching, like the economy, is a complex system, and our fate in both is to muddle through as best we can.

Notes

1. This has also been the case with previous changes in economics, such as the movement from classical to neoclassical economics.
2. In this paper I consider only micro issues. The reasons are that (1) the macro story we tell in the textbooks is less coherent than the story we tell in micro, and (2) there is much more diversity of opinion about what story we should be telling in macro than there is in micro.
3. Whether these changes are good or bad is debatable and not the subject of this article; my point is simply that this is the way it is.
4. I am using "complex" and "simple" in a technical sense here. For a discussion of what is meant by "complex system" see Auyang (2000).
5. These ideas are developed in Anderson, Arrow, and Pines (1988) and Arthur, Durlauf, and Lane (1997).
6. Kreps (1997) discusses the movement.
7. To say that economics has evolved is not to say that it does not reflect its past, and in many ways the changes being made are as small as possible. For example, behavioral economics is moving only slowly away from the deductive foundations and is seldom presented as being part of a broader complexity vision. Most of the published works make only small deviations from standard models. Similarly, most economists think of what they do in reference to what they were taught. It is at the margin, with new professors, that the changes are largest.
8. Examples of issues that are not discussed include the experimentally determined results that sunk costs and fairness often do enter into people's behavior, and that the utility gained from consumption is often determined by one's consumption relative to what others receive, not by the absolute amount one receives.
9. The efficiency story has not always been the central story of economics. It developed in the 1930s and was structured in its current form in Lerner's *Economics of Control* (1944), which is why I call it the economics of control story.

Lerner had a gift of seeing everything in simple terms, and of designing teachable black and white models that others saw in shades of gray. For Lerner theory was a blueprint upon which policy could be built.

10. Solow (1964: 7, 8) has used similar reasoning in justifying the teaching of some high-level models that also do not reflect how economists think. He writes: "In economics...I like a man to have mastered the fancy theory before I trust him with simple theory. The practical utility of economics comes not primarily from its high-powered frontier, but from fairly low-powered reasoning. But the moral is not that we can dispense with high-powered economics, if only because high-powered economics seems to be such an excellent school for the skillful use of low-powered economics."

11. Some advocates of a complexity approach have argued that accepting that the system is complex means that we must give up equilibrium because the economy is continually changing. I do not agree. Once students see models as tools, not blueprints, equilibrium as a state of the model does not tell them anything about the state of the economy, and it can be very useful to use equilibrium models as reference points for thinking about possible basins of attractions, which, in multiple equilibria models, serve the function of equilibrium in unique equilibrium models.

2

Caveat Lector: Living with the 15% Rule

In my discussions of principles of economics texts, I often refer to the 15% rule, a rule of thumb dealing with the question of how much a major principles text can deviate from the "standard" principles text. The rule is: although a new book or a new edition of an existing book has some leeway in the presentation of material, it cannot differ from the standard presentation by more that 15% and still be seen as a mainstream book.[1] The reason behind this 15% rule is easily discernible. Changes greater than 15% require professors to change their notes and presentations by more than the large majority of professors are willing to do. Thus, there is little demand for a book that violates this rule.

The 15% rule is an invisible rule in the sense that no one directly enforces it. Authors are free to write what they want, and, in fact, in the initial contract-signing discussions, potential authors are generally encouraged by publishers to develop their different ideas, and to differentiate their texts from the existing texts. Were it otherwise, many authors would never have agreed to write the book to begin with. But, as is often the case, these high hopes for change are often dashed by the reality of the market. By that I mean that the process through which a book is developed, and through which the author's ideas are translated into the published text, usually eliminates many of the grand hopes of the author, leaving the author with a decision: to continue with less grandiose hopes, or to give up the project.

Generally, if an author does not agree to scale down his changes, he or she will find that the book is classified as a niche book, and the book will receive little marketing support from the publisher, or the book is never published.[2] Numerous famous economists have signed on to do a principles book that has never been published.[3]

There are actually two processes through which a book is brought into line with the "standard" presentation. One is the reviewing process that all textbook publishers use to guide the author and the publisher. A new economics text will have sixty or more reviewers, who, to a large degree, are front-line teachers, already using books with which the new author's book is seen as competitive. They are not specialists in the field who can say whether the material being presented is an acceptable pedagogical simplification of the advanced story the profession is trying to tell. They are economists whose primary focus is on teaching and whose conception of what economics is is very much intertwined with the current texts. Many have only a slight acquaintance with new developments in the field, and thus little of the reviewing process concerns how well the text conveys new developments. Any book that makes it to publication must have gained general acceptance from these reviewers and have had a hard core subgroup of reviewers who strongly favored the changes being made in the book.[4]

Later editions of texts still face this reviewing process, but are more likely to be guided by the market test in which "reviews" are the changes in sales between the last edition and the current edition. If sales are up, the reviews are positive. This market test generally leads to a corollary to the 15% rule, which can be called the textbook convergence rule. This corollary states that as a textbook moves from edition to edition, it will deviate less and less from the standard. The reasons for this corollary are that (1) the standard changes as successful innovations are copied by the other books and become the new standard, or (2) if the standard does not change, the book will change in the direction of the existing standard; if it does not change it will become a niche book.

The 15% rule does not mean that textbooks as a whole do not evolve; they do. Although professors do not like significant change, they do like to feel that what they are teaching is keeping up with the developments in the field. They want a book that is both easy to teach and that keeps up with the developments in the field. Of course, these two criteria often work against each other, leading to a tendency of the texts to emphasize superficial changes occurring in the profession—the fads—while avoiding the more substantive changes that raise deeper questions about the underlying model being presented. For example, the Keynesian AE/AP model has remained in many texts long after Keynesian economics has essentially disappeared from graduate training. What the 15% rule means is that an author who hopes to introduce change, and who also hopes to remain a player in the textbook market, has to choose his battles carefully, often retreating from an attempted deviation either in the prepublication stage, or in the revision stage as the book goes through various editions.

Let me now give examples of how I, in my principles text, live with the 15% rule, and of how my hopes of what I could do in my text have evolved. First, I briefly discuss some general changes that I had hoped to make, but which never got past the reviewing stage. Second, I discuss a specific change that made it through the initial reviewing stage, but that I have backed away from in later editions while still maintaining a slightly different presentation than is found in the standard. Third, I discuss a specific change that I am currently trying out under the 15% rule, and which may or may not survive the market test.

Changes Not Made

Before I wrote my first text I was not told about the 15% rule. I entered into textbook writing with grand ambitions of changing the way the texts presented economics, only to discover that change is much more difficult to introduce than I had imagined. Thus, I have numerous examples of changes that I hoped to make, but which were never made, or which were significantly reduced in the reviewing process.

My initial vision for my book was one that focused much more on the development of economic thought, institutions, and the development of those institutions, than did the "standard" book. My initial manuscript had a strong historical and institutional focus; the manuscript that emerged from the reviewing process had about two-thirds of the initial discussion removed. As the book has gone through additional editions, the elimination process has continued, although at a much slower pace. There is still more discussion of history of ideas and institutions in my book than in the "standard" book, but now it is a much smaller difference than I had initially hoped for. I have converged toward the standard. Why have I converged? Because the large majority of reviewers have clearly stated that that they don't want that discussion in the text. Unfortunately, with less and less economic history and history of economic thought being taught in graduate school, this trend will likely continue, since professors like to teach what they have been taught in graduate school.

Another change that I had hoped to make when I started writing was in the presentation of costs and pricing decisions of firms. I had originally hoped to change the standard model of the firm from a "short-run first" presentation to a "long-run first" presentation. Specifically, I wanted to focus initially on the long-run pricing and production decision, and then to move on to the treatment of short-run issues as an adjustment issue. Such a change was consistent with my institutional focus. I thought that if the change was made, it could alter the focus of price-setting discussions to a much more classical position in which the primary focus is on a model where costs determine price. Demand issues, involving short-run fluctuations around that price, would be presented as a side theme. This change never made it through the initial reviewing process, and was completely abandoned by the third round of manuscript reviews (out of a total of five reviewing rounds—and more for some chapters—before publication). Reviews improved enormously after I switched to the standard presentation of costs. Even though I had done significant work on the history and practice of cost theory, many reviews of the manuscript questioned my understanding of costs because I wasn't presenting the issue in a standard way. After I reverted to the standard, by following a composite presentation found in the other books, reviewers thought my presentation was extraordinarily strong.[5]

A third change that I have not made is significant integrating the implications of the ongoing complexity revolution into the text. In my research on the profession, and on how best to understand the economy, I have become convinced that the economy is best understood as a complex system. My research is focused on considering the implications for economic policy of taking seriously the complexity of the economy. This change would shift the focus of analysis from the analysis of idealized agents—economics as the study of infinitely bright agents in information-rich environments—to the study of realistic agents—economics as the study of reasonably bright individuals in information-poor environments.

Ultimately such a change would involve a major change in the way economics is presented to students. It would switch the presentation to a more inductive approach, with the deductive models that are now central to economics playing a much smaller role. It would also lead to much more nuanced policy views, which I have characterized as "muddling through." Despite my interest in this area, in my text I make no attempt to switch from the standard presentation to what might be called a complexity presentation. Instead, I attempt to integrate the insights from my considerations of complexity in much smaller doses in my text presentations, leaving the text more complexity-friendly than other texts, but far from a presentation of the economics from a complexity viewpoint.

Changing the AS/AD Model: Not

Let me now turn to a consideration of a specific issue that made it through the initial reviewing process, but that has been significantly reduced in later editions. My treatment of this issue continues to differentiate my text from the competition, and hence is a change on which I am spending some of my 15% flexibility. That issue is how the macro model is presented. I've never been a fan of aggregate demand/ aggregate supply analysis. If I had my way, I would eliminate it from the texts. The reason is simple: as an economist trained in a Marshallian tradition, in my view, supply/demand analysis belongs in partial equilibrium considerations, not in considerations of the aggregate economy. In the aggregate the variables we talk about are so intertwined that we cannot assume "everything else constant." That said, even in my wildest dreams I never felt that I would be able to eliminate the AS/ AD model from the texts; it was too ubiquitous. So my initial approach was to spell out in my text what the complete analytics of the AS/AD model were. I felt that a full presentation of the analytics would make it impossible for students to think of AS/AD as supply/demand analysis with a big P and a big Q. It would bring home to students the sense that AS/AD is a reduced form relationship that follows from a much more complicated analysis.

My first edition was distinctive in its AS/AD presentation. It presented the analytic foundations of the model in a consistent way that allowed students to see the relationship between the Keynesian AE/AP model and the AS/AD model. To accomplish that I distinguished an aggregate equilibrium demand curve from an aggregate demand curve, and showed the relationship among the assumptions in both models. Getting these changes through the reviewing process was difficult, but I did it.

My book was a success, not because of my presentation of the macro model but in spite of it (as the publishers had argued in the reviewing stage would be the case). The reason wasn't that my presentation was wrong; that wasn't the issue. The issue was whether the market wanted the presentation changed. I got the change through the initial reviewing process because I browbeat reviewers into admitting that my presentation was more logical and rigorous than the competition's, and because I told my publisher that the book would not come out unless that model was presented the way I wanted it presented.

Why did I hold out? Because I believed it was an important pedagogical innovation that would catch on as soon as people saw the underlying logic of my alternative presentation. In my dreams my model would become the new standard. I was wrong. Strike one against my dream was that very few professors were willing to study carefully the model I presented and try to decide whether or not it was a better way of presenting the material. That's not the way textbooks are chosen.[6] Eventually that problem of getting professors to consider it might have been overcome, but my model had another strike against it: an increasing number of professors were not interested in teaching the AE/AP model, and hence were not interested in whether the AS/AD presentation was consistent with the AE/AP presentation. The third strike against my presentation was that a number of those who did present both models felt that the class should focus on policy discussion, not on models, and thus were unwilling to spend the time to teach the analytics of both models to students. Put succinctly, the change violated the 15% rule.

I am stubborn, but I am not beyond learning. With each successive edition, my presentation of AS/AD has evolved and become nearer the standard. I stopped distinguishing between the aggregate equilibrium curve and the aggregate demand curve, and simply defined the aggregate equilibrium demand curve as the aggregate demand curve, as the other books do. I also significantly reduced the analytic specifications of the model—assigning the remaining analytics to appendices where they could be avoided. Now, the only difference between my presentation of the AD curve and the standard presentation is that I explicitly name the multiplier as a determinant of the slope of the AD curve, and as a factor that increases the size of autonomous shifts in aggregate demand, and the standard books do not, although the standard presentation draws the AD curve in a way that the multiplier must be playing the explicit role I have in my book. They simply don't mention it.

The publishers have pushed me to remove even that small difference, but I have refused, since I still believe the explicit inclusion of the multiplier is needed to give students a clue about the underlying derivation of the AS/AD model, and how monetary and fiscal policy can have effects that are larger than the actual change in autonomous spending. In my view, not to point out the role of the multiplier is to invite students to think of the AD curve as a big partial equilibrium demand curve, and that I will not do.

Has my fight made a difference in the standard? The answer is yes, but the difference is very slight. All books are now careful to state that the AD curve is not equivalent to a partial equilibrium demand curve, and all books that present the AE/AP model generally relate the AE/AP model to the AS/AD model in the fashion that I believe originated with my book.[7] But the fact that the standard books are not explicitly discussing the multiplier in their presentation of the slope and shifting of the AD curve means that my success has been limited.

My inclusion of the multiplier as a determinant of the slope of the AD curve can stay in my text, because it falls under the 15% rule. In some of my broader writing on pedagogy I continue to attempt to get the profession to change, but unless something happens in the economy where multiplier effects need to be raised pedagogically more than they currently are, I have little hope that my exposition will change the standard. My inclusion of the multiplier as one of the determinants of the slope of the AD curve is seen as an acceptable Colander quirk, rather than the logically correct exposition that professors will demand as part of the standard.

Failures of Market Outcomes: Maybe

A second specific issue on which I am currently spending some of my 15% flexibility involves the policy framework we provide students in microeconomics. The current standard is what might be called the "market failure" standard. Using that standard we teach students that government should consider intervening in those cases where there is a market failure due to an externality or some restriction on trading.[8] In my text I am trying to include "failures of market outcomes" as an alternative reason for government intervention to supplement the standard market failure justification. By failure of market outcome I mean a case in which the market is doing everything it is supposed to be doing, but society is still unhappy with the result.

I am pushing for this change because I believe that by not explicitly addressing failures of market outcomes economists open themselves up to the complaint that we are unfairly advocating market solutions by not addressing issues where markets do not solve society's problems in a way that is acceptable to most people.

Including failures of market outcomes as a reason for government intervention allows one to include (1) the interplay of moral issues and efficiency; (2) questions of consumer sovereignty; and (3) questions of the interrelation between measures of efficiency and income distribution, which raise technical issues about drawing policy implications from our standard allocation theory in the discussion of policy. Each of these raises important questions about applying economic reasoning to policy issues that are usually not discussed in the standard economics textbook.

If we don't deal with such issues, we fail two different types of students. First, we lose the interest of the thoughtful students who recognize these issues and want some guidance in how such issues can be integrated into their policy thinking; these thoughtful students drop out of economics and go into ecology, philosophy, or sociology. Second, we make our less thoughtful students think that policy is easier than it is. They come out of the course thinking that policy is an easy task if only people listened to economists and understood economic theory.

As I discuss in that other paper, the recognition that there are failures of market outcomes is not novel with me. Good economists of all political persuasions recognize that the policy choices they make involve broader issues than are allowed within our current market failure framework. My point is that the current principles textbook standard encourages professors to avoid the issues by selectively choosing examples, and focusing policy discussions on issues that are consistent with the conventional moral view.

In Chapter 7 I discuss these issues and give three examples that can be discussed in this broader framework, and cannot be discussed in the narrower market failure framework. Let me consider one of these: how morals interplay with efficiency. An example would be a consideration of whether society should limit individuals selling babies if there is a willing supplier and a willing demander. All the standard arguments for non-intervention hold. Some people have a comparative advantage in producing babies, so to achieve efficiency, individuals should be allowed to specialize and trade, making both those who want babies but have a high cost of producing babies, and those who can produce and sell babies at a low cost, better off. You have a willing buyer, a willing seller, and a clear case of comparative advantage. Selling babies is efficient—in the normal way we interpret efficiency. Yet, most people, including most economists, would oppose such "efficient" solutions. The current standard presentation does not make it clear to students how one arrives at that opposition.

It is not only far-fetched ideas where the issue of morals may enter into policy discussions. It is also in more mundane issues. For example: whether it is appropriate to recycle. In discussing this issue the standard text argues that efficiency should rule. It suggests to students that not to accept the "efficient" solution is to impose their own normative view on the issue, whereas the economic solution avoids making any moral judgment, and hence avoids imposing its normative views.

But avoiding moral judgments is impossible. All policy discussions must begin with Hume's Dictum—that a "should" only follows from another "should." To come to policy implications of theory one must specify one's goal. Efficiency is not desirable for its own sake, but instead involves achieving an outside-specified goal as cheaply as possible. Only after we have specified what the goals are can we talk about efficiency in achieving them.

Another issue that I think needs more careful discussion than the standard text provides is the subtlest type of failure of market outcome with which economics must deal. That issue is that consumer surplus measures are based on the existing distribution of income. Let me discuss one example of how the problem manifests itself. In the standard textbook presentation there would be little consumer surplus to be gained from supplying AIDs drug cocktails to Africans since there is little demand for the drug as measured by consumer surplus. (If you don't have income you can't have a demand for the good.) It follows that the "efficient" solution to the AIDS problem in poor African countries is that the poor should die since in our current textbook supply/demand market failure framework it would be "inefficient" to supply the medicine to them. The standard textbooks don't make the argument in favor of such an "efficient solution" in medicinal drugs because they know that the result would be unacceptable to most students and teachers. But in not making it, they miss the opportunity to show students the more general limitations of a policy that focuses on efficiency and on policies designed to maximize consumer surplus.

As I stated above, none of these issues I raise here is a deep insight of mine; they are well known and many professors present them in their classes in various ways. My point is that the standard text presentation does not raise these issues, and I believe that it should. So I am willing to spend some of my 15% flexibility on pushing for the change. I am hoping that other books will follow my lead and that the standard will change. But I have learned. I present my alternative failure of market outcome approach in three pages in a chapter that can be skipped, so as not to violate the 15% rule. It's there for those who want to teach it, but it's unobtrusive enough to be avoided by those who do not. The reviews on it to date are mixed—some rave about it, others can tolerate it. Future reviews will determine whether it stays. I am happy to say that in the review that matters most to publishers, sales, my book is doing well; sales are up from the previous edition. If they remain up, I expect that other texts will look at this presentation and consider adopting it as an alternative standard.

Conclusion

The process I am describing is not unique to me. I suspect that all textbook authors recognize the nature of the process and choose different places to spend their 15% flexibility. Sometimes they are successful; sometimes they're not, and over time the texts evolve.

So what does all this mean for the user of a text? It means that a text is not a direct expression of what the author believes, but instead is a combination of a much more complicated set of considerations in which inertia and process, not intellectual or even pedagogical validity, play central roles. Perhaps it can be no other way, but users of the books should be aware that that's what principles of economics textbooks are, and should structure their teaching and learning accordingly, adding context to the discussion whenever possible. In reading textbooks, the parallel to caveat emptor is caveat lector.

Notes

1. There are, of course, exceptions, but any exception must reflect changes that are occurring in graduate school, and must be accompanied by a major marketing campaign. Greg Mankiw's introductory book is the best example of an exception to the 15% rule.
2. The degree to which authors are subjected to meeting this reviewing process depends on the author; the general rule is: the better known the author the less he or she is made to adjust to this reviewing process.
3. One need not feel too badly for them; usually, assuming they deliver a manuscript, they are not required to return the advance, even though often contractually they are required to do so if they do not submit an "acceptable" manuscript.
4. The changes I have introduced in my principles of economics book would not have been made were it not for a subgroup of anonymous reviewers who strongly advocated the changes I was making.
5. I also am the author of a social science text that covers all the social sciences and which is now in its 12th edition (Hunt and Colander 2005). With this social science book the reviews are generally more positive on my discussions of the social sciences where I am not

a specialist, and have used texts in the various social sciences as the basis of the presentation, than they are of my discussions of economics, where I do consider myself a specialist.

6. My publishers tell me that most professors flip through a text and come to a quick decision based on that quick perusal.
7. At least I hadn't seen it in any other books when I wrote my book.
8. Actual intervention requires taking government failure into account as well.

3

*The Art of Teaching Economics**

Most academic economists are simultaneously teachers and researchers, although they often consider themselves one or the other first. Those who consider themselves researchers first tend to think of teaching as a necessary annoyance, and research on economics education as not real economic research. I strongly disagree with that view and in my work on the profession I have chided those who consider themselves primarily researchers, arguing that they should take teaching more seriously. This chapter is directed toward a different group of economists—those economists who consider themselves teachers first, but who maintain a research agenda by doing research related to economics education, those economists who read and contribute to economics education journals.

The chapter is based on my observations at, and discussions with attendees at, numerous teaching conferences, which, because I have an economics textbook, and a strong interest in teaching economics, I attend regularly. At these conferences much of the research presented is on delivery rather than content, and various "new approaches" to teaching, such as active learning, the new paradigm of teaching, and cooperative learning, are put forward and discussed. While I agree with much of what is said in these conferences, I cannot help coming away from them with a word of caution; the purpose of this chapter is to explain the reasoning behind that word of caution.

That word of caution is to remind those of us concerned with teaching not to fall into what might be called the "education school dilemma." Ultimately content, not delivery, determines whether one is or is not a good teacher. No matter how well you deliver it, if you do not have something to say, you are not going to be a good teacher. In thinking about this issue I remember a quotation that Joseph Lowman included

* For helpful comments on earlier versions of this paper I would like to thank my colleagues, referees, attendees at the Teaching Economics Session at the Canadian Economics Association, and attendees of the University of Richmond Teaching Workshop and the University of Kentucky Teaching Workshop where earlier versions of this chapter were presented as the keynote address.

in his essay, "What Constitutes Masterful Teaching?" It was: "What all the great teachers appear to have in common is love of their subject, an obvious satisfaction in arousing this love in their students, and an ability to convince them that what they are being taught is deadly serious" (Lowman, 1984). When I think back to teachers with great delivery and lousy content and those with great content and lousy delivery, it is the ones with content that I remember—the ones who convinced me that what they were doing was important. John Rawls, William Vickrey, and Edmund Phelps all had horrendous delivery, but had great content, and changed my life.

Where I think the U.S. educational system has gone off the deep end with delivery is in high school teacher education. There, until a recent backlash, the educational focus was so strongly focused on technology and delivery that it lost contact with content. In some education schools, you did not need to major in math to teach math, but you had to study a whole variety of teaching methods courses. And in the United States you do not need to have taken economics in college to teach economics, even supposedly college level AP economics, although you do need to have taken a combination of teaching methods courses.

We have not, as yet, fallen into that problem in college teaching. However, the focus on teaching methods rather than on content is pushing us in that direction, and that research focus on methods makes it easier for other economists to dismiss research on economics education, and not see it as an integral part of general economic research. So I reiterate: in my view the content of what we teach is absolutely central to what we are doing, and we should not lose sight of that as we do research on economics education, and as we write about the technology of teaching. I am a reasonably good teacher not because I have good delivery; I do not. But I am a reasonably good teacher because I have a love of economics, and a strong belief that students will be much better off studying economics, and learning the lessons economics provides, than they will be studying a wide variety of other subjects.

I am a consumer, not a producer, of the literature on educational technology and delivery, which encompasses much of the research on teaching methods. My main area of research in economics is on how we translate the latest advancements in economic thinking into digestible discussions and models that students can understand. Thus, I spend much of my time thinking about what I call "content" issues of teaching—Does the AD curve say what we want it to say? Is our treatment of sunk costs and fixed costs consistent? How do we relate the models we teach to policy issues? What is the appropriate degree of uncertainty about policy to convey to students in the models we teach? In short, for me, the key teaching issues are: What is the content of what we are teaching; what role does that content serve; and should the content be changed?"

The New Paradigm in Teaching

To give you an idea of what I mean by an over-focus on delivery, consider Table 1, which is adapted from an article on the "new paradigm of teaching." (Smith and Waller, 1997; the first, second, and fourth columns are from their table). In that article the authors contrast the new and old paradigms of teaching. While there are a number of variations of this new paradigm, the version they present is consistent with the views I usually take away with me as the lessons being advocated at teaching conferences.

My problem with this new paradigm is primarily one of emphasis. My view is that as long as the new approaches are seen as spice, they're nice, but when the spice becomes the main course you've got problems. The main course in issues of teaching has to be content. Thus, in my view, while much of what Smith and Waller present as a new paradigm of teaching is nonobjectionable, there are some objectionable hidden, and not so hidden, agendas that show up in the discussion and application of the "new paradigm" and undermine the content issue.

To highlight my objections, in column 3 I add a third comparison— what I call the "common sense" approach. This common sense approach combines content and delivery issues; it is a synthesis of the approaches in columns 1 and 4, and is the approach that the silent majority of professors follows. The approach doesn't get much exposure precisely because it is the common sense approach; it is hardly worth writing about. All too often in the discussions of teaching methods, I see one side or another creating a straw professor, whom they can then thrash.

Let me now turn to a discussion of the various components of the new paradigm as set forth in Table 1.

Knowledge and Students

These new paradigm entries of first and second rows, labeled Knowledge and Students, are what I consider two "anti-content" components of the "new paradigm." If the professor has some content that is being taught, then knowledge is not being jointly constructed. A

Table 1: A Common Sense Approach to Teaching

	Old Paradigm	Common Sense Approach	New Paradigm
Knowledge	Transferred from faculty to students	Faculty leads students into a previous constructed knowledge while pointing out that it is not necessarily truth; emphasizes critical thinking	Jointly constructed by students and faculty
Students	Passive vessel to be filled by faculty's knowledge	Active vessel to be filled by faculty's knowledge, but still a vessel to be filled	Active constructor, discoverer and transformer of knowledge
Mode of Learning	Memorizing	A combination of learning terminology and relating	Relating
Faculty Purpose	Classify and sort students	Develop students' competencies and talents; inspire, force, connive ways to get them to learn	Develop students' competencies and talents
Student Goals	Students strive to complete requirements, achieve certification within a discipline	Students strive to complete requirements and achieve certification and maybe become interested in broader learning	Students strive to focus on continual lifelong learning within a broader system
Relationships	Impersonal relationship among students and between faculty and students	Respect by students for faculty; personal relationship among students and between faculty and within confines of the class	Personal transactions among students and between faculty and students
Context	Competitive/Individualist	Combination of cooperation and competition	Cooperative learning in classroom and cooperative teams among faculty
Climate	Conformity/cultural uniformity	Sufficient conformity to make the class work	Diversity and personal esteem/cultural diversity and commonality
Power	Faculty holds and exercises power, authority, and control	Faculty has the authority and power, but uses it with restraint and understanding	Students are empowered; power is shared among students and between students and faculty
Assessment	Norm-references (i.e. graded "on the curve"). Typically multiple choice items; students rating of instruction at end of course	Norm referenced grades, with clearly defined requirements. Teaching environment determines the type of exam used	Criterion-referenced; typically performances and portfolios; continual assessment of instructions
Ways of Knowing	Logico-Scientific	Uses the logico-scientific narrative, with acknowledgement of its limitations	Narrative
Epistemology	Reductionist; facts and memorization	Abductive, combination of inductive and deductive	Constructivist; inquiry and intervention
Technology Use	Drill and practice; textbook substitute; chalk and talk substitute	Class size and available technology determines the use of technology	Problem solving, communication, collaboration, information access, expression
Teaching Assumption	Any expert can teach	Content comes first; teaching comes second. An expert who cares can convey that to students	Teaching is complex and requires considerable training

The second and fourth columns are from Karl Smith and Alisha Waller, "Afterward: New Paradigms for College Teaching," in David Johnson, Roger Johnson, and Karl Smith, *Active Learning: Cooperation in the College Classroom*. The middle column is my synthesis of the two.

good teacher indoctrinates a student; the student and teacher are not on a joint voyage of discovery.

Where I think the new paradigm makes some sense in teaching economics is in how much truth we suggest the models that we teach have. I think we need to emphasize to the students more than we do that the central models we teach in economics are simply models—what I call "calisthenics of the mind." These models are useful in some instances, and not useful in others. The monopoly maximization model exemplifies what I mean by calisthenics of the mind. This model only loosely relates to reality and the decisions firms make. But learning it requires the student to use mental energy, and working through problems and exercises with it gives her or him a better grasp of the meaning and application of constrained maximization.

An example in macro of where I believe economists go wrong is in not discussing enough how potential income is an immeasurable concept, and how all models that use potential income as a knowable concept make macro policy look more certain than it actually is. An example in micro is the way we focus on diminishing marginal returns and upward sloping cost curves in our discussions of applications. That presentation goes way beyond what is believable and students need to be told that. They need to be shown how the reasoning process carries over into real-world situations where there are multiple margins, and diminishing returns are not central to the decision at hand.

Mode of Learning

The new paradigm sees faculty relating to students on a one-to-one personal level. I do not relate to many students on that level. Quite frankly, I do not think many 18-20 year olds are much into that type of relating with a nerdy middle-age economist such as myself. Good teaching has more to do with motivating than it does with relating. Much of the problem of teaching economics has to do with getting our students to exercise their minds, which, for most students, needs enormous calisthenics, just as my body does. To learn, some things just need to be done over and over again, and others need to be memorized.

For example, when Ptolemy I, the king of Egypt, wanted to learn geometry, Euclid told him that it would take long hours of study and memorization. When the king demanded a shortcut, Euclid responded, "There's no royal road to geometry." To that I would add, "there's no relating road to learning economics." Obviously, a professor should relate to the students as much as he or she can. Professors are not up above, and students down below. Students are people, and professors can and should talk to them as people. In my principles of economics book, I emphasize a conversational tone because it puts students at ease and helps them relate to economics, but I try to be careful not to replace teaching—in which the faculty is conveying to students a set of knowledge—with relating—in which both are exploring their feelings as they jointly construct knowledge.

I am not advocating teaching a lot of facts. We are teaching some facts, and we are teaching some general reasoning, writing, and computer skills, but in economics we are not teaching specific skills. This is explicit in a liberal arts college, such as the one where I teach, where we pride ourselves on teaching nothing of practical use for students. (It would be impossible to get a marketing course through the curriculum committee.) But to say that we should not be teaching facts or specific skills does not mean that we do not need to get students to learn specific skills and facts. I think that any discussion of teaching must take into account that most learning does not take place in class, or in students' reading of the texts. The key to getting students to learn is to get them to discuss economic issues together in bull sessions, to get them reading about the economy on their own. Much of my teaching strategy is designed to accomplish that.

For example, I assign *The Wall Street Journal* and each week I give my students a 5-minute quiz on the main ideas in the articles relevant to what I am teaching that week. These quizzes count for 10 percent of their grade. Thus, when I teach macro I have them following what is going on in Argentina, with the Fed, in Japan, with EU fiscal policy, or whatever relevant events are occurring that fit what we are talking about. Initially, they often do not know what is going on, or what the institutions are, in the articles they read, but by the end of the semester, almost by osmosis, they have picked up enormous amounts of terminology and institutional knowledge, without my teaching it at all. Generally, the discussions in the newspaper do not fit the textbook models. But that is because the textbook models make far too many assumptions about what is remaining constant. Students need to recognize that and become familiar with analyzing issues where everything is changing. But they also need to learn the specifics of the model, because without that, there are just too many things changing to even start to understand the issues.

I am not an especially good lecturer.[1] Despite this reality I am a reasonably good teacher, who succeeds because I get my students to learn—to teach themselves. The average workload in my principles course is over 10 hours per week outside of class, and attendance, because of the quizzes, is high. And, despite my lousy delivery, the students usually give me high evaluations because I convey to them that the content—the reasoning process—of what I am teaching them is important, even if it is not directly applicable.

Faculty Purpose and Student Goals

My views about faculty purpose and goals (rows 4 and 5) are similar to those views associated with the new paradigm, but I do not know many professors whose views are not. None of us like classifying and sorting students. That said, I think there are many types of students, and how one teaches has to fit the student body one has. We need to judge our teaching success by the value we have added, not by how much the student knows at the end of the course.

The new paradigm seems to make the assumption that the student is self-motivated—that he or she wants to learn, an assumption that seems to be shared by many attendees of teaching conferences with whom I speak. When you have students like that, it's wonderful. But, that's not most students, even at top schools. My perception, based on 30 years of teaching and discussions with both students and faculty, is that most students are in college not because they are deeply interested in gaining knowledge, but because they are interested in getting a sheet of paper that will allow them to do other things. In many ways the students are simply responding to real incentives; having the college degree credential is more important to their success than what they know. If holding that in front of them can motivate them to work harder, I say fine.

The mistaken belief of many professors that students are self-motivated occurs because there is a self-selection bias in who decides to become a teacher, and who focuses his or her research on teaching. "Good students" (and by that I mean those few self-motivated students who want to learn for learning's sake) are the ones most likely to decide to become teachers. Most students do not become teachers, and would not want to teach.

Much of the success in teaching involves motivation—motivating students to learn. The first thing I say when I go into my class is that I am not going to teach you anything, but I am going to do everything I can to get you to learn. And I structure my course to do that. To get students to read the chapter before the class, I give 5-minute quizzes to see if they have read the chapter. Before the quiz I allow questions, and often in those questions, most of the issues I would have raised in my class come up. The difference is that the issues arise in a dialog with students; they are not presented as a lecture.

To get students to focus on the discussion, I do not let students take notes. I tell them to put down the pen—that what I say is too important for them not to be focusing on it entirely, and when something is being covered that will be on the test, I tell them—now it's time to pick up the pen and put this down as a short note marked: important—going to be on the exam. When you are teaching from a textbook, notes are redundant. Read the executive summary at the end of the chapter, or the margin notes. The lecture has been already summarized for you. When you are not teaching from the text, notes are much more important, but in principles of economics, most of the teaching is from the text.

Relationships

While I do not believe that faculty should concentrate on having "personal transactions with students" I do believe that students learn better when they have a bond with faculty—where the students respect the faculty and the faculty respect the students. It works even better when the students feel able to question the professor's arguments, and discuss them together. Where I teach, it is just assumed that that is the case. It is when people are at universities, and are teaching because they have to, not because they want to, that there are problems with faculty availability and interaction with students. That problem, however, does not describe professors who attend sessions on teaching at economics conferences, or who read journals devoted to the teaching of economics.

Context, Climate, and Power

The new paradigm pushes cooperative learning (rows 7, 8, and 9), and I am all for it. But I am also an economist and one of the lessons I have learned from economics is that cooperation can only take us so far, and that successful institutions have developed that put individuals in competition with others. Now, I think that the standard economics presented in the texts often pushes the benefits of competition too far—

greed is not good; Adam Smith was very clear about that. It is why he wrote the *Theory of Moral Sentiments* before he wrote *The Wealth of Nations*, and the lessons in *The Wealth of Nations* can only be understood in the context of the *Theory of Moral Sentiments*. The new work on evolutionary game theory is finally getting that into the core of economics. The reality is that good economic institutions, and good educational approaches, find the right mix of cooperation and competition. Ultimately, the teacher is not a student's buddy; he or she is their teacher. Student self esteem comes from learning what the teacher has to convey to the student, and showing the teacher that he or she can jump the hurdles the teacher has set up, not because the teacher has empowered the student.

Assessment

Assessment is something that depends on the structure of the course. Where I teach, we have small classes, and do not give multiple-choice tests. With three or four classes of seventy students each, multiple-choice tests can be a necessity; portfolios, and even short essay tests, are out of the question.

Grading is another key element of the new paradigm where I part company with the new paradigm. In the new paradigm grading on a curve is wrong, because it puts students in competition with other students rather than bringing out cooperation. I grade with a curve—not a precise one, but a loose one, where exact numbers do not mean anything. My students do not need a 95 percent on a test to get an A. Often 50 percent can be an A. I would go further than that and argue that we are doing our students a disservice when we do not grade on a curve, because, by using a 95 percent standard, we instill in them a belief that in order to know a subject they have to know much more than is possible to know.

Economists know only a small amount of what there is to know about the economy. To require students to get 95 percent of what we ask them right is to ask for far more than what we as economists deliver. Economists are lucky if we beat the averages. In economics we are not teaching a well-defined set of knowledge, and our grading procedures should acknowledge that. We are teaching an approach to looking at issues. Unfortunately, the content of the models we teach often conveys to students that issues are more clear-cut than they are.[2]

Assessing students in a way that encourages them to think that they can know 95 percent of the material being presented suggests to me that the material being presented is not the right material. It suggests a serious problem of content of what we teach. We need to teach students how to approach problems with a combination of imagination and rigor, and often there are three or four approaches that are reasonable. Our exams and our grading should reflect that need. But that often is not the case.

In a way there is a parallel of grading with content. The models that we teach focus on decision making in a rich information environment—where 95 percent knowledge, or even 100 percent knowledge—is necessary to make the correct choice. That is not the way the world works, and is what constitutes my biggest complaint with the content of what we teach, which is why I am focusing much of my recent writing on complexity and the teaching of economics. My argument is that the model of policy that we teach students—the economics of control model— is the wrong model, what we should be teaching students is an "economics of muddling through" model.

We, as economists, understand only about 20 percent about the economy. Business people often understand only 10 percent of a problem before they make a decision. I want students to come out of my class feeling comfortable making decisions with far less than perfect knowledge, to be as comfortable as possible with understanding only a small part of a complex issue, and recognizing that success generally depends not on fully understanding an issue, but on understanding it better than the next person. What I am teaching is how Marshall saw economics: not as a body of concrete truth, but an engine for the discovery of concrete truth, and my assessment tools reflect the lessons I am trying to teach.

Ways of Knowing and Epistemology

For me the new paradigm presents a false dichotomy between ways of knowing and epistemology. (rows 11 and 12) In my view what the new paradigm calls "logico-scientific" cannot be contrasted with narrative; "logico-scientific" is simply the narrative upon which economics is built. Research in economics is designed to improve that narrative. I agree that there are problems with our narrative, and my research on the profession has been meant to highlight the problems I see with the narrative we teach.

All knowledge is integrated into a rhetoric. What we teach is not the truth, but simply the approach we use. (McCloskey 1985, 1994) We should teach students that; we can justify the approach by pointing out that ours is an approach that has been useful to others in the past, but that is a quite different justification than teaching students that it is the truth.[3]

I have a very pragmatic view of what we, as economics professors, are supposed to be doing. In my view the economics major is designed to produce "general information processors"—students who, when they graduate, will be able to process general information and come to reasonable conclusions. This requires students learning to organize issues into more and less relevant categories, and to integrate quantitative and qualitative analysis into a decision. To do that they need to know the logico-scientific narrative, but they also need to know that it is a narrative.

To do that we teach a set of exercises and concepts that society has found it useful for these general information processors to have worked through. In my view those exercises are not perfect for achieving the desired end, but they do instill in our majors an approach to processing information that is not instilled by other majors. Our outputs—our graduates—are viewed favorably by businesses and organizations that hire our students, and thus, despite my critical view of what we are teaching, I caution care in changing it.[4]

Technology Use

The teaching of economics is evolving on many fronts, both in terms of content and delivery technology. All teachers face severe constrained optimization problems: Which front should they keep up with? For me keeping up with the changing content in economics is more than a full-time job. The approach I use is to try to keep up with changing content, and to wait until the information technology department has simplified the technology so much that I can use it with little effort. The appropriate tradeoff depends on class size, one's technology quotient, and the effectiveness of the college's or university's information technology department. In my view, the error in the uncertain optimization should be made on the side of keeping up with changing content, not technology. Failure to keep up with changing content will undermine one's effectiveness as a teacher, regardless of one's knowledge of changing technology.

Once a delivery system has been developed so that it can be used with little effort, then adopt it. Currently, assignments and basic information can be made easily available to students on the web, or in class folders on the college server, and communication with students by e-mail has become essential. These delivery systems have progressed to where they are user friendly. Whether a teacher's web content is Flash compatible or includes multimedia is less of a concern.

Teaching Assumption

The contrast between the old paradigm, "any expert can teach," and the new paradigm, "teaching is complex and requires considerable training" (row 14) is too sharp for my tastes. Teaching is complex, but it is an art, and like most arts, is, in many ways, too complex to teach. Some discussions of teaching are important, as is conveying to faculty the need to be concerned about his or her teaching. But beyond that, I suspect that there are highly diminishing returns to studying teaching and teaching methods. Obviously, teaching is complex and "any expert" in content cannot do it; however the position I hold is that students are very forgiving. With some concern about their students, a good economist with solid content can survive in the classroom, and convey the excitement of economics to the students. The opposite is not true; an economist without good content will not be a good teacher; such economists might get good teaching evaluations, but they will not be good teachers. To be a good teacher one must have something to teach, which is why I believe content comes first.

Conclusion

Content is important: journals of economic education, and economists interested in research in economics education, should spend more time researching how we can translate the latest developments in economics—evolutionary game theory, complexity theory, non-linear dynamics, and psychological foundations of economics—into teachable concepts, than on looking into the delivery of teaching and teaching technology. I would rather see the majority of teachers of economics spending their time keeping up with the changing *content* of economics rather than with the changing *technology* in the delivery of knowledge to individuals.[5]

Stark contrasts between new and old paradigms inevitably portray one or the other side as more strident in its views than supporters of that approach actually are. There is a common-sense approach to teaching that maintains a middle ground between the old and the new paradigm, and which most professors would be comfortable with as an ideal, even though in practice it may not be achievable. This middle ground is consistent with an active learning approach, but does not make a fetish of it. It sees the professor as the authority, not a joint constructor of knowledge, but it sees him or her using that authority with restraint and understanding, and conveying the limits of our knowledge as well as its strengths. It teaches the "logico-scientific" method as narrative, not as truth. It takes the user-friendly technology that is available, rather than trying to be on the leading edge of technology. It accepts that competition is part of the system, and uses teaching methods that combine competition with cooperation to motivate students.

I would not push my points in this chapter too far. Any "common sense" synthesis is probably consistent with what the holders of both sides of the synthesis felt that they were really purveying, and that the reader has misinterpreted them. And they are probably right. The problem is that the holders of the different views often do not interact, and that lack of interaction fosters such misinterpretation. It is my hope that this chapter will help in reducing those misinterpretations and misunderstandings, and move the debate in economics education journals more toward content.

Notes

1. When my youngest son was 11 he attended one of my major lectures and asked me: "Dad, do you have to put so many ah's in your lectures, and could you please finish all your sentences?" It was devastating.
2. For a curve to work, it must have a wide spread, and the students must know how it was constructed and that it was not arbitrary. The spread of grades in my classes is large. In the principles course I most recently taught, the grades normed to a 100-point scale ranged from 27 to 78 with the grades spread over that range. A grade above 72 was an A, and any grade over 40 was passing.
3. I agree that in economists' "logical-scientific" rhetoric, statistical significance is often misused, and various sources of gathering knowledge are not given appropriate weight in economic analysis. (McCloskey and Ziliak 1996) We should pass that information on to students, but in doing so we should not lose sight that we are teaching them that "logico-scientific" narrative.
4. My critique is that the current content of the economics curriculum provides students with too little practice in operating in an information-poor environment, because (1) it concentrates too much on teaching about decision makers in information-rich environments, and (2) the testing of knowledge concentrates too much on having full information about a specific set of issues, and not enough on the use of economic reasoning as an engine for discovery. Whenever possible in my text, in my teaching, and in my teaching methods, I attempt to switch the focus to practice on information-poor environments. But to say that is not to say that the exercises we teach are not highly valuable and more than justify the principles course.
5. In Colander, Holt, and Rosser (2004) we discuss the changing content of economics.

4

Thinking Like an Economist:
A Consideration of the Economics Major in
American Higher Education

In 1991 a commission on economics education was set up to consider
the economics major (Siegfried et al. 1991) and to write a report on the
economics major. The authors of that report were teachers in the true
sense of the word. The ideal economics program they described, and
the proposals they made, were highly compatible with what most
economics departments at liberal arts schools attempt to do. Because I
teach at a liberal arts college, it should not be surprising that I generally
support the proposals and the sensibilities embodied in the report. Had
I been on the Association of American Colleges Commission, I would
have signed on.

But, I was not on the commission, which leaves me free to complain
about where it leaned too far in one direction or another, or took a
commission's way out and avoided or papered over a difficult issue. This
essay is my complaint.

Thinking Like an Economist

The report's central theme—the purpose of the economics major is
to teach the student to think like an economist—is a wonderful goal for
a commission report. It is superficially satisfying and politically neat,
because every economist's interpretation of thinking like an economist
is that it means the way the economist himself or herself thinks. The
desire to get young minds to think like oneself is, I suspect, the reason
most of us went into teaching in the first place; it is a goal about which
few will object. It is a perfect commission goal.

I can agree with the report because, as I interpret it, it implicitly
assumes an economist's thinking process that is very much like the
thinking process I picture as mine—one that stresses creativity, deals
with fuzzy problems, structures questions, asks tough questions, and, in
short, uses economic analysis but simultaneously recognizes the limitations
of economic analysis.

Perhaps in some far-off time my interpretation of the commission's implicit assumption of what thinking like an economist means fit, or will fit, reality. But I do not think it fits now. So my fundamental problem with the report is that it does not sufficiently address the question: Do economists think the way the commission implicitly assumes they do? I contend that many do not. How could they, when the skills the commission advocates are not taught in graduate school?

The current structure of graduate education weeds out, in the first two years, many of the individuals who have such skills. They go off into business where they can make a lot more and be more appreciated. Because it is difficult to teach something you have not learned, the issues of graduate education and undergraduate education are closely related. Structural reforms of undergraduate education will not work, and will not be undertaken even if they would work, unless graduate education in economics is reformed.

Given the current structure of graduate education, thinking like an economist requires an uncritical mind that accepts far-out assumptions without questioning; does not ask, what's the purpose of what I'm doing?; leads the student to do what the current institutionally structured incentives guide him or her to do; and requires the use of formal empirical techniques to address questions that those techniques cannot answer.[1] In short, graduate schools are creating economists who, having little or no experience in dealing with real-world problems, uncritically accept models and do not worry about the intuition behind those models. These graduate students become the undergraduate teachers of the future.

The commission's choice of the goal, thinking like an economist, allows its report to avoid the politically difficult discussion of whether economists teach undergraduates what the commission wants taught. It allows the commission to talk about the positive things we want to do in undergraduate education. The reality is that what is taught in undergraduate economics, and how it is taught, is intricately tied up with what is taught in graduate school and what the profession does. You can ask someone to teach critical thought, how to frame questions, and how to apply economics to reality. But you will not succeed when what the teachers learn in graduate school is how to solve explicit problem sets and how to structure formal proofs. Similarly, you will not succeed in getting someone to teach undergraduate economics the way the report proposes when the incentives for research are to do something quite different. People have a strong incentive to teach what they learned in graduate school and what they are researching. As long as the goals desired for undergraduates are not the goals that the professors are taught and are striving for in their research, those goals will not be taught. Thus, I am far less sanguine about the prospects for improving teaching of undergraduates than is the commission report. Specifically, I do not think the reforms the commission suggests will significantly affect what is taught, or how it is taught. I am not against the reforms; I simply do not see them having much effect. To be effective, reforms must confront much more fundamental issues.

Let me give an example of where I believe the nature of the profession will undermine the commission's recommendations. The commission suggests that departments take control of intermediate courses and determine their content and urges more use be made of outside examiners. How easy will it be to find outside examiners who share the commission's sensibilities and goals? Or, even if the department shares those goals, to find one that will collectively put in the time to achieve those goals? Given the current reality, I believe that those reforms would not work the way the commission hopes they will but will lead to more formalism and focus on technique. Economics is primarily embodied in the activities and ways of thinking of current practitioners, not in the structure of the courses or the examination of those courses.

Let me now turn to a specific example where I believe the report implicitly accepts activities that, I am convinced, work against the commission's goal of getting students to think the way the commission wants economists to think— the use of models by economists.

A natural manifestation of the focus on technique is that, all too often, economists accept models uncritically. That is what they are taught to do in graduate school. Although the report, in places, tends to agree with me, in other places it implicitly accepts the uncritical use and testing of models and theories that have become commonplace in economics. For example, the report suggests that thinking like an economist involves "using chains of deductive reasoning in conjunction with simplified models, and testing alternative hypotheses" (Siegfried et al. 1991, 199). This definition and similar discussions in the report take the position that models are accepted on the basis of empirical evidence. The commission states:

Understanding economic relationships is the central goal. This involves formulating hypotheses to explain these relationships, constructing models that capture their essential features, assembling empirical observations bearing on these relationships, and testing the hypotheses using quantitative techniques. Such testing not only increases the understanding of economic phenomena but also promotes ever more effective predictions of the consequences of changes in our evolving world. (ibid, 200)

The Commission then modifies that statement by saying:

In essence this form of scientific method is used in many disciplines, but economists usually must conduct their hypothesis tests without the luxury of controlled experiments. (ibid, 200)

This general discussion is unobjectionable, but it leaves the impression that all models must in some way be testable by quantitative techniques. That is not true, yet I believe most economists believe it to be true.

To avoid such an impression, the commission report would have had to expand significantly on this modification. It could have stated:

Many models used in economics are not formally testable, and thus they must be chosen on the basis of judgment and knowledge of the economy. For this reason, common sense and a good working knowledge of economic institutions and of the highest level of theory are essential skills for any economist. The level of economics that undergraduate students learn is not, and cannot be, based on a technical understanding of a formal model that exists independently of a knowledge of the workings of the economy.

This modification would have made it clear that theories that are not formally testable still have a role in economics. If economists accepted that proposition, they would be far less inclined to test what is untestable and to draw more from the data than can be drawn.

Let me consider briefly alternative roles for nontestable theories. I call one such role the hurdle-role. Analyzing models and drawing logical relationships from models is a useful exercise even if the models have no direct relevance to anything. Many of the models that undergraduates learn serve this purpose; they should not be tested against reality because they do not fit reality. They still should be learned. Logical thinking develops with practice; modeling and working with theory can vivify that development. Dealing with ambiguous, dialectical concepts is a much more complicated task than is dealing with neat formal mathematical models. That is why it makes sense to start students out with formal models. If a student cannot deal with formal models, there is no way that student is going to be able to deal effectively with the far more difficult, hazy reality with which real-world economics must deal.

The student should not be misled into believing that understanding models that serve a hurdle function is anything more than what it is—the equivalent to doing calisthenics—or that models that serve a hurdle-role are relevant to reality in any way other than the broadest sense. In fact, it is often best that the models do not relate to reality, so that the student's logical facilities, not knowledge of the economy, can be exercised. Models of fictitious economies help students understand modeling better than models of the real world do. Robinson Crusoe has a role in economics.

Because the commission report does not specify this hurdle function of models, the report can be interpreted as a call to apply existing models to reality. It is far better to talk about make-believe worlds of widgets and wadgets than to talk about the computer industry as if it were a perfectly competitive market.

Hurdle-role models should not be tested formally, or directly applied to reality. Yet in many introductory and intermediate textbooks, because the hurdle function of models is never explicitly stated, continual attempts are made to apply such models to reality. Books that pretend to discuss the real world using models that do not fit the real world are doing students a disservice. For example, in the monopoly and the monopolistic competitive models, firms set marginal costs equal to marginal revenue to determine output and price. These models serve a very useful hurdle function but do not describe how real-world firms classified as monopolists or monopolistic competitors set price or quantity. These models are also untestable, but they are still useful in getting students to understand constrained optimization. But students should also be taught that real-world constrained optimization is much more complicated than is described by these models and that these models cannot be directly applied to reality. Often students are not told that.

A second example is the short-run production analysis based upon diminishing marginal returns. The standard model of the firm we teach serves a wonderful hurdle function, but it is almost irrelevant to the real world of sequential decision-making in a dynamic context with multiple margins and large numbers of nonconvexities. And yet, in an attempt to pretend relevance, textbooks apply the standard models to reality. These attempts at relevance start a consistent pattern of separating common sense from modeling. Those students who have common sense find that they do not do well on exams and drop out of economics because it is intellectually unsatisfying.

The Pretence of Relevance

If economics is to be more relevant, much of the current pretence of relevance of what we teach at the undergraduate level must be removed. To have helped in that process, the commission report should have put much more emphasis on the argument that hurdle models (which include most of the models taught in introductory and intermediate microeconomics and macroeconomics) should be taught but should not be formally applied to analyzing observable reality, just as models of Newtonian physics should not be applied to understanding movements of atomic particles. Economic reality is extraordinarily complicated, and students should not be led to believe that it can be described solely by any of the neat, simple abstract models that exist in undergraduate textbooks. But they are led to believe that, even at good liberal arts schools.

Ask good students how real-world firms set output and prices of goods, and they will say, "Firms will equate marginal revenue and marginal cost." Even the simplest real-world firms consider 8 or 10 interrelated margins. Even if real-world firms wanted to apply this multiple-margin prescription to reality, they cannot. Even if the firm is using the most advanced cost accounting procedures that currently exist and has the latest computer on which to do the calculations, the necessary information for implementing this prescription is too costly to collect. That is why real-world firms set prices by rules of thumb that have some loose relationship to the simple monopoly model but are not directly related to it.

As another example, ask good students the questions: "Why do real-world short-run marginal cost curves slope upward?" and "What will happen to average costs if a firm increases production?" To the first question, they will say, "Because of diminishing marginal returns." To the second question, they will say, "Average costs will tend to increase as output is increased." In both cases, the students will also be wrong.

Empirically, diminishing marginal returns are not a big element in many firms' considerations, because those considerations are for periods in which all the relevant inputs are somewhat variable and the nonvariable inputs were chosen so as not to impose a constraint on production. Those diminishing returns that do exist are overwhelmed by nonconvexities of the production process and indivisible inputs. For those same reasons, most firms' average total costs fall as output increases. These observations do not imply that the standard model is wrong; only that its assumptions do not fit reality. I am not arguing that the standard model of the firm serves no purpose; it serves a very useful hurdle function. What I am arguing is that the standard model of production does not directly relate to modern production.

To motivate people to do the kind of calisthenics that are necessary for a sport, one must at times give them a sense of fun—of playing the sport for which they are training. That, I believe, is why so many attempts are made to apply the undergraduate model to reality. Unfortunately, we have done it so much that we have lost sight of the object of the real sport—to understand a reality that exists, not to see how many innovative ways we can make reality fit a model known not to include many of the relevant factors that shape that reality.

Undergraduate economics education is primarily the equivalent of physical conditioning; yet textbooks so often pretend that conditioning is the sport and that students never progress beyond the contrived game that textbooks have made out of what should be conditioning. Real-world applications of specific current undergraduate models should be seen as a pleasant diversion necessary to keep students interested, not as the goal of what is taught. While the general implications of the models have enormous relevance, and should be discussed constantly (I have my students read the *Wall Street Journal* and I spend part of each lecture explaining where general economics principles shed light on what is happening in the economy.) actually applying the models we teach is usually impossible. Reality is full of color and multidimensional; our textbook models are black and white and two dimensional.

The hurdle-role is not the only nontestable role that a model can play. A second nontestable role that many models in economics play is the role of logical organizer. To talk about reality, one must organize one's thoughts about that reality. Models, even models that are not testable, serve that purpose.

Good examples of models that serve such roles are the supply and demand model and the Keynesian model. The supply and demand model cannot be formally tested. That does not make it a bad model; it serves an important role in helping to organize one's thoughts about reality logically, and in placing in perspective a whole set of real-world phenomena. What is testable are third- or fourth-hand logical derivatives of that model that are based on many additional assumptions. Failure of these empirical tests will not, and should not, lead to giving up our core supply and demand theory; at most, it will lead to giving up the peripheral assumptions. Supply and demand theory is a metaphysical theory that allows structured thought; it is not a formally testable theory. The relevant empirical question is not how much does reality conform to supply and demand theory; rather it is how much, and in what ways, does reality differ from the supply and demand model.

How many students would answer that the role of supply and demand theory is to supply a logical organization to one's thoughts? I believe not many. Unless students are taught that metaphysical theories are allowable, they will believe that all theories must be testable.

Bringing the Models to the Data

The same argument about formal testability can be made for many of the concepts in economics. The Keynesian model is not a formally testable model. It is a model that, at best, structures some general relationships in unknown time periods and presents relationships that influence the direction of the aggregate economy. Or alternatively, consider the concept of elasticity of demand. Empirical estimates of the elasticity of demand are included in every micro textbook I know, including mine.

No textbook that I know of gives students a sense of how arbitrary the estimates of these elasticities are. Yes, most books include discussions of how the elasticity of demand increases over time, and some include both a long-run and short-run elasticity of demand. They do not, however, relate that discussion to the dynamics of price adjustment over time and the limitations of comparative static supply and demand analysis. If it is true that the elasticity of demand increases with the length of the time period being considered, what is meant by elasticity of demand with no time specified? An elasticity exists only for a specific period of time and for very explicit assumptions about expectations. But no undergraduate textbook discusses the time periods over which elasticity of demand estimates are measured, or discusses the structure of the expectations they are assuming. Yet without this information, the elasticity estimates are of little practical use.

The econometric techniques necessary to properly measure a changing elasticity based upon explicit assumptions about expectations are extraordinarily complicated and beyond what can be discussed at the undergraduate level. Yet undergraduate students are taught that one should empirically measure elasticity with undergraduate statistical techniques. They measure it, and when they get a significant result with the right sign, they think they have measured elasticity. For example, a senior thesis student in our department had worked for an oil tank production company, and, for his senior paper, he decided to measure elasticity of demand for oil tanks. He began his thesis by explaining that there was an enormous shortage of oil tanks and that there was a six-to-nine-month wait for an oil-tank order to be delivered. He then took the price and production data and estimated a demand curve based on the number of oil tanks sold. He came up with a correct sign, and the estimate was significant at the 1 percent level. When I asked him how his earlier discussion of disequilibrium related to his empirical estimate, he was at a loss. An implicit assumption of almost all undergraduate econometric work is that the market is in some type of comparative static equilibrium, even though there are strong arguments that real-world markets are in various states of disequilibrium much of the time. As should have been apparent to my student from his initial discussion, the equilibrium model did not apply. He was measuring garbage—and finding it significant.

My student's failing was simply a blatant example of what economists do all the time. As Leamer (1983, 1988) and Basmann (1990) point out, many empirical economists do not really do useful empirical work at all. They go through the motions and come up with formally impressive results, which are convincing to nonspecialists but which have not estimated or tested what the economists say they are estimating or have tested.[2]

It would be far more honest if undergraduate students were taught that with the techniques available to them, elasticities are formally unmeasurable. Then, they could be taught ways of informally intuiting what the elasticity of demand is and how to make a rough check of that intuition, using the computer to manipulate numbers. There is nothing wrong with data-mining, as long as one recognizes what one is doing.

By emphasizing these alternative roles of theories I am trying to put economic theory in proper perspective. For students to respect the power of formal empirical testing, they must understand the limitations of those tests, as well as the limitations of the theories that are being tested. I would suggest that early in every economics course a variation of the law of significant digits should be taught. The law states that one should round off all numbers to the level of the least significant digit because the result can be no more accurate than that. The variation of the law states that when the concepts one is dealing with are vague, and thus themselves approximations, as is the concept of elasticity, formal empirical testing is not possible.

My comments about these models are not meant to demean those models or to demean formal empirical testing. They are meant to strengthen the underlying foundation of both. By carefully specifying the limitations of the model and the difficulties of testing the versions of the model that can be presented at the undergraduate level, the instructor can foster students' respect for the model and for meaningful formal empirical testing. Students can thus be shown the state of knowledge as it is, not some idealized version of what cannot be.

Conclusion

The above discussion has been, I suspect, highly controversial and slightly irritating to many economists. The commission report was, by comparison, relatively uncontroversial and soothing to most economists. My tendency to be irritating is, I suspect, why I am not on many commissions. But in this case of the economics undergraduate major, I think irritation is what is needed. The problems of the economics major are much more deeply rooted in the practices of the profession than the report lets on, and unless a discussion of those problems is accompanied by a severe irritation, only superficial reforms will be made. Had I been on the commission I would have pushed for a more irritating report that placed the problems of economics in perspective. I doubt whether I would have succeeded. Commissions do not arrive at irritating reports.

I could go on about other areas of the report about which I disagree, but doing so would convey a sense of the report quite different than the sense I actually have. As I said, had I been a member of the commission I would have signed on. Like real-world firms, commissions have extraordinarily complicated objective functions and constraints that govern and shape the final report. This report reads like a report written by economists who have a mission similar to mine but who better recognize the political realities, and maximized subject to what might be called "commission constraint." Given that constraint, it is a solid report.

Notes

1. This essay was written in 1991; since then my assessment of what is taught in graduate education has improved somewhat but my view is that it is still far from desirable. See Colander (2005b).
2. I am happy to say that empirical work in economics has improved significantly since this paper was first written.

5

A Capstone Course in Economics: To What, and For Whom? *

Capstone courses are currently popular in the economics educational community. A capstone course is generally designed as a culminating research experience in which self-motivated students integrate, apply, and extend the body of knowledge gained in the major. In thinking about the capstone course, it is helpful to think about the capstone metaphor. The metaphor comes from architecture where a capstone is the stone placed on a set of pillars, tying the pillars together. The capstone course is thus designed to be the "crowning achievement"—the course that connects the pillars of the undergraduate major.

This paper offers some words of caution to those economics departments thinking of a mandatory capstone course, especially those in a liberal arts setting without a business program. It highlights some of the problems that are likely to arise with a single, mandatory capstone course and suggests that economics departments should worry more about providing pillars, not capstones, for the majority of students.

Problems with a Capstone Course

Capstone courses are problematic for three reasons. First, it is not clear that a mandatory capstone course is appropriate in any discipline. Educators have a tendency to picture students as they themselves are—highly motivated, thirsting for knowledge, mature enough to recognize the pleasures of independent research, and recognizing that a future in academia, even at lower pay, is the path to self-fulfillment. Most students are not like that; most students see college as a stepping-stone to a job they want, or to a better future generally. They see a college degree as a union card—one that allows them access to a better set of jobs. They do not see themselves as scholars now or in the future. These students are not open to a capstone course because it requires more independent research and thinking than they are willing to do; in their minds, the

* This essay was written jointly with Jessica Holmes for a presentation at the Southern Economic Association Meetings. We would like to thank Gail Hoyt and participants at those meetings for helpful comments on an earlier draft.

intellectual costs of completing a capstone course exceed the intellectual benefits.[1] Capstone courses are most appropriate for young future scholars, which is not the vast majority of our students.

It is particularly difficult to justify a capstone course in a liberal arts setting. Students at liberal arts institutions are learning to be general information processors, not specific information processors. Their major generally makes up about one third of their courses, and, if one were talking about an appropriate capstone experience for them, it would be a capstone to their college experience, not to their major. This total capstone course would be one that tied together their disparate courses in all the various fields—English, history, political science, science, and math. At one time, colleges offered "contemporary civilization" courses that attempted to do that, but colleges have generally moved away from that approach, as teaching has become organized around field-specific departments and graduate education has become more specialized.

Second, even if one believes that capstone courses generally have merit, it is not clear that the capstone course is appropriate within the economics discipline. Capstone courses are most appropriate for those fields of study in which what students are being taught will become central to their lives in the future, either in their everyday life, such as is the case with many English or literature majors, or in their career, such as is the case with many of the science majors. In economics, however, that is not the case; only a very small minority, about 2% of all majors, will go on to do graduate work in economics, and almost none of the majors will do economics for pleasure once they graduate. The majority will move into law, business, government, or a variety of other professions in which economics will be one of many educational pillars in their professional life.

Third, the current set of courses in economics is not capstonable. The reason is that the economics major is organized to be part of a broader educational experience, not as a pathway to graduate work in economics.[2] Let us explain. The economics core is set up with three pillars, which, combined, are designed to expand students' theoretical, empirical, and substantive understanding of economics. The standard core of the economics major consists of a micro block, a macro block, and a statistics block, usually consisting of two courses each. The micro sequence teaches them opportunity costs and how choices are made under conditions of scarcity. It teaches students concepts of efficiency and the policy reality that there is no such thing as a free lunch. The macro sequence introduces students to the workings of the aggregate economy, gives them a sense of a modeling approach to problems, and gives them a working knowledge of monetary and fiscal policy. The statistics sequence provides students with a basic understanding of probability theory, data collection and analysis, and a sense of the importance of understanding statistics in making decisions.

A true capstone course would tie these three pillars together. But what capstone course would successfully tie all three together? As the courses are currently taught, micro and macro are not designed to be tied together; they focus on different issues, and often, at least in the undergraduate presentation, use fundamentally different approaches. The capstone metaphor is potentially more appropriate to the statistics pillar being tied to either micro or macro. Thus, if one were to have a capstone in economics, it would have to be a dual capstone. But even this dual capstone approach presents problems. To start, it is difficult to see how the statistics that most students are taught can be capstoned with the macro that they are taught. In terms of coverage, the standard statistics courses do not come close to touching on the issues in dispute in modern macro theoretical discussions, and the chance that even the best students are going to be conversant enough to enter into those debates is unlikely at best. Some issues are complicated, and to expect an undergraduate major to be able to put such issues together, when the profession is still struggling with them, is more than optimistic. Thus, it seems that if there is to be a capstone course, it will have to be a limited capstone that ties micro and statistics together.

But even if one reduces the capstone to serve this limited role, there are still problems. The way micro and statistics are currently taught, it is not clear to us that the classes are meant to have capstones. In both, the students are still only at the beginning of their studies. As pillars, the two sequences are incomplete, and at best support a tin roof, not a massive capstone. Pushing students too early into research generates bad research habits, just as pushing students too early into doing sports generates bad athletic habits. Learning involves calisthenics, and much of what we teach in both micro and statistics is better described as calisthenics of the mind. As they are currently taught, the core courses in microeconomics and statistics are not meant to prepare students for doing formal economic research.

Both the micro and the macro that we teach are quite different than the research we do. In macro, we teach the IS/LM model, while much of the work of macro economists consists of forecasting, using a variety of statistical techniques that are not mentioned in either the introductory or intermediate courses. Modern research in macro centers on the dynamic stochastic general equilibrium model, a model that is seldom mentioned to undergraduates, even in top intermediate courses. Empirical work in macro often turns on sophisticated distinctions between various restricted VAR models, and cointegrated time series econometrics, topics that are often not touched upon even in advanced econometric courses, let alone the core statistics and intermediate econometrics courses.

In the micro core sequence we teach variations on supply and demand, focusing on logical implications of rationality assumptions and optimization subject to constraints. It is designed to teach students the efficiency story, and how individual optimization relates to social optimization. But the empirical micro research that we do often only tangentially relates to such theoretical issues. Most research in micro is the advanced use of statistical techniques to tease information out of data; it is research that uses the micro theory that we teach undergraduates only to the degree that it assumes incentives matter. Another aspect of micro research relates to game theory, and theoretical work in evolutionary game theory, but again that only has a tangential connection to the core micro that is taught.[3] What comes closest to research is the statistics and econometrics that students learn, but here, the core courses often focus on theoretical issues and asymptotic properties of distributions, and spend little time on the problems of doing applied econometrics. They seldom discuss the large number of assumptions that must be made before one even reaches the issues addressed in these courses.

Now one could argue that being pushed into doing research excites students even though they do not understand the theoretical issues involved. We agree; it does. Moreover, with STATA or SPSS, there is no limit to the tests that students can do, and the "analyses" they can undertake. Students can come up with results. But excitement is not necessarily consistent with good teaching. To push students too early into research without their having learned the fundamentals and skills necessary to do good research can incorporate bad habits into research approaches that are difficult to eliminate. Economists' loose ways with regression analysis, and with distinguishing statistical from economic significance, recounted by McCloskey and Zilaik, (1996) is a case in point.

Serious research is serious work, and a good researcher must do more than type in commands in STATA and read the results. After two courses in micro and statistics, most students are not ready to undertake serious empirical research.

We have no doubt that one could structure courses in micro and statistics so that they lead to research. If the goal of most economics departments was to train economics researchers, the courses would have evolved differently. But as currently designed, the economics major is a pillar of a broader liberal arts training. In terms of that broader liberal arts training, the current economics major makes a lot of sense, but it makes sense only if the courses are seen as pillars in that liberal arts education, not pillars for economics research.

In many ways field courses are meant to shore up the micro and macro theory courses and combine them with statistics. These courses are directed courses, where the students are led through a variety of exercises and are shown how economic theory is applied in specific instances. However, most students are only required to take two or three field courses to complete the major. Given the wide range of sub-fields in economics (the *Journal of Economic Literature* broadly defines eighteen), the majority of students would gain more from taking an additional field course than from taking a capstone course for which they are not prepared. In other words, let's add another pillar rather than a cap to a weak structure.

Now, one could say that if our premises are true, then the pillars in economics should be made stronger, so that the core undergraduate economics courses would better prepare students for what is done in economics. But that, in our minds, is an inappropriate strategy since most students are not going to pursue a career in economics. We agree that, for a small minority of highly motivated, self-disciplined, undergraduates who have strong pillars, and are capable of original research, a capstone experience might be a success. But just about any experience will be a success for these students, and since there are so few of these students, we propose that schools establish an independent research program for this small minority. In very few programs will that small minority fill an entire class.

Giving Students a Real-World Research Experience

Many capstone course supporters would probably agree with the above arguments, but would point out that they are not arguing for such a capstone course; rather, they are arguing for a course that gives economics students a research experience. In part we agree; much of the discussion of capstone courses in economics is more appropriately seen as a call for a more real-world research focus in seminar-type courses. The research advocated by capstone supporters is not research that builds significantly on the core courses in economics, but is instead research that uses common sense, hard work, and very simple expositional techniques. In many ways such research is independent of the core courses in economics.[4] Appropriately defined and qualified, and without consideration of a budget constraint, we would strongly support the economics major including such a research component, and in fact we are working hard to expand its importance in teaching at our school. However, we would not characterize such an "applied research" course as a capstone experience in the economic majors (that is, a crowning achievement that connects the pillars of the undergraduate major) since such a course could be taken successfully after completion of only two economics courses (for example, micro and statistics).

Departments considering adding a course with a real-world research focus should carefully consider the difficulties associated with mounting such a course. First, the decision involves serious budget constraints: guided research courses of any type are heavily labor intensive, very difficult or impossible to standardize, and very expensive to provide. Their cost makes them of questionable appropriateness for all but the wealthiest colleges.[5] Second, the courses require highly motivated teaching-oriented professors and very small classes.[6]

The current structure of the economics major must be understood in the context of budget constraints. The current structure can be likened to assembly-line education; it provides well-defined hurdles that students are made to jump over. Although these hurdles are in many ways simply calisthenics of the mind that have little direct relevance to policy issues, they have much indirect relevance. Students who have done those calisthenics are much better prepared to deal with real-world issues. Our concern about capstone courses is that devoting resources to a capstone course would likely reduce the resources devoted to these calisthenics, much to the detriment of a majority of economics majors.

But even if the resources exist, and the capstone course is thought of as a real-world research experience, it is still not clear that the course makes sense, because graduate work for the economics Ph.D. involves little or no training in doing simple, real-world research; graduate training focuses on high level, highly technical research. If a simple "real world" research course is what one is advocating, why should the people teaching it have Ph.D.s in economics? If one's interest is in simple applied policy research, wouldn't it make more sense for such teachers to have a two- or three-year apprenticeship at a consulting firm or government agency than a Ph.D. in economics?

Some Qualifications

Our attack on the capstone course has been strident, probably more strident than we ourselves believe the concept calls for. We are not arguing that departments should change existing capstone courses; there is far too much change in educational structure. In our view, given the high costs of change, it is generally better to work within the existing structure, whatever that may be. With the right professor, and small enough classes, a capstone course will work. But with the right professor, and small classes, so will just about any course. The structure of the major is, in our view, far less important than the content of the courses. Good courses push students a bit past their limits and challenge them, and then pull back enough to let them breathe a bit, and then challenge them yet again.

If a capstone course already exists, it can be taught not as a capstone, but as a senior seminar or an upper-level field course that leads students in one particular area. Students can do a research paper as part of this course, but that research would be the type of research appropriate for the student, not what is appropriate for a capstone in economics. For most students the appropriate research paper would involve developing an interesting and feasible research plan, generating and/or locating suitable data, and making a reasonable and consistent argument about an economic issue, perhaps using statistics and simple regression analysis. This is what they will be doing in their future jobs, and such training will serve them well. The papers of these students could cover a variety of approaches, and may or may not tie different economics courses together, but it would tie their liberal arts training together.[7]

However, if a capstone course does not already exist, we would discourage departments from establishing one in the hope that it will improve economics education. Changes in structure seldom improve the educational experience for the majority of students independent of who is teaching within that structure. What is ironic is that the professors who generally push for capstone courses are often the dynamic teachers who reach students and who do a superb job educating students. They don't need the capstone course to do that; they will reach students in almost any structure.

Conclusion

One of the lessons of economics is that you cannot be all things to all people; there are always costs to go along with the benefits. The economics major is currently organized as a diverse set of courses that provide building blocks for a liberal arts education. It is not structured to provide pillars for future economists who will conduct economic research. A capstone course in economics does not fit the current structure of the economics major, and thus will not add to the educational experience of the large majority of the students.

Notes

1. We are not saying that they are unable to do independent thinking; they can and do. In fact, rejecting academics' conception of a fulfilling life is evidence of their independent thinking. All we are saying is that they are highly unlikely to direct their independent thinking into a capstone course.
2. It is because the economics major does not prepare students to do graduate work in economics that the undergraduate major is not required of incoming graduate economics students.
3. The new field of experimental economics offers more opportunities for undergraduates to do research, but teaching economics as an experimental science would require some major modifications to the undergraduate core, and is not consistent with the deductive way that the core micro is currently taught.
4. As one seasoned educator pointed out, calling such a course a capstone experience can serve a useful purpose within the educational bureaucracy, since administrators are more likely to approve the course.
5. That is why much of the discussion of capstone courses has occurred at private liberal arts schools, where budget constraints are often softer.
6. Some schools give two teaching credits for capstone courses limited to a small number of students. Even there, few professors want to teach the course.
7. Papers involving sophisticated empirical analysis are appropriate for only a very small minority of majors destined for graduate work in economics.

6

"Little Think" Economics: Is That All There Is?

A while ago I received a letter from some graduate students at a top-ranking school asking me for some ideas about what to study so that they might learn some real economics. The letter reminded me of Peggy Lee's old song, "Is That All There Is?" Is it really true that the esoteric problem-solving toolkit (whose relevance and whose validity is highly questionable) that one learns in graduate economics classes is all there is to economics?

I suspect that the answer they were hoping to get from me was that there's more to economics, and here's some exciting new work that will give you purpose, show you the relevance of what you're studying, and turn your life around. Alas, that's not the answer they got. The answer they got from me is that graduate economics education is a slog; it is meant to be a slog, and unless you stay highly focused on the toolkit, you won't get through graduate school. So my advice is to forget "big think" for now and study the tools you are being taught.

Having given that advice, I have to admit that I had the very same feelings when I was in graduate school. And when I asked essentially the same question of a top dissident economist I got essentially the same advice. He said "Don't spend too much time thinking about what you're doing now—just do it—or you'll never make it through graduate school. Save all that big think stuff for presidential addresses in the future."

Having given them that advice, I should also admit that I didn't follow it—that was back in the 1970s when no self respecting student would follow the advice of any older (over 30) person. But it was good advice then, and it's good advice now. The reality is that the graduate economics educational system is designed to weed out "big think" students who don't mind their existence proofs and quasi-logical exercises. That isn't all bad. Learning the techniques and tools is a good exercise of the mind; knowing them will be useful in doing meaningful research in the future. Once students become professors and get tenure they will be allowed the freedom to address some "big think" issues, if they haven't been co-opted, or lost their identity, in the process.

Let me explain my position. Most of the techniques that students learn in graduate school are useful; the techniques developed because they solved problems that serious researchers grappled with. The problem with grad school for me is not the techniques; it is that students aren't provided a context for using the techniques. Students are generally told to study techniques for technique's sake, and are not told the reason why those techniques developed.

Different people have different levels of toleration for learning techniques for technique's sake. "Big think" low tolerance students need some side reading to cleanse their palette and keep them going; these readings give them a counterweight to prevent their sinking into the seemingly infinite Sea of Technique. As long as the side reading remains side reading, and complements rather than substitutes for the study of techniques, it probably won't hurt too much. What follows are some suggestions of counterweight readings for low-tolerance students.

In micro, Nicholas Georgescu-Roegen comes to mind. I remember reading his *The Entropy Law and the Economic Process* (1971) in grad school and being completely blown away; it opened up lots of new ways of thinking. In grad school I had a Chicago-style micro course. Perhaps that is the reason that I am less convinced than is Deirdre McCloskey that Chicago-style textbooks are the way to learn microeconomics. In my view the Chicago approach is simply a useful way of thinking and approaching policy issues.

If you have not been introduced to Chicago-style economics in your classes, (and fewer and fewer students are—it's not even being taught much at Chicago any more) getting some flavor of it is worthwhile. But I wouldn't suggest reading Chicago-style textbooks as an introduction to the Chicago approach as Deirdre often suggests doing. Instead I'd read George Stigler's *The Economist as Preacher* (1982) or Stephen Landsburg's *The Armchair Economist: Economics and Everyday Life* (1993). I'd also read some of Gordon Tulluck's pieces; he's often much more biting than any of the Chicago authors.

If you are susceptible to the Chicago bug, I'd read some Richard Thaler (perhaps his *Quasi Rational Economics*, 1994) as an antidote, and as an interesting introduction into behavioral economics, if you're not getting any of that in your micro class. I'd also read some Albert Hirschman [for example: *The Passion and the Interests* (1977) or *Exit and Voice* (1997)] to keep some broader perspective.

In macro, I remember reading G.L.S. Shackle's (1972) and Paul Davidson's (1972) works to give me some perspective. They remain relevant today. However, in general I have a much harder time suggesting counterweight readings in macro. The problem is that many of the complicated models learned in macro classes are so lightweight in "big think" space that any "big think" reading quickly sinks the model, making it hard to stay focused on learning those models. If you're in a particularly destructive mood, you might look at some of Allen Kirman's (1992) work that calls into question much of what is done in the aggregation procedures in macro. Then try to go back and do some representative agent, rational expectations modeling. (Actually, wait until you've passed the macro prelims before you read any of these.)

In my view macro issues are best approached through a study of complex systems. A good place to begin thinking about complex systems is in the writings of Hayek. His book, *Abuse of Reason*, (1952) his article, "Use of Knowledge in Society" (1945) along with much of his later writing on constitutional law issues have convinced me that there's much more to Hayek than I originally thought. If you haven't been introduced to complexity, and want a readable popular book that pulls you in, take a look at Waldrop's *Complexity* (1993); it is a fun read. The actual complexity work is much more of a slog, but you can see some of it in a digestible form in *The Economy as an Evolving Complex System* (edited by Philip W. Anderson, Kenneth J. Arrow, and David Pines, 1988).

A reasonable justification for taking a complexity approach can be found in Duncan Foley's "Complexity and Economic Education" (2000). It puts into perspective what most students want, but aren't getting out of their classes.

As a counterweight to what is learned in most econometrics courses, reading Deirdre McCloskey is a definite must. Her *The Rhetoric of Economics* (1985) is worth reading, but the *Journal of Economic Literature* article of the same name may be a more efficient introduction to her views. Also see her *JEL* article on standard errors with Steven Ziliak. (McCloskey and Zilaik 1996) You also might take a look at Tom Mayer's *Truth vs. Precision in Economics*, (1993).

As a counterweight to the sometimes almost irrelevant policy discussions in many classes, I'd read Amartya Sen's work (for example, *Development as Freedom*, 1999). You can find a number of references in his Nobel Prize Lecture. That lecture provides as careful a summary of where we are in social choice theory as I have seen. Sen thinks deeply about actually applying economics to real-world policy within a formal setting, and about designing new tools and concepts that will make that application possible. Good stuff, and good ideas for dissertations.

Finally, some general books with interesting articles about economists include *Passion and Craft: Economists at Work* (edited by Michael Szenberg, 1998) and *A Guide to How to Do Economics* (edited by Steven Medema and Warren Samuels 1996). My two collections, *The Lost Art of Economics* (2001) and *Why Aren't Economists as Important as Garbagemen?* (1991) are easy reading, and make a few useful points. A book that I have just finished rereading is Ronald Coase's *Essays on Economics and Economists*; (1994) it had some thought-provoking insights.

But let me leave you with a final warning. "Big think" reading can be bad for your grades if not your health; it should only be approached once you have exceeded your "little think" toleration threshold. Until you have gotten tenure, it's far better to take my earlier advice, and assume that "little think" is all there is.

Part 2: Micro

7

Integrating Sex and Drugs into the Principles Course: Market Failures vs. Failures of Market Outcomes *

The introductory economics course has become an institution, propagated by a set of textbooks that determine course structure. In turn, these textbooks reflect the desires of reviewers who must teach the course, and these desires generally reflect the structure of existing textbooks. This makes any change in the textbooks gradual, and generally leaves the basic structure almost unchangeable. The overall structure has developed for a variety of reasons: pedagogical simplicity, need to fit in current issues, and a consensus of what elements of economics are best taught to principles students. Changes in theoretical viewpoints that show up in graduate schools enter into the principles course only with a long lag.

The central argument of this article is that the current micro principles course is structured around an approach to policy that avoids many of the controversial, but central, issues of policy. These include (1) the interplay of moral issues and efficiency—that's where the sex comes in; (2) questions of consumer sovereignty—that's where the drugs come in; and (3) questions of the interrelation between measures of efficiency and income distribution, which raise technical issues about drawing policy implications from our standard allocation theory. I argue that all three of these issues should have greater prominence in the standard micro principles course than they currently do. The reason is twofold—(1) discussing them makes the course more interesting to students, and (2) discussing them is necessary to relate economic thinking to real-world policy debates.

More generally, my argument is that the current policy-organizing framework of principles of microeconomics textbooks—what I call the market failure framework—excludes discussion of a broader set of failures

---

* I would like to thank Beth Bogan, Hirschel Kasper, and the referees for helpful comments on this article.

of market outcomes: failures in which the market is doing everything it is supposed to be doing, but society is still unhappy with the result. By not addressing issues where markets do not solve society's problems in a way that is acceptable to most people, we open ourselves up to the complaint that we are unfairly advocating market solutions. In this article I suggest a dual "market failure" and "failure of market outcome" policy framework. I argue that this dual framework provides students with a more useful policy framework than does the market failure framework alone.[1]

Let me begin with a story I have in my principles textbook (Colander 2006) that raises a "failure of market outcome" issue. It is a story about Lady Astor and Winston Churchill.[2] In it Churchill asks Lady Astor if she would sleep with him for one million dollars. They know each other quite well, and she contemplates the offer as part of a broader intellectual game they played. After some thought she responds, "Yes, if the payment could be guaranteed." He counters, "Would you sleep with me for $1?" To which she replies, "Of course not, what do you think I am, a whore?" He responds triumphantly, "We've already established that; now we're simply negotiating about price."

Even though reviewers generally liked this story, my publishers were concerned about my including it in my principles book; they felt it might hurt sales with both the religious right and with feminists. They strongly urged me to remove it. In this case I resisted, and kept it in, but in the majority of cases the publishers win out, and textbooks avoid offending anyone.

Now, why did I want to include this story? I clearly have no desire to reduce sales, nor to alienate the religious right or feminists. I wanted to include it because I believed it raised important questions about applying economic reasoning to policy issues that are usually avoided in economics textbooks. Specifically, I wanted to raise such questions as: How should policy makers deal with the tradeoff between moral issues and efficiency? Is that tradeoff lexicographic; or so incomparable that the tradeoffs are considered only outside the range of feasible prices? These are messy questions, but they are questions that should be raised in a policy-oriented principles course that deals meaningfully with actual policy issues.

If we don't deal with such issues, we fail two different types of students. We lose the interest of the thoughtful students who recognize these issues and want some guidance in how they can be integrated into their policy thinking; these thoughtful students drop out of economics and go into ecology, philosophy, or sociology. We make our less thoughtful students think that policy is easier than it is. They come out of the course thinking that policy is an easy task, or would be if only people listened to economists and understood economic theory.

Now let me be clear about what I am proposing. In my role as a teacher I don't know, and don't care, what positions my students take on such moral questions. But I do want students to think seriously about such issues and to understand that policy issues must be decided within a broader moral framework. To do that we do not need to spend a lot of time discussing such issues. We simply need to create a policy framework that acknowledges their importance. One way that I have found to do so in my classes is to devote some discussion to policy views of heterodox economists such as libertarians and Marxists. Translating their views to textbookese, which means that the ideas are forced into a simplicity that belies the subtleties of positions, but which are testable (that is, they can be made into test questions) and which are easy to remember: Libertarians tend to believe that most everything should be for sale; Marxists tend to believe that almost nothing should be saleable. Marxists view the labor market as a type of temporary slavery; libertarians believe that if consenting adults want to sell something, it is immoral for government to say they can't.

I don't agree with either of these moral positions, but they are logical and reasonable positions for an economist to hold. I want students to understand that, and to understand that before we can talk about policy we must decide our moral stance on such issues.

The argument I am making is not novel. Good economists of all political persuasions recognize that the policy choices they make involve broader issues than are allowed within our current market failure framework. But the current framework of principles textbooks encourages professors to avoid the issues; they are presented as asides, not core topics. Textbooks accomplish this by selectively choosing examples, and focusing on those policies that are consistent with the conventional moral view, which means that the moral issues don't show up in the discussion. Conventional policy proposals don't highlight the moral issues in the same way that more unconventional policy views do because they are based on policy compromises that do not push moral buttons for a majority of the population. Good politicians carefully avoid policies that push the boundaries of conventional morality. In my view good teachers should take an opposite approach. They should focus on policies that push the boundaries, because it is by pushing the boundaries that students develop a deeper understanding of issues.

When the discussion concerns less conventional policy issues—a radical animal rights advocate's, or an ultra-property rights advocate's, view of environmental issues—the market failure framework is no longer sufficient. That's why I spend a lot more time than most economists talking about unconventional policy proposals. When students struggle with these issues they become better able to deal with the shades of moral gray that actually characterize most policy issues.

The Dual Policy Framework

Let me briefly summarize what I see as the "market failure" policy framework that structures our micro courses. We present supply/demand analysis, social and private costs, opportunity costs, and externalities, and drill students on their understanding of how policy can correct externalities by equating marginal social costs with marginal private costs. That framework is excellent for shedding light on many economic policy problems where broader issues are of secondary importance, but it is not useful for shedding light on policy problems where moral, psychological, and distributional foundations of efficiency issues are critical. Because these three issues are important for many policy issues, but do not fit our current framework, I propose a dual policy framework that includes the standard market failure but also includes a broader category that includes the possibility of "failures of market outcomes."

The dual policy framework provides a much broader framework for discussing economic policy. For example, if you morally believe that markets are wrong, then the correct social policy is to not allow markets. The market failure framework has no room for morally questioning markets. If you believe that people don't make choices in their own interest, then you may need policy to direct people to make choices "in their interest." That, too, doesn't fit in the market failure approach. And if you do not believe that the existing income distribution is fair, or that tastes are relatively homothetic, then market prices in the absence of externalities do not necessarily represent socially desirable outcomes.

This dual framework that I am proposing has two types of justifications of intervention in the market: the traditional market failure and failure of market outcomes. With a failure of market outcome, the market is doing precisely what it is supposed to be doing—supply equals demand—and there are no externalities. But the market outcome is nonetheless seen as undesirable by society. In the dual framework society must determine its moral stance on issues before policy positions can be arrived at, something our current "market failure" framework does not require.

Let me now briefly discuss each of the three issues that I believe belong in the broader policy framework.

Moral Issues

In the introductory section of my principles textbook I raise a number of moral issues such as the selling of babies and human eggs, as well as the Lady Astor story mentioned above. They always provoke student interest and involvement in the class. I can do this in the beginning because there I am talking more broadly about economic policy, and have not yet developed the formal framework. But presenting such issues becomes more difficult when I get into the formal presentation of micro, because such issues don't fit into the market failure framework. Once I have developed that framework, I can't raise such issues without undermining it. Where's the market failure in selling babies? You have a willing buyer, a willing seller, and a clear case of comparative advantage. It is more efficient—in the normal way that economists interpret efficiency—for individuals to specialize into baby producers and baby consumers. Yet, most people would oppose such "efficient" solutions. The same argument holds for indentured servitude, prostitution, and the selling of body parts.

Textbooks generally avoid discussing the problem that such issues pose for the market failure framework. They stick to issues such as smoke pollution that, for many, do not raise the moral flags that the above issues do. But even with pollution there is a problem. The reality is that a large percentage of the population believes that pollution has a moral dimension—that it is morally wrong to pollute, and that it is morally wrong not to recycle. The typical principles book, generally implicitly, dismisses such moral arguments in discussions of the policy solutions it presents, and argues that efficiency should rule: Because pollution permits or pollution taxes balance costs and benefits and can reduce pollution, these solutions are preferable to outright bans, or other alternative solutions. Market-based solutions leave individuals free to choose the amount of pollution they will generate, as long as they internalize the cost of that pollution. The implicit presumption of the textbooks is that moral issues should not enter into discussions of pollution. The textbooks suggest that not to accept the "efficient" solution is to impose your own normative view on the issue, whereas the economic solution avoids making any moral judgment, and hence avoids imposing any normative view.

That, in my view, is a clear misunderstanding of how normative issues fit into policy, and is a violation of the normative neutrality that economic policy tries to maintain. It is not for economists to say whether moral issues should enter in; economists' job is to provide a framework within which economic issues and normative issues can be considered. Baumol (1982; 1006) nicely captured this sentiment when he commented that "as a profession committed to the position that we should not tell people what they ought to want, and that the utility functions, which we usually accept as given data, are what would enter the social maximand, it ill behooves us to reject such beliefs out of hand. If people feel that putting a price on something demeans it, then we cannot tell them that it should not. In positive economics we simply accept their views." His point, which I agree with, is that if individuals believe that there is a moral dimension to pollution, it is not for economists to tell them they are wrong. Our job is to figure out policies that best achieve their desired goals, given the moral preferences of society.

Many situations will get students to think about these issues. One is the giving of gifts for Christmas. Using the standard economic policy framework, Christmas is inefficient. This follows because people are receiving gifts that were chosen by someone else, and hence are unlikely to receive what they would have chosen. The result: dead weight loss of 20 percent or so of the value of the gifts (Waldfogel 1993). Using the efficiency framework suggested in the texts would lead students to conclude that giving money would be much more efficient. And it would, but would it provide a better outcome? Would we really be better off without Christmas? Most people believe that the answer is no; they believe that Christmas should be judged on criteria that go beyond the standard economic interpretation of efficiency.

Examples can be expanded widely, but the point is that moral elements, and the methods of allocation—gift or market— play an important role in people's judgments of the value of goods. Hence they need to be considered carefully in any policy discussion.

Psychological Failures

A second cause of failure of market outcome is psychological failures. The example I use in my book is of Joe Drunk, an alcoholic. He spends all his money on booze. He is unhappy, but he is freely making choices. The standard framework says that to put any such restrictions on his ability to buy booze decreases efficiency. And it does, as long as one accepts that what he chooses is, by definition, in his best interest. But is it a reasonable assumption? Is he doing what he really wants to do?[3]

Similar issues arise with smoking, eating chocolate, or any of our infinite other minor vices. If there are psychological failures it is possible that a person would be better off if his choices were constrained. A large percentage of society believes that individuals do not always do what is in their best interest; and it is not for economists to tell society that that view is wrong. We can try to show them through experiments, but when we have done experiments, we find that people often act in ways that violate our rationality assumptions.

The possibility of psychological failures means that we must consider the possibility of endogenous tastes in our discussion of policy. The reality is that people's tastes are not fully exogenous; they are partially endogenous, and with endogenous tastes, all bets are off as to what policy is the best policy. How do I know that tastes are endogenous? The market tells me so: When I see firms spending billions of dollars on ads to change people's tastes, I have a clear indication that tastes are endogenous. Marketing campaigns ("Wassup," "The power of Cola," and "Just do it") have become central elements of our culture.

Endogenous tastes undermine the efficiency argument in favor of markets. Businesses are not fulfilling given wants, but are creating wants and then filling those created wants. Now, we economists know the difficulty that dealing with this issue raises—who is to say what people want if we do not accept their revealed preference? But do the textbooks discuss that? No. They avoid the issue, and in doing so, do not give students a framework for thinking about the policy issues that might follow if we decide that tastes are not fully exogenous.

The point is that there is a set of policies that follow from semi-endogenous tastes—sin taxes, such as the high tax on smoking, and policies that supercede those of the market—and encourage the consumption of merit goods and discourage the consumption of demerit goods. To talk about such policies meaningfully we need to specify those goods where tastes reflect basic needs (primitives), and those goods where tastes are more socially constructed. Only after having done so can we talk about policy.

A range of policy issues are currently being discussed that fits under a psychological problem heading—taxes on cigarettes, subsidies of the arts, and positional, or conspicuous consumption, luxury goods. Students are thinking about such issues; the principles textbooks should provide a framework for dealing with them.

Now I am not arguing that justifications based on psychological problems are correct; I am an economist, and share with most economists a strong belief in consumer sovereignty—that's why above I argued that we had to consider people's moral beliefs carefully. But I believe that in our teaching we should be neutral in our presentation of policy, and not let our views shape the way we present issues to students. There are legitimate arguments about consumer sovereignty that need to be discussed when talking about policy options. But these arguments do not fit into the market failure framework. Frank's (2000) positional goods (and Veblen's earlier conspicuous consumption goods) offer the possibility of a twofer—a tax that improves people's welfare without reducing someone else's welfare. Such win-win policies are impossible with standard economic assumptions, but can be found in a variety of places when psychological problems are considered. As demonstrated in the work of economists such as Robert Frank, modern micro is considering such issues. What I am arguing is that we need a textbook policy framework that allows us to present such issues as legitimate.

Income Distribution/Efficiency Problems

I saved distribution/efficiency problems for last because they are the subtlest type of failure of market outcome with which economics must deal. We all know how we handle income distribution problems within standard welfare theory: we assume that costless lump-sum transfers are possible and preferences are homothetic. So much for income distribution problems. The former means that we have a policy tool that solves the problem, and the latter eliminates the preference problem for efficiency when the market does not solve the distribution problem. But we also know that such assumptions do not fit reality, and that distribution is a central policy issue in many policy discussions. Most principles books discuss such issues. But most do not discuss the implications of an existing undesirable income distribution for measures of efficiency.

The market summation of preferences that the market builds into decisions about what to produce, and into the social surplus measures we teach students, weights the importance of preferences of various individuals by the existing income distribution. Alternative income distributions could lead to a quite different set of social preferences, and the efficient result, to which the market leads, given the existing income distribution, could be one we abhor. Consider the following example that I present in my textbook concerning the demand for the AIDs drug cocktail. That cocktail can stop AIDS from killing people; thus the desire for the AIDs cocktail among individuals with AIDs is high. The desire for the drug among those without AIDs is minimal.

In some African countries, 30 percent of the population has AIDs. Because consumer surplus reflects desire, a student might think that in Africa the consumer surplus from the desire for the AIDs drug cocktail would be enormous. But it isn't. Most people in Africa cannot afford the cocktail. In fact, for a large majority the price of the cocktail exceeds their total income, so, technically, they get no consumer surplus from the cocktail at all. In our current textbook supply/demand market failure framework, it would be "inefficient" to supply the drug to them. In the supply/demand framework one can only have a demand for a good if one has the desire and the income to pay for it. Most textbooks don't make the argument in favor of such an "efficient solution" in medicinal drugs because the result would be unacceptable to most students and teachers. But, by avoiding the topic altogether, textbooks miss the opportunity to show students the more general limitations of a policy that focuses on efficiency and on policies designed to maximize consumer surplus.

Notice that the problem here is that according to most people's social welfare function, income is not acceptably distributed, and preferences are nonhomothetic. In such a case market prices do not reflect social values even when there are no externalities. The issue is not a market failure; the market is doing precisely what it is supposed to be doing. The problem is a failure of market outcome: Most people don't like the market result.

The Dual Policy Framework and Pedagogy

As I stated before, none of these issues are deep insights of mine; they are well known and many professors present them in their classes in various ways. My point only concerns pedagogy; it is that our current textbook policy framework does not make the presentation of these issues easy. One must present them as outliers, and as outliers they are usually given little coverage. In a dual policy framework, it will be much easier to introduce these issues. Goods and issues can be arranged along a spectrum of the three issues that they raise. Goods that raise few such issues fit nicely within our market failure framework. Goods that do not must be dealt with in the broader failure of market outcome framework.

I am not suggesting enormous changes in the way we teach micro principles. Essentially, what I am suggesting is the addition of one lecture on failures of market outcomes, with examples of each type, and a recognition of such issues in other discussions. In my principles textbook, it means that I have devoted five pages to it. In my class, as a class exercise, I have the students classify policies that raise significant moral issues and those that don't, and in doing so get them thinking about these broader issues.

I want to be clear about what I am proposing by emphasizing two points. First, I am not saying that we should spend lots of time discussing these broader issues—we have neither the expertise nor the time to do so. What I am saying is that the policy framework we present students should be broad enough to let them know that all policy answers do not come from economic theory alone. My suggested dual policy framework does that. Second, I am not saying that more government intervention is good. To make such decisions it is necessary to discuss government failure and failures of government outcomes. If one believes such government failures are major, then little intervention is called for even if failures of market outcomes exist. But the justification for nonintervention is government failure, not the fact that the markets automatically lead to desirable results. It is a choice between undesirable alternatives, and government intervention leads to even worse results than the market. In this argument public choice moves front and center into the policy debate, which is where I think it should be.

How We Got to Where We Are

In an attempt to understand how we came about teaching the way we do, I've been studying the evolution of welfare economics. As economists struggled with moral issues, and distinctions between normative and positive issues, we started focusing on a subset of issues where it was felt that economics could shed some light on the problems.

We narrowed the focus of microeconomics to allocation theory. If you go back to Classical economics you will see such broad issues discussed; Adam Smith set the framework for *The Wealth of Nations* with his *Theory of Moral Sentiments*; Mill structured his policy discussions within a much broader discussion of morality. But moral issues are fuzzy, and as we attempted to avoid the fuzziness, and formalize welfare theory, we limited the domain of the field. Initially we did so with appropriate caveats about how the domain was being narrowed. Good policy economists understand these caveats well. But somehow in the pedagogical presentation of policy issues to students, the pressure of teaching the technical issues pushed aside these broader caveats—and the micro presentation came to focus on teaching students an allocation framework where those issues are not discussed.

Initially, that focus worked, because it was taught as a technical constrained optimization issue, and was not related significantly to policy. But over the years, there were calls for relevance and policy applications, which the textbooks tried to follow. The textbooks focused less and less on technique, and more and more on policy. As they did so the problem developed, because they were forced to fit policy into a narrower framework than was possible.

If we were only teaching a technical constrained optimization course, and were not teaching a policy oriented course, this would present no problem, because that cost-benefit framework is an extraordinarily powerful tool, which I strongly believe all students can usefully learn. I want every student to know that there is no such thing as a free lunch; that everything has a cost, and that constrained optimization is a useful framework to analyze issues.

But market pressures force textbooks to do more than that—students want policy relevance, so professors and textbook writers are continually applying the tools to policy issues. Herein comes the problem: a large number of policy problems are not market failure problems—they are policy problems that include some degree of failures of market outcomes. One cannot adequately relate the tools to the policy unless one acknowledges these broader dimensions of policy.

Conclusion

Goethe said that all theory is gray; to that I suggest adding the addendum that all policy is even grayer. Policy issues are seldom easy or clear-cut. To present them as easy or clear-cut is to do an injustice to one side or another. If we are going to teach policy issues in principles, and I think we should, we should do it within a framework that is open to issues that society thinks are important. Only by engaging those issues, and placing economic policy discussions within a framework that allows them, can we provide students with a framework that can actually deal with policy issues, rather than with a subset of issues. We should make the economics we teach as simple as possible, but not more so.

I make this argument both for those professors who believe deeply in the market and for those who are highly skeptical. If one's goal is to indoctrinate students with the view that markets are generally good, then the dual policy framework will not be useful. But if one's goal is to show economists' reasoning about markets, and place that reasoning in a context where students can make their own decisions about what issues should go within the market, and which should not, then it is a preferable framework. I strongly believe that the purpose of the principles course is not to indoctrinate students into believing in the market; the purpose is to teach them about the benefits and costs of markets.

The dual policy framework allows us to discuss policy issues that present conundrums, and that are not fully worked out. Doing so helps seize students' attention, and creates a passion for economics. It gives them puzzles to think about: where do markets work, and where don't they. The current framework in principles texts directs the student to problems where markets work, which gives the skeptical student a sense that we're stacking the deck. The dual policy framework gives students an unstacked deck, and, by doing so, gives them a better sense of both the strengths and weaknesses of markets.

Notes

1. The issue here is the textbook framework, not what teachers actually do. Many principles teachers already incorporate these issues within their courses.
2. This story has been attributed to a variety of other protagonists as well.
3 See T. Schelling (1999) for an insightful discussion of such issues.

8

Complexity and the Principles Course

Teaching economics is telling a story, and in economics there are two stories that we tell. One I'll call the complexity story line; the other I'll call the efficiency story line. Both are important in understanding the theme of the principles course—which concerns markets and their role in society—and both come to the same bottom line: Markets are pretty good institutions that do some marvelous things. But both focus on different issues, and get to the bottom line by entirely different routes.

The Efficiency Story

The efficiency story is a story about the state of competition. It is a static story, which nicely fits into a calculus (especially LaGragrangian multiplier) framework. While few principles students completely understand the full efficiency story line, they do get a number of examples of it—the effect of taxes, the effect of quantity restrictions, price ceilings, and price floors on efficiency, and the way in which the economy adjusts, or does not adjust, efficiently to expansions in government spending, expansions in the money supply, or sudden changes in tastes.

It is a story taught as analytic exercises centered around graphs. One has the production possibility curve, supply and demand curves, and a variety of cost curves, all of which convey the strength of constrained maximization analytic techniques. Students learn how to maximize some function (utility, profit) subject to a constraint. Students also learn that under appropriate conditions individual maximization will lead to social maximization, although, to be honest, few principles courses students come away from the course with a deep understanding of that. They are usually struggling with the simple individual optimization story.

The Complexity Story

The complexity story is a story about the process of competition. It is based in a dynamic framework; it is an evolutionary story of an economy operating over time—drifting along on a slowly moving river with occasional rapids, none of which are directly controlled, or controllable. The complexity story tells how the invisible hand of the market takes

97

what should be chaos, and turns it into an elegant complex structure that fits together, not efficiently, but sustainably. The resulting system is not admired for its efficiency, although in some loose sense one might argue that it is efficient, but for its very existence.

In this complexity story the market isn't desirable because it achieves some grand sense of efficiency, and government isn't seen as something that can tweak the result in an analytic way. The market is more integrated with the entire whole, and tweaking one aspect can change another—a butterfly flapping its wings in China can change the weather pattern in the United States.

In principles of economics we primarily tell the efficiency story because the complexity story is so difficult to tell. Brian Arthur gives the following example of a discussion at the first Santa Fe conference on complexity that gives one a sense of why the story is so difficult. Arthur was talking with one of the physicists there. Arthur brought up the problem of including increasing returns in the economic model. The physicist remarked that increasing returns is like spin rotation and that therefore economics with increasing returns is very much like physics. The physicist went on to say that since there are more atoms than people, physics must be harder than economics. But Arthur changed this physicist's view by pointing out that in economics one has an additional complication. To make the analyses comparable each atom would have to be assumed to have a will of its own, and each is trying to take advantage of the other atoms. With that the physicist agreed that economics is much more difficult.

Students' Reactions to Economics

Students with mathematical backgrounds have varying reactions to this story. Many have just enough mathematics to follow it, and to find it challenging mathematically, and thus find it acceptably hard. Students with weak mathematical backgrounds find it almost impossible to understand. But these same students are often attracted to the complexity story because it fits their intuition, and seems wonderfully magical. They are not trying to deal with it mathematically. So, while the mathematics associated with complexity is far too complicated for most professors teaching principles, let alone students, it is a story that, for many students, intuitively fits the economy, and thus they find it enjoyable. Since, at the principles level, the complexity story is told in English, not mathematics, it is much easier for the students to understand. Of course, that makes the complexity story difficult to teach.

The Evolution of the Story We Tell

Both story lines are beautifully interwoven in Adam Smith's *Wealth of Nations*, which is why it was such a popular book. In many ways, it would be nice to teach principles of economics from that book, but, unfortunately, the prose is too difficult for students to follow easily. So we teach economics from principles textbooks. These principles texts have evolved from early texts, with Alfred Marshall's *Principles of Economics* being a key text. In it Marshall developed the supply/demand story, and in doing so he developed a mechanical framework that was appropriate for the efficiency story. But throughout the book he also made continual reference to the complexity story, which he stated better fit in a biological framework.

As the principles texts have evolved, the efficiency story has been given more and more space, and the complexity story less space. Paul Samuelson's principles text, which forms the template for most modern textbooks, concentrated almost entirely on the efficiency story line. It moved from the "one thing at a time" approach of Marshall, which left the larger coordination issue up in the air, to a general equilibrium approach like Walras', which extended the efficiency story line to the explanation not only of the small issues, but also to the large, general equilibrium, issues.

Important reasons why principles texts have focused on the efficiency line are the teaching technology available and the institutional structure within which economics is taught. The efficiency story fits that technology and institutional structure; in fact they have coevolved. The complexity story is much more ambiguous and much more difficult to define and test knowledge of with a clear-cut set of questions. Since the large classes where principles of economics is generally taught require clear-cut questions and answers, to make grading easier, the complexity story has been downplayed in the texts. Thus, the complexity story did not fit the technology and institutional structure, and for the most part disappeared from the course.

A Comparison of the Elements of the Complexity Story and the Efficiency Story

In the book I edited on complexity and economics (Colander, 2000a) a number of authors considered the complexity story line in some detail, and some of the implications it would have for the teaching of economics. In that book I presented a table Brian Arthur created that distinguished

100 The Stories Economists Tell

the old economics (the efficiency story) from the new economics (the complexity story). Going through this table, and noting the differences, gives one a good sense of how the complexity story differs from the efficiency story.

Articles draw out

Old Economics	New Economics
Subject seen as structurally simple	Structure seen as inherently complex
Decreasing returns	Much use of increasing returns
Society as a backdrop	Institutions come to the fore as a main decider of possibilities, order, and structure
Discovery of immutable laws Language: 19th century math, game theory, and fixed point topology	Laws change Language is more qualitative
Based on 19th century physics	Based on biology
Technology given	Technology fluid
Based on marginality and maximizing principles	Other principles than marginality and maximizing possible
Preferences given	Formation of preferences is endogenous

The efficiency story of economics is built into the standard definition, "economics is the allocation of scarce resources among alternative means," that we find in most principles texts. That definition presupposes scarcity, and directs us to think about constrained maximization, given appropriate assumptions. It places broader issues outside the realm of economics, and suggests that economic problems are separable from social and political problems.

The complexity story of economics sees these issues as much more interrelated. It uses a definition of economics that focuses more on coordination of individuals and continued existence of the economy as observed phenomena needing to be explained. In the complexity approach the key question is not whether the economy operates efficiently; who knows whether it does or does not? In the complexity approach the key question is how the economy operates at all. One would think that six billion people each doing his or her own thing would lead to chaos. But it does not; we somehow manage to muddle along. Looking at that question directs the analysis toward institutions that restrict individuals' action, and that shape individuals to fit society's need for its continued existence. The efficiency story doesn't touch such issues.

Much Use of Increasing Returns

The efficiency story is premised on nicely behaved functions and appropriate second-order conditions. In presenting the models we slide in the standard assumptions: "Let's assume that individuals have a diminishing marginal rate of substitution and that costs are increasing at an increasing rate"... The complexity story spends much more time focusing on situations with "inappropriate" second-order conditions. What happens when there are increasing returns? How does competition work in those cases? What happens when there is learning by doing, and when people's preferences are non-convex? Somehow, all these non-convexities seem to work out, and do not cause the economy to implode or explode. Competition still rules, but it is an ongoing process, not a static concept. The complexity story explores how that happens.

One of the things I like to ask my students when introducing them to the complexity story is to intuit an average and marginal cost curve for producing a car. What they get are average and marginal cost curves that slope downward. I then ask them to contrast that with the cost curves presented in the textbooks. After doing that I have them talk about cost curves for lumpy decisions: building a new plant or developing and marketing an idea. In all these, diminishing marginal returns shows up very little, yet in our texts we emphasize diminishing returns as central to the story of costs. The complexity story would emphasize increasing returns, learning by doing, and network externalities.

Institutions Come to the Fore

The efficiency story is essentially a mathematical story, part of whose beauty is in its generality. Constrained maximization and shadow prices are central; institutions are simply constraints that define the particular application of the general analysis. Institutions play a much more fundamental role in the complexity story. They evolve and are a central part of the story. In the complexity story efficiency cannot be discussed separately from institutions. Institutions shape individuals; they are not only constraints; they are also the building blocks of an effectively working economy.

Laws Change

In the efficiency story there is a push to discover specific laws—the law of supply, the law of demand, the law of diminishing marginal utility, the quantity theory of money, which hold for all times. Thus, the economic system that students are presented with is one in which these universal laws are always working, and it doesn't matter whether one is in one society or another—the laws will still be the same. The complexity story is far less concerned with finding immutable laws, and more concerned with finding patterns that can be helpful in dealing with certain problems. An example is the treatment of potential income in macroeconomics. In the standard approach potential income is assumed to change only slowly due to specific microeconomic causes one can specify. In the complexity story, potential income can change suddenly as some slowly moving variable hits a critical point and changes the perceived nature of the system.

Language is More Qualitative

The language of the efficiency story focuses on calculus, game theory, and, in more technical stories, fixed-point topology. The story is essentially deductive in nature, starting from first principles, using logic and formal language to extend those principles to broader insights. It relies on either/ors and logical deductive language, and tends to be very formal. The complexity story uses a more inductive approach. Complexity economics is based on observed reality and observed patterns. Individuals are thought of not as logical deductive machines, but as fast pattern-completers. For these fast pattern completers formal proofs are less necessary. A sense of something can be conveyed without a full formal proof of its existence, which makes the language much more qualitative.

Based on Biology

As I stated above, the efficiency story is essentially a mechanical story—telling how pieces of the economy fit together. The complexity story is more about evolution and continual change, which makes it fit better into biology than in mechanics. For example, the complexity story sees the economy in much the same way as an evolutionary biologist sees an ecosystem—as an intricate, evolving life form, which can take on a life of its own quite separate from the life of the components.

Technology fluid

Technology is appended to the efficiency story. It is hidden in the assumption of a given production function, and most of the formal analysis of production takes place with a given technology. While technology can be added back as a residual, it is not the focus of the analysis. In the efficiency story there's no consideration of how technology affects preferences, or even how technology affects the way we analyze issues. In the complexity story, technology is center stage. Technological lock-in becomes an important issue, as does the way in which technology influences choice.

Other Principles than Marginality and Maximizing Principles Possible

The workhorse in resolving the plots in the efficiency story is marginality: If the marginal benefits exceed the marginal costs you are in disequilibrium; if they are equal you are in equilibrium. Marginality brings resolution to the efficiency stories. In the complexity story equilibrium is far less important, and will not necessarily be based on marginal conditions because of increasing returns and nonconvexities. Instead, principles such as sustainability become much more important.

Formation of Preferences is Endogenous

In the efficiency story, we are born with certain tastes, which we then go out and fulfill. Given tastes are central to the conclusions of the efficiency story: markets work. In the complexity story, we are not born into this world with a complete set of tastes; many are imprinted upon us by society. In the complexity story what tastes are inherent—that is, deeply imprinted and thus unchangeable—and what tastes are determined by society is an empirical question. The complexity story would look at this question; it is not addressed in the efficiency story. This leads to two different analyses of advertising. In the efficiency story, advertising provides information or possibly disinformation. In the complexity story the purpose of advertising can be to change tastes. In the complexity story line, advertising gets more discussion than it does in the efficiency story.

Conclusion

What does all this mean for how we teach principles of economics? In the short term, not a whole lot. The principles course is an institution and it cannot be changed quickly without a sudden shock from the outside or a major technological change. Some supporters of the complexity approach may see this as a problem, but I do not. In my view the efficiency story the books tell is an important one, well worth learning. The lessons learned from it, compared to the lessons learned in most other classes, make the principles course, as it is currently taught, an essential course for students to take. It is practical, gives students new insights, and plays a central role in a solid liberal arts education. In an evolutionary sense it is stable in the short run.

In the long term, however, I think the work being done on complexity means major changes for how we teach economics. There are two reasons why. The first reason is that the complexity approach is now getting much more discussion in graduate school and advanced work. In the short run the texts, and the principles course, will only add tidbits about the complexity approach as we go along, but in the long run what is taught in graduate school guides what is taught in undergraduate school. The second reason is changing technology. The complexity approach is much more conducive to computer presentation, which can deal with agent-based models and simulations. As technology swings from a print-medium presentation to a computer-medium presentation of the course, the complexity story will get more and more time. Eventually, it will be the central story told, and the efficiency story will be a minor sub-story. At that point, if I am still around, I expect to be defending the need for the principles course to give more emphasis to the efficiency story, rather than leaving it as a sidelight.

Notes

1. There are other story lines that I do not discuss here. One that is seldom even mentioned, but which would fit into a complexity story and not in an efficiency story, is the pre-Classical economics story of how markets divert people's attention from destructive passions to the relatively benign pursuit of material interests, and thus help hold society together. (See Albert Hirschman, 1997.)

9

Complexity, Muddling Through, and Environmentalism*

In *The Worldly Philosophers* Robert Heilbroner tells a story of a dinner John Maynard Keynes had with Max Planck, the physicist who was responsible for the development of quantum mechanics. Planck turned to Keynes and told him that he had once considered going into economics himself, but he decided against it—it was too hard. Keynes repeated this story with relish to a friend back at Cambridge. "Why, that's odd," said the friend. "Bertrand Russell was telling me just the other day that he'd also thought about going into economics. But he decided it was too easy." That story captures two typical reactions that students often have to economics. For some it is too easy; for others it is too hard.

In this chapter I argue that both these reactions are reasonable, depending on what economic story one is trying to explain. I distinguish two stories that economists have in their mind when they think of economics—one is a story of efficiency and control that has its foundation in the work of David Ricardo and Leon Walras. The other story is a story of complexity and muddling through; its roots are in the work of Adam Smith and John Stuart Mill. I argue that the new work in sustainable forest management, and in the environmental literature more generally, is part of a broader trend that is occurring in economics— switching from the efficiency and control story to the complexity and muddling through story. As such it is associated with current changes going on at the cutting edge of economics.

Two Alternative Stories

One of the reason economics can be viewed as both easy and hard is that it is a highly complex subject, which, for pedagogical reasons, has to be simplified to a basic story line. Some tangents are allowed, but ultimately those tangents must interweave with the main story line, or

* Parts of this chapter come from early drafts of a book I am currently working on with William Brock entitled *The Economics of Muddling Through*. At this point I alone am responsible for the arguments presented here.

they do not appear. I suspect that Planck and Russell differed because they were referring to different story lines.

Russell was likely thinking of the story line currently used in the micro texts, which is what might be called the efficiency story line. The efficiency story is a story about the state of competition. As I discussed in the last chapter it is a static story, which nicely fits into a constrained optimization framework. Students learn variations of the partial equilibrium efficiency story line such as the effect of various restrictions on efficiency or the way in which the economy adjusts to sudden changes in tastes.

Students are also presented with the general equilibrium efficiency story—that under appropriate conditions individual maximization will lead to social maximization, although, to be honest, few principles of economics students come away from the course with a deep understanding of that broader story. They are usually struggling with the simple individual optimization story. It is beyond most students to carry the analysis through to the aggregate level and understand the welfare implications about markets of that social optimization story. In fact, most of those welfare implications are negative—the arguments cannot be carried over to social maximization under reasonable assumptions. We tell it nonetheless because it is a useful story in organizing thinking about very complicated policy issues.

One of the reasons this social maximization story makes an acceptable textbook story is that it provides space both for economists who prefer government action, and for those who oppose it. While, under the "right" set of conditions the market maximizes social welfare, those conditions are often not met; externalities can upset that market-based social maximization. But, not to fear; the government can offset those externalities through appropriate tax policy. Thus, the efficiency story line has the needed neutrality to sell to a wide market—a necessary attribute of any textbook story—and fits with the reasonable proposition that there are costs and benefits to government regulation. The story neither opposes nor favors government action. Moreover it can be spun in a variety of ways to fit individual instructors' biases.

Many students have a hard time understanding the efficiency story because, even though it is highly simplified, it is still difficult. That's because the stories are often told graphically and algebraically, languages that are difficult for many principles students to understand. In fact, many students never get around to learning the ideas of economics; they spend all their time learning math.

This maximization cost/benefit story line, which is a key element of the efficiency story as it relates to policy, is very useful for students to learn, and to remember for the rest of their lives. Since principles of economics is only one of about 35 courses that make up students' training in college, it seems a reasonable story to teach. But, as with all things, it comes at a cost, and that cost is that many students are never introduced to other important stories that economists could tell. One of those alternative stories involves developments that are currently ongoing in the economics profession. That alternative story line might be called the complexity story line.

As I have argued in the previous chapter (Chapter 8) the complexity story is a much more complicated story than the efficiency story, and is the story Planck was likely referring to. It is about the process of competition; it is based in a dynamic framework and is a story in which the economy evolved, and is not directly controlled, or controllable. The complexity story is an almost magical story, one in which the invisible hand of the market takes what should be chaos, and turns it into an elegantly complex structure that fits together, not perfectly or efficiently, but sustainably. Patterns and pictures develop out of nowhere. The resulting system is admired not for its efficiency, nor for any of its static properties; the resulting system is admired for its very existence. Somehow the process of competition gets the pieces of the economy to fit together and prevents the economy from disintegrating into chaos. Observed existence, not deduced efficiency, is the key to the complexity story line.

While the complexity story line has its origins in the economics of economists such as Mandeville, Smith, and Malthus, its more recent development is to be found in the work of evolutionary biologists such as Edmond Wilson and John Maynard Smith. Both stories are centered around constrained optimization, but whereas the efficiency story line structures the story so that it comes to an answer, and, in principle, a set of policy recommendations, the complexity story line is a never-ending story in which every answer simply raises new questions, and the hope of control gives way to a realization that the best we can hope for is to muddle through.

Environmental Sustainability and the Two Stories

Environmentalists have had a hard time communicating with economists, and the reason, I believe, is economists' focus on the efficiency story. Recognizing the existence of these two stories helps explain the neglect of issues of sustainability in economics and provides a broader framework within which the emerging work in sustainable forest management can be understood. Traditional work in environmental economics falls within the efficiency story line. For example, the standard literature in forest management, the tradition started by Faustmann and Ohlin, considers the problem of optimal forest rotation assuming fixed tastes and homogeneous super rational, independent, agents, and shows what would be efficient, and what would not.[1] That work does not deal with the question of whether efficiency is society's goal in forest management, or whether it should be.

Looking at broader issues in social welfare theory, it is very clear that that work is contextual—it can only be understood within a much broader framework of thinking about institutions, social well-being, and social welfare. Within the broader contextual framework found in the Classical economics of John Stuart Mill and the grand tradition of liberalism, it is clear that efficiency is not an end in itself; it is a means to an end. Efficiency only has meaning when one specifies the goals, whose goals they are, how the goals are to be weighted, and what method we have of resolving conflict among goals. The textbook presentation of economics avoids this broader discussion, as does the traditional work in environmental economics. I see the work in sustainable forest management as one of the many movements currently going on in economics that is bringing back these broader issues.

Sustainability in the efficiency story is reduced to a question of aggregate existence. Since that efficiency story is generally told in reference to a unique equilibrium model, the presumption of the model is that markets have a natural way of achieving sustainability. We all know the story: Scarcity leads to price rises, which leads to conservation and substitution of the scarce resource, which leads to sustainability. The system simply changes to maintain sustainability; as forests decrease, we switch to other means of providing the services that forests provided—plastic trees, photosynthesizing machines, whatever. In the efficiency story substitutability will solve any problem of scarcity, so why even discuss sustainability? To discuss sustainability means you don't truly understand the scarcity story.

The gross substitutability answer to sustainability, such as that presented in Goeller and Weinberg (1976), is a reasonable one, but is not the concept of sustainability that most people have in mind when they discuss sustainability. They have a different idea in mind, an idea that does not fit in a unique equilibrium model. The sustainability literature fits into models with multiple equilibria, with equilibria selection mechanisms, and with some equilibria being preferred to others. The model that sustainability advocates have in mind has multiple dimensions—one in which a world of rows of neatly organized trees is not the same as a world of old-growth forests where ecological competition has prevailed. Such multiple dimension nonlinear optimization issues quickly go beyond the mathematical abilities of the students, and indeed of even the brightest mathematicians. So, once the models are expanded to include such issues, it becomes clear that economists' models no longer provide answers. Instead, they provide, at best, a heuristic solution, not a formal solution to the problems most individuals are interested in. To avoid getting into such issues, the texts, and much of the research in traditional economics, avoid discussing sustainability.

Another reason that the term "sustainability" is not used in the texts is that it conveys to many economists an integration of normative judgments into the analysis. Such a normative use of the term involves not only an interruption of the efficiency story, but a complete incompatibility with it. The efficiency story has struggled to keep such normative judgments out of the reasoning process being taught, even though almost every economist, if pushed, will accept Hume's Dictum that you cannot derive a should from an is, and that policy necessarily involves normative judgment.

It is for these two reasons that if you look at principles of economics texts you will see very little discussion of sustainability of any type. In fact, among Rust Belt economists (Chicago/Rochester and their satellites) the very mention of the term "sustainable" makes their eyes roll in a signal to other Rust Belt economists that "Here we go again; we are talking with another of those wishy washy environmentalist tree-huggers, who are trying to instill their values in others." For Rust Belt economists, sustainability simply isn't an appropriate topic of discussion for proper economists.[2]

Sustainability fits much better into the complexity story. In models of complex systems one doesn't talk about equilibrium; but rather about basins of attractions. Nonlinearities are accepted, and phase transition jumps are expected as the system evolves. Sustainability means keeping within the existing basin of attraction, and not going to another that is considered less desirable. Within a complex system a "rational choice" is much harder, and indeed impossible, to specify. It is multiple levels of the system, not only the individual, that are optimizing. So, the individual, the result of lower-level optimization at the physiological level, is himself optimizing, and is a component of higher-level systems that are themselves optimizing, and competing for existence. Everything, including agents, is coevolving. Even if one can specify non-contextually what one means by "rational choice," the systemic forces rewarding "rational choice" are often weaker than they are in simple systems. This means that instead of weaving the textbook story around a predetermined equilibrium that must finally be reached if the system is left to its own devices, as is done in the efficiency story, the complexity story is woven around the dynamic process through which one basin is reached temporarily, but where other forces are building up to push it into another basin; the story is never-ending.

Generally, complex systems will have no single equilibrium; but instead a collection of possible basins of attraction, with some basins more likely than others. One can only discover the likelihood of certain basins of attraction by considering the evolution of the entire system with either a heuristic or formal simulation. Instead of thinking of equilibrium, one thinks of replicator dynamics, which drive the system forward in a variety of possible ways. By the replicator dynamics I mean the way in which the aggregated decisions of the agents in the system have a tendency to lead to certain outcomes often not foreseen by individual agents, and possibly not predictable by any agents in the system. Because of the multiple paths, and the potential complicated dynamics, complex systems are generally analytically indeterminate. To gain insight into a complex system one must think within an evolutionary framework in which many different paths are possible, some more sustainable than others.

In the complexity story the market isn't desirable because of some grand sense of efficiency, and government isn't seen as an entity that can tweak a market process result in a certain way to achieve efficiency. Because the market is seen as fully integrated with the society, tweaking one aspect of the market process can create a major change in another aspect—the proverbial butterfly flapping its wings in China that changes the weather pattern in the United States. Sudden shifts of the system from one basin to another become part of the analysis, and thus the sustainability of a particular basin, which in the complexity literature generally goes under the name resilience, becomes an interesting issue.

This complexity story conveys a quite different sense of what is happening to an economy than does the efficiency story. It sees change as an evolutionary process occurring at many levels simultaneously. There are interdependent, slow and fast moving variables, and policy is affecting all of them. Since one does not see the effects on the slow moving variables in the short run, short-run empirical measures of the effects of policy may be highly misleading. Not only do you have to look for optima, you also have to look for early indicators of switch points, such as what level of phosphorous will fundamentally change the nature of a lake.

The policy problem of complex systems is exponentially complex, and pure theory provides far less guidance than it does in simpler systems. There is no one model, so model uncertainty must be part of analysis. Policy must take account of multiple levels of optimization occurring at different speeds. For example, the selection of a certain policy can change tastes, so any policy built upon current tastes may be less than optimal. Policy that does not take account of the cumulative process of policy change can miss important elements of what is really going on. Moreover, in a complex system optimizing likely involves nonlinearities and kinks, making first-order conditions of little use in drawing out robust global policy conclusions.

It is into this complexity world that sustainable forest policy is stepping. Ironically, the concern about stepping into that new world tends to be the reverse of the various sides' concern about sustainability. Traditional economics is not concerned with sustainability of the system but seems to be very concerned with sustainability of traditional economics. Traditional economists' argument for not dealing with the true complexity of the system is that to do so would threaten the current research environment in which researchers are comfortable; it would take them out of the theoretical and methodological terrain that has made economics the queen of the social sciences. If we give up our efficiency model, and start dealing with the complexity model, it will be hard to differentiate us from other sociologists. We might even be mistaken for sociologists!

Sustainable forest management advocates take the opposite position. They argue that our current research terrain is too restrictive, and doesn't allow economists to reach their full potential. They suggest that economists should step into an area where economists have little training, and where the comfort level of tradition and well-worked tools is gone.

Both sides have a point: Who knows—if we go there, will there be an economics profession left? Will we destroy the good that economics does, as we try to deal with these more complicated questions? Isn't it better if we stick with what we know, and have explored, and reach out ever so tentatively and cautiously? Will the economics profession be sustainable in the new uncharted territory?

The sustainable forest management answer to them is essentially the same one that efficiency advocates give to sustainability concerns: don't worry; extending beyond where we are will make things better; economists will have more to offer; we will not have to give up our current benefits to extend the analysis. Of course, economics will be sustainable; we'll just be doing things better.

By temperament, I find myself very much in sympathy with the brave new world view. But I think that the potential of entering that brave new world has to undermine economics must be admitted, and accepted. In academia there may indeed be multiple basins of attractions, and some of them may not include economists as we know them today. Traditional economists lack a spirit of personal adventure for themselves even as they embrace a framework that advocates it for the economy as a whole.

It is that same feeling of adventure that places me in opposition to many of the views of those who argue for sustainability as a key goal of society. To say that sustainability of the environment is a potential concern of the system is not to say that the way in which sustainability is used by researchers is not subject to implicit, unstated value judgments, ambiguity, and assumptions that are not in accord with empirical observations. As I read popular articles on sustainability it is often unclear to me precisely what the authors mean by sustainable. When I look at the empirical and historical evidence, I find that the system has continually adjusted much more than sustainability advocates predicted. But just because not all individuals who use the term have cleared up the definitional ambiguity, and just because the term does not neatly fit into the efficiency story, does not mean that sustainability is not a relevant topic for economists to consider, nor a highly relevant topic for public policy. I believe it is both.

Now that I have spelled out my arguments, let me return to Planck's and Russell's different reactions to economics. Judged from the perspective of a Planck, or a Russell, the efficiency story is a piece of cake; it involves elementary algebra and calculus. To Russell that story was too easy to study. The complexity story, however, is formally untellable (at least at this time), and is far more difficult than particle physics. It requires mathematics not yet developed in Keynes' time, and is only today beginning to be developed. For Planck, that story was too hard to even contemplate studying.

Why the Complexity Story Isn't Told in the Texts

I am both a textbook author and an economist, so I feel the pull between the two stories. As an economist, I direct most of my thoughts toward the complexity story, trying to understand the work that is being done on it. But little of that work shows up in my principles text. There are two reasons why. The first is the sheer complexity of the complexity story. I believe there is a story there, but I'm not sure I can tell that story in a meaningful way to students, or even to myself. A second reason is that I believe the complexity story and apply it to all my decisions. Applied to textbooks, it makes me, and I suspect authors of other successful texts, reluctant to change what is working. Currently textbooks are working and serving a useful purpose. I believe that the story we are telling in our teaching of economics—the efficiency story—is a useful one for all students to learn; it is far more useful than the stories they learn in most of their other classes. I want every student to come out of college with a strong understanding that there is no such thing as a free lunch. Telling the efficiency story achieves that end, and thus seems justifiable, so it is only reasonable to be hesitant to change that story.

The underpinnings for a major change in the story economists see themselves studying, are, however, being built; eventually the transition will occur. As the complexity research continues, the complexity story will become more and more tellable, and, as the current texts die out, new texts that make the change to the complexity story will eventually replace the older texts. But I suspect that because the change involves a totally different story line, the change in stories will be a sudden shift rather than a smooth movement. (Colander 2000c) In the meantime, by which I mean the next 20 to 40 years, the real cutting-edge changes will be made in research in particular fields such as forest management. In most of these field areas researchers have already fully mined the efficiency arguments, and have extracted much of the insight from that model. Thus, they have an incentive to explore alternatives, such as the complexity approach.

The Changes Currently Going On in the Profession

While all the field courses are proceeding on their own path, there is sufficient similarity in the changes to suggest the common nature of these changes. It is a change in the allowable assumptions, from the (holy trinity of rationality, greed, and equilibrium) to a broader set of allowable assumptions, which might be called a new holy trinity of purposeful behavior, enlightened self-interest, and sustainability.

The acceptance of these changes by the profession can be seen in a variety of theoretical work, such as work in behavioral economics, evolutionary game theory, agent-based modeling, experimental economics, and new institutional economics. In this new work utility maximization is enriched by insights about the individual from psychology and neuroscience. Behavioral economics is the most developed. It is considering issues such as reference-dependent preferences, the replacement of expected utility with prospect theory that seems to capture individuals' decision process much better than simply utility maximization, the development of hyperbolic discounting arguments, the formalization of cognitive heuristics, the replacement of theories of self-interest by theories of social preference, and the development of adaptive learning models.

Once one accepts that the behavioral foundations of choice are important, one is directed to experiments, and experimental economics is another expanding area. Experimental economics provides an almost endless set of possible dissertation topics using a methodology that is quite outside the efficiency framework. It provides a method of choosing among assumptions, and an alternative to statistical empirical testing. Economists still have a long way to come in experimental work, but that work has the possibility of significantly changing economics.

The acceptance of behavioral economics also leads to using evolutionary game theory as the setting for a foundational theory of economics. Evolutionary game theory allows one to redefine how institutions are integrated into the analysis and to develop a social dimension of individuals, which was previously lacking in the current textbook story of economics. The movement is slow, but it is happening, and is reflected in the recent allocation of awards in economics. For example, Daniel Kahneman and Vernon Smith recently won a Nobel Prize for their work in experimental economics, and Matt Rabin won the John Bates Clark medal for work on behavioral economics. Because of these changes, today one can no longer describe modern economics as neoclassical economics. (Colander 2000a)

I do not want to overstate how these changes are currently affecting economic research. The research of most economists are variations of what they were taught, and so does not change significantly. "Same economist" research changes only slightly. But the economics profession is not a static group; it is a set of sequential cohorts. So the research changes with the evolving composition of cohorts, with younger, newly trained economists coming in, and older economists going out. Thus the evolutionary hiring and retirement process affects research.

As time passes, younger, differently trained, economists replace older economists, and the average image of what economics is and of how one does economics changes. Since the profession replaces itself every 35 years or so, the rate of change is only about 3% per year. However, even that rate may over-estimate the degree of change in the initial stages of a cycle of change, because most students choose to work with established professors in established methodologies; the newer methodologies and techniques are risky. Initially only a few risk-preferrers choose that path. So, at the beginning of a cycle of change, the rate of change toward a new acceptable approach is smaller, probably closer to 1%. However, at some point a critical mass of work is accumulated, a shift point occurs, the new approach becomes the hot approach, and students flock toward it. At that time the rate of change increases to greater than 3%.[3]

Where Are the Changes Leading Us?

Ultimately I see these changes leading to a change in the basic story we are telling in economics from the current efficiency story in the texts—the story of infinitely bright agents in information-rich environments—to the complexity story—the story of reasonably bright individuals in information-poor environments. Another way of describing my thesis is that the vision of the economy will evolve from its previous vision of a highly complex "simple system" to a highly complex "complex system."[4] Simple systems, no matter how complex, are reducible to a low dimensional set of equations, making it possible to model the system analytically. A complex system is not, and must be represented in another fashion—through simulation, or through insights gained with replicator dynamics. One can never have a full analysis of the entire complex system.

As I stated above, the steps the profession is currently taking toward a complex systems approach are minimal, but the ultimate result of these steps is a movement from telling the efficiency story to telling the complexity story in their research and eventually in the texts. The acceptance of this complexity vision of the economy involves a shift in economics that is far more fundamental than anything associated with the movements away from the holy trinity made so far.

Why Now?

Heterodox and heuristic economists have long argued that economics should deal with broader issues. So the questions arise: Why is the change occurring now? And: Why didn't it occur previously? My answer to these questions is that what has changed is not the recognition that these broader issues are important; that's always been there; what's changed is the belief that economics may have something to bring to bear on these broader questions. The reason is twofold. First, economists now believe that they have something to bring to these questions because of changes in the analytic and computing technology. Second, theorists have an incentive to branch out because the efficiency model, which is structured around the holy trinity, has been well-developed, and the low hanging fruit has been picked. In short, the changes will take place because they offer exciting dissertation topics to graduate students and research possibilities for young researchers, not because of any new insights into the nature of the problem. The efficiency model will die because, given current technology, it's too simple to generate the dissertations and articles that are the underbelly of the profession in the current institutional structure.

From a technical standpoint, the mathematics involved in the efficiency model is really quite simple; the efficiency models assume away path dependency, non-linear dynamics, and many similar complicating features that could well characterize real world processes. Schumpeter (1954) made the assumption of a unique equilibrium as a necessary component of a science of economics. The complexity approach begins with the belief that a unique equilibrium is unsupportable as an assumption, which undermines the efficiency vision of how markets lead the economy to a social optimum. If, however, uniqueness was a requirement of science, studying complexity could not be science.

With the higher level of mathematics being taught in graduate school, and with the greater mathematical sophistication of those entering the profession, that restriction is no longer necessary, which is an important reason why these more complicated issues are being explored. Modern economists have come to believe that by understanding the processes that guide the economy in its evolution that they can gain insight into the economy and into the future direction of the economy, even if they do not know what its ultimate equilibrium will be.

As soon as one moves to these more complicated mathematical approaches, neat analytic solutions are far less likely to be forthcoming. This leads to another change that is occurring in the profession, and is likely to be the most significant change in the more distant future—the movement from analytics to simulations. The reality is that advances in computing power have fundamentally changed technology, reducing the value of deductive theory. If one can gain insight through simulation, there is far less need to gain insight through deductive analytic theory. As long as computing power continues to double every 18 months, agent-based simulation will become more and more important in economists' tool kit, and will eventually replace deductive analytic theory and the supply/demand framework of the current texts.

In these agent-based models the researcher "grows" an economy, letting simple algorithms describing agent behavior (algorithms developed in behavioral work) compete with one another, and see which wins out.[5] Agent-based simulations are fundamentally different than simulations designed to solve equations. In agent-based modeling the system is analyzed without any equations that describe the aggregate movement of the economy; one simply defines the range and decision processes of the individual actors. Multiple simulation runs provide insight into the likelihood of certain outcomes and of the self-organized patterns that emerge from the model. As computing power becomes cheaper and cheaper, such modeling will likely take over the profession. Ultimately, I see virtual economies being created in which policies are tested to determine their effectiveness in the same way that virtual designs are currently tested.

Is such agent-based modeling still economics? I believe it is: It keeps much of standard economics—it sees individuals as purposeful, although the precise nature of purposeful behavior is derived from the model rather than assumed. It assumes individuals interact and trade, and that successful individuals continue what they are doing; unsuccessful individuals do not. But to be honest, it is likely that the simulation-based economics will be more like social science generally, and fall under a general "cognitive science" discipline.

Policy Implications of the Two Stories

What relevant policy lessons for students come out of the complexity story is far less clear to me, and I think to the entire profession, than is the fact that changes are occurring. In thinking about the policy implications of the complexity story, Hayek, an early advocate of the complexity approach, initially pushed the implications too far, and seemed to be saying that there was no room for policy activism—that the economics system should be left alone.[6] I see a more nuanced policy view coming out of the complexity story, in which the theory is neutral about general policy prescriptions in the same way that the current textbook efficiency story is neutral. There are reasons for government intervention and reasons for laissez faire. They just are not necessarily the same reasons as those found in the efficiency story, and they are much harder to pull neatly out of the analysis. Determining a firm foundation for the implications of the complexity story for policy is a long way off.

In my work with Buz Brock I am trying to develop that sense of policy nuance in my work on what I call the "economics of muddling through," which I contrast with the efficiency story's "economics of control" approach. In the economics of control, one can, at least in principle, state the optimal action for each agent, and the optimal policy for the policy maker. In the economics of muddling through, specifying the optimal action for the agent and the optimal policy is far beyond the capabilities of the modeler. The best agents and policy makers can do is to muddle through.

Instead of controlling the economy, the goal of policy makers is to muddle through toward broadly defined goals as effectively as possible, perhaps improving the workings of the economy in certain specific instances, but with no grand vision that one is going to suggest an optimal policy. In the economics of muddling through there is no such thing as a free lunch, but once in a while you can snitch a sandwich. Policy work is designed to snitch as many sandwiches as possible. I am pleased with this "muddling through" policy story, and believe that eventually it will be the way economists think of themselves and policy. But it is still in development and is not yet ready for prime time.

I do not claim that muddling through is a breakthrough in our understanding of economic policy issues; it simply is <u>recognition of the limitations of our knowledge of the effects of economic policy</u>. The limitations of the current theory are well known, and the policy implications of any model theoretical economists have developed have always been far more nuanced, and considered in a much broader framework, than are policy discussions found in the texts. However, to make the story simple enough for the texts, the policy presentation has to be simplified, and it is that simplified version that students learn, which reporters present as economists' views, and which economists sometimes fall back on when they are pushing an idea, or simply being lazy.

<u>Muddling through is conducting policy without an ultimate set of plans</u>. So not only are the agents of the new economics operating in an information-poor environment, so are the policy makers. In such a situation policy becomes problem driven, not theory driven. Economics becomes not a single theory that guides policy, but a set of tools—statistical tools, modeling tools, and heuristic tools—that when incorporated with knowledge of the institutional structure can help the policy maker achieve the solution to problems posed by agents in the system.

This <u>muddling through approach</u> is a quite different view of policy economics than the view that is presented in the texts, where economists know what policies will achieve global efficiency. In muddling through, global efficiency is beyond what one can hope to achieve. One can still talk about efficiency, but it is defined locally in relation to existing institutions, and means producing what one is currently producing within existing, or only slightly modified, institutions, at the lowest cost. The muddling through approach is useful only in analyzing incremental change, where issues of sustainability are minimal. Used in this limited sense the implicit assumption that one's normative goals are little changed, and can therefore be left implicit, can be seen as a reasonable simplification.

Broader, less locally defined efficiency, is much more difficult to either define or use in policy discussion. Policy work in muddling through must make one's goals and assumptions clear. Thus, more generally, in muddling through efficiency is not a goal, but a condition imposed by the analysis about the costs of achieving whatever goal has been specified. It is achieving given ends as cheaply as possible, and only has meaning in regard to those ends. In this muddling through framework you hire an economist, tell him or her your goals, and he or she will bring his or her expertise in modeling and data analysis to help achieve those goals at the least possible cost.

It will be a long time before textbooks tell the story of muddling through; it is too radical a change in vision. Initially, changes that are least challenging to the textbook story will find their way into the texts. The field of behavioral economics that is exploring the meaning of the "purposeful behavior" assumption is offering the type of modifications that will show up in the texts soon. These modifications offer a slight change in the policy prescriptions that follow from the analysis. An example of what I have in mind is <u>Cass Sunstein and Richard Thaler</u>'s (2003) concept of "libertarian paternalism."[7] It proposes a set of policies that are consistent with the standard economic policy prescriptions that follow from the efficiency story, but which take into account agents' ill-formed preferences, one of the insights that follows from behavioral economic work.

The e<u>xistence of ill-formed preferences</u> means that individuals' choices are influenced by default rules, and libertarian paternalism is designed to take advantage of this fact. For example, say the policy maker believes that individuals will be better off with more forests in the world. If a policy that allows individuals to direct a part of their taxes to forests is made the default option, the policy maker can increase participation in the program significantly while still letting individuals choose. Doing so does not take away the individual's choice since the individual has the same choice in both situations, but the behaviors will be quite different.

Applying even this small implication of behavioral economics to policy is a major step. It means that economists must accept that normative judgments become part of the policy process. But a full acceptance of the policy implications is a much larger step. If tastes are endogenous, then normative issues become a central role in economic policy and cannot be escaped or ignored.

Conclusion: Economics and Sustainability

Let me conclude with a few brief comments about the implications I see this shift having in a specific area: forestry research. Many people have a sense that it may be a good goal for society to have the economy move to an equilibrium that is characterized by more land devoted to forests than they believe is likely to be the case under existing institutions.[8]

In dealing with this debate the efficiency story is not especially helpful, because it excludes many of the issues upon which the debate is based. By being more open to alternative assumptions, the complexity approach to economics brings economists back into the broader theoretical and policy debate. Rather than defining the model and policy questions that can be asked, economic reasoning can be used as an input into broader more inclusive policy models. That, in my mind, is a plus for everyone involved. I disagree with those economists who fear this movement; to fear it means that one does not believe that the policy insights of economics will be able to compete with the insights from other disciplines and from other approaches. I believe that economic insights are strong enough to survive, and even prosper, on this expanded terrain. The complexity approach gives up the pillars upon which our welfare economics is built and in doing so it gives up the almost theological sense of what is right, which is often associated with that view. In doing so economics loses some influence. But by engaging the larger debate, and letting economic ideas procreate with other ideas, it gains influence, and becomes stronger.

In the complexity approach we will not have theory to rely upon to say what policy is right or wrong. We will have tools that can add insights about how to arrive at the desired ends. Will "certification" actually increase the amount of forests, or will it have unintended effects? Are there other ways to achieve that goal? Can trees be made into an "image good" so that individuals can gain pleasure from the existence of trees? Can land trusts be expanded, so that people have a method of changing their notional demand for forests into a real demand that can be revealed in a satisfactory way? Can we structure institutions so that our society is more forest friendly? For example, I have often wondered about the wastefulness of cemeteries and the granite monuments to death that somehow have been built into our culture. Why couldn't we have found a basin of attraction that, whenever a person dies, instead of being buried in a cemetery, that person is buried in a sacred cemetery forest, which will be kept for generations and generations? I'm not sure what the answers to these questions are, but in asking them, and others like them, the research in forestry is moving to the new complexity story approach to economics that will eventually take over the way economics is done.

Notes

1. I will use forest management as an example, but the argument applies to many environmental areas where economists are currently widening their approach.
2. Steve Landsburg in *The Armchair Economist* (Landsburg, 1993) provides good examples of the approach taken by Rust Belt economists.
3. That is close to happening in behavioral economics in certain fields such as finance. As Richard Thaler has said: Once, people asked what behavioral finance was; now people ask what other type of finance is there. A leading indicator of the changes that are occurring is the hiring priorities of top schools. In the early 2000s behavioral economics is seen as a hiring priority; experimental economics is not yet a totally accepted hiring priority, and agent-based modeling is hardly on the horizon.
4. For a discussion of what is meant by "complex system" see Auyang (2000).
5. For a discussion of agent-based modeling see Robert Axtell and Josh Epstein (1996) and Robert Axelrod (1997).
6. In his later writings, he modified these views and focused more on the importance of institutions and law. For a discussion, see contributions on Hayek in Colander (2000b).
7. I include a discussion of libertarian paternalism starting in the 6th edition of my principles text.
8. While I tend to agree with that normative view, I also believe that what one means by forest is often ambiguous. What can be called a forest, and how to weight different types of forests, are difficult problems and can lead to much confusion in the debate.

10

On the Treatment of Fixed and Sunk Costs in Principles Texts

Recently X. Henry Wang and Bill Z. Yang (2001) proposed an alternative textbook convention concerning the treatment of fixed, variable, and sunk costs. They argue that in the standard model fixed costs should be divided into two components—sunk costs and avoidable fixed costs. They base their argument on the existence of inconsistencies in some textbooks.

As a principles textbook author, who wants to provide as clear a presentation of costs as possible, I seriously considered adopting their usage, but in the end decided not to do so. The reason I decided against using it was that it did not pass the KISS (Keep it Simple, Stupid) and CLAP [Change As Little As Possible (from the standard presentation)] criteria that are standard for any textbook revision. Instead, I maintain that the current presentation in my book (which is the same convention that most other principles books currently use, although they may not always be consistent with that convention). I argue that this current convention is acceptable. Correctly followed, it does not have the logical difficulties to which Wang and Yang refer, and allows us to maintain the proposition that "in the long run there are no fixed costs" as well as the other aspects of the model that are based on a single category of fixed costs.

Let me begin by saying that I am highly sympathetic with the point that Wang and Yang are making. One of the reasons I wrote my principles text was a desire to present cost analysis clearly to students. Initially, I had grand hopes of clearing up the presentation, and making it compatible with advances that were then being made in cost accounting and optimal control presentations of decision theory. When I wrote my first draft of the first edition, I tried to provide a new presentation of cost analysis. I presented costs in an optimal control framework in which there was a planning horizon (the long run) and an adjustment horizon (the short run). The short run was an adjustment decision to a long-run planning decision and any short-run adjustment would be characterized by its cost of adjustment. Adjustment costs, not fixed inputs or fixed costs, became the central concepts of short-run analysis. In this alternative model there were no fixed or variable inputs; costs of adjustment, not changing marginal productivity, was the explanation for the shape of the short-run cost curve, and there was a range of inputs that varied by their costs of adjustment.

None of that presentation made it into the first edition. Reviewers universally panned it, and I quickly learned an important lesson in Textbook Writing 101: Once a model exists, deviate from it at your peril. Thereafter, I struggled to fit my views into the existing framework, and arrived at the convention that my principles textbook, and most other principles textbooks, currently use. It is compatible with that broader optimal control vision, but deviates from the standard fixed/variable cost model as little as possible.

The key to the current convention is that in the standard model all fixed costs are assumed to be sunk costs. This does not mean that in the real world all fixed costs must be sunk, in the same way that in the real world not all "fixed inputs" are fixed; it simply means that, for purposes of the model, that is the assumption that is being made. What Wang and Yang call avoidable fixed costs are thus excluded from the standard model, as are many other issues.

Because changing from the current convention involves significant coordination issues among different textbooks and among standardized tests such as the AP exam, to argue for a change from the current convention one must make a stronger case than "Had an alternative convention developed, it would be preferable." One must argue that the current convention is logically wrong, or is hurting students' understanding of the issue. The current convention does not suffer from those problems.[1]

Wang and Yang are right to point out the importance of a convention to textbook presentations of costs. Some convention is necessary because costs do not divide up into neat fixed and variable categories; most costs are somewhere in between the two; they are quasi-variable, or quasi-fixed, and can be adjusted at a cost. By pointing that out, and reminding teachers of economics that that is the case, Wang and Yang have made an important contribution to pedagogy.[2]

Problems with Their Convention

Their proposed convention distinguishes two types of fixed costs—one sunk and the other avoidable. I have two problems with this convention. The first is that it complicates the presentation and requires revising a number of standard propositions, including the "in the long run there are no fixed costs" and the "shut-down point" analyses. These are both deeply integrated into the teaching of the course, and switching from them will involve much confusion. For example, to use their conventions, a new curve must be added—average sunk costs—to analyze shut-down points, and the short-run supply curve must be redefined because it would no longer begin from the average variable costs. Such changes, while reasonable, are substantial, and the expected gains from those changes would have to be significant to warrant introducing them into the texts. In my view that is not the case. By simply being clear that in the model fixed costs are assumed to be sunk, one can avoid those changes. Doing so maintains the logic of the current presentation, although it does not prevent discussion of the broader issues of quasi-fixed costs as an addition to the model.

A second, more serious, problem with their proposed convention is that their distinction between sunk and avoidable fixed costs is far too confining. It suggests to students that the problem of lumpiness and partial adjustability that underlies this convention exists only at the zero level of output. That is not true. The problem is much more general. Most costs are partially adjustable not only at zero output, but at all output levels. To see this, consider the example they give of the existence of short-run, avoidable fixed costs. They write:

> A lawyer has signed a lease to rent an office from a landlord. Monthly rent is a short-run fixed cost for his or her business. Suppose that the lawyer decides to shut down the office for a couple of months or immediately get out of the business after the lease has been signed. In this case if he or she can sublet to someone else or pay the financial penalty for breaking the lease, at least some of the monthly rent can be avoided. Only that unavoidable part of the rent or penalty fee is sunk cost. (Wang and Yang 2001: 181)

This example is quite reasonable, but it does not go far enough. It is not only at zero output that costs can be avoided, but at various levels of output. For example, if demand is lower than expected, the lawyer can rent out one of the rooms of the office to someone else. Or he could share it with another lawyer, lowering his costs. In that case, what had been considered fixed costs are partially avoidable not only at zero output, but also at higher level of output. The reality is that many costs classified as fixed are partially avoidable, and there is no reason that they are avoidable only at zero output, as suggested by Wang and Yang.[3] The problem with the Wang and Yang convention is that it integrates this insight only into one place in the model, and, in doing so, makes it harder to present their insight as a general limitation of the model.

Justification for the Alternative Convention

In their presentation, they agree that the current convention of many books (and the one I am supporting here)—making fixed costs a synonym of sunk costs—provides a logically consistent convention. They argue against that convention for three reasons.

The first is that it can potentially confuse students and instructors into looking for a difference between fixed and sunk that does not exist. They argue that if sunk costs and fixed costs are the same, why have both terms? My answer is that the term "fixed" is associated with the term "fixed input" in the standard model. It is part of the current convention, and might be described as a "sunk" term that we have to work around. The cost associated with the fixed input is the fixed cost; the input cannot be changed, and has no other use, which makes it a sunk cost. The cost associated with the variable input is a variable cost, which, by assumption, can be varied costlessly.

Now, I am not arguing that, had one been starting the presentation from scratch, the fixed/flexible metaphor would have been the ideal one. It would not have been. Neither of these assumptions nicely fits many real-world production processes, but it is the standard model that textbooks use, and the terms reflect the model.

In making all fixed costs in the model sunk, the textbooks are not making the terms synonyms as Wang and Yang suggest; they are simply assuming, for simplicity in the model presented, that the fixed costs of the model are sunk—and the money spent on them cannot be recovered.

A second argument Wang and Yang give for not assuming that all fixed costs are sunk is that such an assumption leads to logical inconsistencies in presentations. Although I have no doubt that logical inconsistencies exist in textbook presentations, I think they overstate the problem and a number of the logical inconsistencies in the texts that they point out are not, in my view, logical inconsistencies. They find logical inconsistencies because of a particular interpretation they give to the statement that "costs do not vary with the quantity of output produced." Consider the following argument they make:

> Some textbook authors interpret fixed costs as the costs that are independent of the scale of production. This is false. This mistake is made in two steps. In the first step, an author correctly notes that there are no long-run sunk costs by stating that there are no long-run fixed costs. In the second step, forgetting that fixed costs meant sunk costs, the author re-interprets fixed costs inconsistently as costs that are independent of the level of output. Then the statement that "there are no long-run fixed costs" becomes false. It is the inconsistency in defining fixed costs that makes it a myth. (Wang and Yang 2001: 179)

They interpret "independent of the scale of output" to mean that costs do not vary for output greater than zero. An alternative interpretation is that costs do not vary for output greater than or equal to zero. The latter interpretation makes it clear that in the model one is assuming that all fixed costs are sunk. Simply by interpreting the phrase "independent of output" as inclusive of zero, all fixed costs have to be sunk, and there is no inconsistency, and there are no fixed costs in the long run. In my principles textbook when I present the concept of fixed costs I explicitly point out that in my example the fixed input can't be modified or used for other purposes, which is why the costs are sunk. As long as one distinguishes a long-run planning period from a short-run adjustment period, this classification works nicely. In the long run nothing is fixed, but some costs are lumpy or indivisible, which means that they will be treated as fixed as soon as they are incurred. These indivisible set-up costs help account for the downward slope of the long-run cost curve. But they are still flexible in the long run. As soon as a contract is signed, the costs become fixed, and one is no longer in the long run; one is in the short run.

A third argument Wang and Yang provide against the current convention is that higher-level books in managerial economics dedicate pages to clarifying the distinction between the two. This, for me, is not an argument for changing the presentation in the principles textbook. Upper-level books rightly expand on the models presented in principles in many ways. As long as the principles presentation is not inconsistent with what is presented in upper-level textbooks, keeping it simple makes sense. Principles students have more than enough to learn already. To prepare students for upper-level courses, I have a section in my textbook on using cost analysis in the real world. This section points out the major simplifications of the model and briefly describes the problems.

In this discussion the distinction between avoidable and unavoidable fixed costs is one of many real-world complications. Other complications include unmeasured costs, joint costs, economies of scope, asymmetries, and learning by doing.

Conclusion

The models presented in introductory microeconomics have many failings. Wang and Yang have pointed out one of them. However, the fact that some principles books may have been sloppy in presenting the cost model does not mean that the basic cost model they use is not logically consistent and pedagogically supportable. Because that model is consistent with propositions that have become built into economic knowledge, and because it is simpler than the alternatives, it is highly desirable to maintain it. The alternative convention Wang and Yang put forward complicates the model significantly and does not offer enough gains to warrant being used.

Notes

1. I want to make clear that the arguments presented in this article only concern principles textbooks, where simplicity and minimal change are more highly valued than in intermediate micro and field courses, where students are expected to explore more complex issues.
2. One can see the growing influence of the *Journal of Economic Education* by the number of reviewer comments I received telling me of the Wang and Yang argument.
3. The parallel to this proposition is that many of the costs specified as flexible have significant costs of adjustment. In fact, in many industries, it is more costly to change labor than to change machines.

Part 3: Macro

Stories Economists Tell

11

Teaching Keynes in the 21st Century

Keynesian economics is being slowly eliminated from the principles course. Some new principles books are treating Keynesian economics as an historical artifact, no longer relevant to current economic events.[1] Others, such as McConnell and Brue, continue to make Keynesian economics the core of students' understanding of macro. I come out firmly on the side of saving Keynesian economics, or at least something similar to what we now call Keynesian economics. I'll explain below what I mean by that. For now, let me present the arguments that have been put forward for dumping Keynesian economics.

Four reasons are generally suggested:

1. As a guide to policy, the Keynesian model is wrong; it teaches students that deficits expand the economy and surpluses contract the economy. But in the 1990s deficits were contracting, and the economy was booming. Thus, we should abandon the Keynesian model and replace it with a presentation of the long-run relationship between deficits, interest rates, and growth. We should teach that deficits have little effect, or contract the economy, emphasizing the Ricardo equivalence theorem.[2]

2. Empirically, multiplier effects aren't very large, and the consumption function is nowhere near as stable as it once seemed. Hence, as a basis for policy, the Keynesian multiplier model is almost unusable. Indeed Robert Barro (1996) goes so far as to argue that the World War II deficit spending isn't even an example of the multiplier working—even though unemployment was reduced from 14 percent to under 2 percent during that time. Barro argues that the economy didn't expand much more than the increase in government spending, so therefore, there was no multiplier effect even then, and by induction, if not then, when?

3. The economy gravitates to a long-run natural rate equilibrium on its own. It is not unstable as suggested by the Keynesian model. Thus, we should teach a model based on a concept of the natural rate of unemployment and its corresponding potential income toward which the economy always gravitates.[3]

131

4. The economy doesn't have cycles any more; hence cycles and
    stabilization policy are obsolete. Thus, the Keynesian model, which
    highlights cyclical fluctuations, is also obsolete and should be replaced
    with a model of long-run equilibrium growth. On the intermediate
    level, that model is the Solow growth model; on the principles level
    it is a general discussion of steady-state growth with essentially no
    formal model.[4]

What Keynesian Economics Should Be Saved?

Although I am arguing that Keynesian economics should be saved,
I want to make it clear that I do not want to save everything that has
been swept under the Keynesian mantle; I am quite willing to jettison
much of what has gone under the name Keynesianism.

I am even willing to admit that a key reason for the decline of
Keynesian economics has been the ambiguity about what is meant by
Keynesian economics and that much of this ambiguity is traceable to
inconsistencies in Keynes' writing. There have been numerous
interpretations of Keynes, all supported by references to the literature.
The debates resulting from these various interpretations have consumed
a large portion of many brilliant researchers' time. I avoid those debates
completely. Quite honestly, I don't care what Keynes said when and I
don't care whether what I call Keynesianism is what Keynes really meant,
and I don't think students care either. I'm not even sure that Keynes
really knew what he meant.

But that said, there was clearly something there in Keynes' writings,
and in what goes under the name Keynesianism in the principles
textbooks, that I believe is worth preserving and teaching to students.
What is that something? To me, it is a vision of macroeconomics that
differs from the vision that has become known as the Classical vision.
Specifically, it is a vision that does not assume that the market economy—
left to its own devices—will necessarily gravitate toward a preferable
equilibrium. That is, it is the acceptance of the proposition that the
economy is complex and that, theoretically, markets may not always
lead to the optimal aggregate results. A person who accepts my
interpretation of Keynesianism accepts that the market can, at times,
gravitate toward an undesirable equilibrium for a period of time long
enough to warrant the consideration of government action to modify
that equilibrium.

Although I was never taught so in my principles course, a subset of Classical economists fully accepted this vision, at least as being a possibility. It was only later, after I became interested in the development of ideas and read the Classics in this light, that I learned that there was much more to Classical economics than I had been taught. What I was taught was that Classical economics was wrong and that Keynesian economics was the truth. What I was taught was a model that demonstrated that the aggregate economy was unstable—that is, if it deviated from its potential income, there was no natural tendency for it to return to that equilibrium. The macro economy needed direct government intervention to stabilize it. Keynesian economics was presented as a scientific truth to be contrasted with the Classical incorrect way of looking at the world. That brand of mechanical Keynesianism ended long ago, and I am pleased that it did.

But, recently, it seems that the pendulum has swung too far the other way. Now it is the subset of the Classical vision that sees the unimpeded market as the solution to all our problems that is being taught as the scientific truth, and it is Keynesian economics that is being relegated to the dustbin of history. It is this tendency of macroeconomics texts to swing from one extreme to another that underlies the joke about the student who comes to visit the professor he had 25 years ago. Looking at the exam the professor is about to give the student remarks that it is precisely the same exam that he was given 25 years ago. The professor responds that that is true; in economics, the questions always remain the same; it's the answers that change.

What I am arguing for is teaching macroeconomics without the pendulum—for us to teach that there is a tendency for the market to work fine on its own, and for private institutions to adjust to the problems that develop. We also need to teach that, at times, the macro economy can experience serious coordination problems that may require government action.[5] To do all that we need to teach both what is currently seen as the Classical model, and simultaneously teach the Keynesian model with the multiplier analysis that shows how reverberations from an initial shock can lead the economy to an undesirable position. Economic theory does not tell us what model is appropriate to what time period. That is a matter of judgment, and in that judgment reasonable economists may differ.

I believe that the large majority of economists would find this middle ground acceptable. But it is hard to stay on this middle ground. One of the reasons is that the two alternative views have not been allowed to coexist on the level of high theory. The debate about which of the two views is correct has filled hundreds of thousands of pages of journal articles, 99.9 percent of which are irrelevant to principles students. Specifically, at the principles level all the debates about what might happen if there were instantaneous price-level flexibility, all the esoteric debates about wealth effects, and all the debates about whether Keynesianism was a theoretical or a practical revolution are beside the point.

Again, Keynes is partially to blame for this state of affairs. To distinguish his view from the Classical economists' view, which also allowed that less than instantaneous wage and price adjustment could cause coordination problems, Keynes made his case assuming a perfectly competitive goods market. His policy arguments would have followed just as well if he had simply stated that, institutionally, wages and prices do not adjust instantaneously, and that these institutions require a price level that does not fluctuate "too much." If you assume that some degree of wage and price level stability is required by the institutional core of a monetary economy, then that debate about what would happen if there were perfect price-level flexibility becomes irrelevant.

In my view, all principles students need know is that there is such a debate, and that economic theory does not lead to a definitive conclusion about whether the economy gravitates toward a unique equilibrium within a politically acceptable period of time. To convey this to students, the principles books need only point out that in the real world wages and prices tend to adjust less than instantaneously and, in such a world, repercussions of effects of one market can influence other markets and lead the economy to undesirable outcomes.

This is not a highly controversial position. Monetarists would agree with it; and many of Keynes' Classical contemporaries—the economists of the 1920s and 1930s—would also agree with it. In fact, about the only people who will disagree with it are a few purely theoretical new Classical and real business cycle economists. Consider the following quotation:

> In the first place my attention is fixed by the inquiry, so important to the present interests of society: What is the cause of the general glut of all the markets in the world, to which merchandise is

incessantly carried to be sold at a loss? What is the reason that in the interior of every state, notwithstanding a desire of action adapted to all the developments of industry, there exists universally a difficulty of finding lucrative employments? And when the cause of this chronic disease is found, by what means is it to be remedied? On these questions depend the tranquillity and happiness of nations.

Who do you think said it? As Petur Jonsson (1995) pointed out, it was Jean Batiste Say, the Say of Say's Law (Say 1821: 2). Keynes set up Say as the straw man of Classical economics, in order to tear Classical economics down, but the actual Say was a subtle writer who fully believed general gluts were possible. Another leading monetary economist of Keynes' time, Denis Robertson, had a sequence model of the economy that arrived at Keynesian-type results, as did Lauchlin Currie here in the United States. It is a textbook fiction initially perpetrated by Keynes that led us to the polar views of Keynesian economics and Classical economics. Keynes wanted to differentiate his product and he did so by painting Classical economists as one-dimensional and as believing in something that many of them did not believe in.

The reality is that Classical economics had an extremely rich and varied tradition that included much, if not all, of what we currently present as Keynesian economics. In marketing his ideas Keynes took that rich and varied tradition and pigeonholed it into a one dimensional line of thought that he centered around Say's Law. As I have argued in *The Coming of Keynesianism to America* (1996: 15), in doing so Keynes unfairly characterized Classical economics. Had Keynesianism not existed, much of what we teach as Keynesian economics would still be taught, only it wouldn't be called Keynesian.

The reason I oppose dumping Keynesian economics has nothing to do with whether or not the profession dumps the Keynesian name. The reason is that, in dumping elements of Keynesian economics, the profession is swinging the pendulum back too far toward an implicit assumption that the market solves all our problems, and is leaving out another important pragmatic dimension of Classical thought—the belief that serious problems can develop. For example, in the early 1930s Frank Knight and A.C. Pigou were both supporting government works programs and deficit spending to expand the economy. Similarly Keynes supported public works programs before he wrote *The General Theory*.

Even the Austrian economist W. H. Hutt, one of the strongest anti-Keynesians, writes, "But once the persistent ignoring of 'classical' precepts had precipitated chaos, and insurmountable political problems obviously block the way to non-inflationary recovery, only a pedant would oppose inflation" (1979: 45).

Most Classical economists didn't believe that theoretically the market was the solution to our problems—that view only developed in the analytic revolution when economists became enamored of math. Most Classical economists believed that, practically, the market was the best way to solve our problems. Generally, I believe that Classical view is right, as did Keynes. But it is not always the case, and students need to be taught that. They need to be taught that the argument for leaving things to the market is an historical argument, not a theoretical argument. It is based on the importance of government failure, not the absence of market failure.

With that background discussion, let me now return to the four reasons for dumping the Keynesian model discussed at the beginning of the chapter.

Reason #1

The first reason was that as a guide to policy, the Keynesian model is wrong. But that view is based on seeing the Keynesian model we present to principles students as a mechanistic, rather than an interpretative, model. The interpretative Keynesian model does not say that deficit spending will always expand the economy. In fact nowhere in the General Theory will you find an argument that deficit spending is needed to keep the economy going.

As I point out in "Was Keynes a Keynesian or a Lernerian?" (1984), Keynes was strongly against deficits. Keynesian economics simply states that at times deficits may be helpful. And that, I think, is true. At times they may be. It isn't only I who believes that. In policy makers' minds, demand management policy, taken broadly, and not as a tool of fine tuning, is alive and well in policy discussions. We are doing our students a disservice if we do not teach them the multiplier model upon which that view is based. If we are teaching what policy makers talk about, which is what I think we should teach, policy makers think that multiplier effects are important. Consider Japan's macro policy discussion in the late 1990s of tax cuts and spending programs. Clearly, policy makers still discuss macroeconomics in Keynesian terms.

What was happening to the U.S. economy in the 1990s is not a contradiction of the Keynesian model; it is an example of it. For one thing, the price level remained constant even as the economy expanded beyond what economists believed possible. Think back; the reason the Keynesian model was dumped was that the assumption it made about fixed prices over a range of output did not seem to hold. But if you look at the data, the economy of the 1990s and early 2000s fits the assumption of the Keynesian model.

Even the expected surplus that was predicted in the late 1990s was consistent with the interpretative Keynesian model. Keynes emphasized the uncertainty in the economy and fully believed that expansions in consumer and investment spending could fuel a substantial boom. And that is what happened. The expenditure function shifted up quite independently, causing tax revenue to increase and thereby causing a budget surplus. Why, when it fits the empirical data, did we dump it?

Reason #2

The second argument is that empirically, multiplier effects aren't very large. The evidence here is ambiguous, especially if monetary and fiscal policy are thought of within a forward looking expectational model. In such a model the mere expectation of the policy can affect decisions and the economy, making it almost impossible to empirically measure what the actual effect of the policy is.

What should be deleted from the model is any underlying certainty about the size of multipliers. That's why I favor teaching the interpretative, not the mechanistic, Keynesian model. The interpretative Keynesian model uses the multiplier model simply to suggest the direction of policy effects. The model is not to be interpreted literally. It is an exercise of the mind, not a model of the economy.

If we don't teach the interpretative multiplier model, students are left with the story that the economy adjusts to shocks and never can experience unwanted booms or busts. That, in my view is not correct, nor is it what policy makers believe.

All real-world econometric macro models have multiplier effects in them. For example, the DRI model is centered around demand equations and cost-plus markups and has an implicit multiplier of about 2. Why? Because that is the model that empirically best fits our economy.

Finally, let me turn to Barro's argument about the size of the multiplier in World War II. It is true that there were no significant multiplier effects beyond the initial spending of government. But the reason why is clear. The government imposed rationing, and a whole set of programs, such as price controls, to stop the secondary effects, because it wanted to focus all the production towards the war effort.

Reason #3

The third reason—the gravitation toward the natural rate argument—also has a problem. We economists simply don't know what the natural rate is, if there is one. Consider our record. How many economists in the early 1990s predicted that in 1998 inflation would be less than 2 percent and unemployment less than 4.5 percent? Few. Let me present some economists' views at the time, emphasizing that these were generally held beliefs of economists, and the economists chosen are only examples. The first example is Robert Gordon who in 1994 advised the Federal Reserve Board that the natural rate was probably 6 percent and possibly as high as 6.5 percent. In 1995 he adjusted that to 5.5 percent, and when the unemployment in the United States went lower, lowered his estimate to 5 percent. Another example is Edmund Phelps who in 1994 was saying that the natural rate was 6.5 percent; he lowered his estimate to 6 percent in 1995 and thereafter made no estimates for the record that I know of.[6] The final example comes from Stuart Weiner, vice president of the Kansas City Fed. The first comes from 1993. He writes

> ...estimates suggest that the natural rate of unemployment is currently near 6.25 percent and could move even higher depending upon the extent and persistence of structural disruptions....Thus, the near-term inflation risk may be higher than generally perceived. (1993: 53)

Fact: Unemployment rate in 1993 was 6.5 percent at the time the article was written. Core inflation rate was about 3.2 percent in 1993 and fell to 2.7 percent in 1994.

In 1994 he was also writing. He states:

> ...the natural rate is currently 6.25 percent. With the actual unemployment rate averaging 6.2 percent in the second quarter, this means that labor markets currently are operating at full capacity. (1994: 6)

Fact: Unemployment rate in 1994 was 6.1 percent at the time the article was written. Core inflation rate was about 2.7 percent in 1994 and 3.0 percent in 1995.

Not to be undone, he writes in 1995 that the natural rate is 6.25 percent and states:

> ...I do not find the skeptics' arguments compelling. If I had to choose just one variable to help me forecast inflation turning points, it would be the unemployment gap. And that gap is signaling that concerns about future inflationary pressures are well founded. (1995: 24)

Fact: Unemployment rate in 1995 was 5.6 percent at the time the article was written. Core inflation rate was about 3.0 percent in 1995 and fell to 2.8 percent in 1996.

No further articles by Weiner on the natural rate appear in the Federal Reserve Bank of Kansas City *Economic Review*. In 1999, unemployment was below 4.5 percent and inflationary pressures continue to subside. I want to reemphasize that Weiner was not alone; he was expressing the view, based on the best empirical evidence available to them, of the large majority of economists in the 1990s. Not surprisingly, after this experience most economists became far more circumspect when talking about the natural rate. My question is: Do we really want to make a fixed natural rate the centerpiece of our presentation of macro?

Reason #4

Finally, let me turn to the fourth reason: The economy does not have cycles any more; we are on an upward growth path that will continue into the indefinite future. In response I simply cite the 1998 Asian crisis and the U.S economy's experience in the early 2000s. The Asian crisis was not an experience of economies on their natural rate growth path; it was a crisis of confidence that caused recession in those countries.

I, for one, would not want to go on record as saying that the U.S. economy is recession-proof. The reality is that there is a lot we don't know about the macro economy—generally it is relatively stable, but because it is based on financial stability, which is based on trust and expectations, that stability can disappear quickly.

Conclusion

There's a lot we don't know about the macro economy. We should not be embarrassed by that. The macro economy is complicated—very complicated—and it is not surprising that we have a poor record of predicting. But given that we don't know a lot, shouldn't we be honest with our students, and not present macro economics as understanding more than it does?

What concerns me about the direction of principles of economics textbooks in the United States is that in the attempt to simplify, they are presenting economic knowledge as more certain than it is. In doing that they are giving up teaching the economic method, and instead, concentrating on teaching what the policy answers are. The truth is we don't know for sure what the policy answers are. U.S. economists did not predict the growth the U.S. economy experienced in the later 1990s, and we have been horrendous in predicting which areas would grow.

In thinking about what to teach there is another legacy that I think we can usefully gain from Keynes. Specifically, Keynes was well known for his changing views. Hence the famous joke—if you have four economists you will have four different opinions, unless of course one of them is Mr. Keynes'—then you will have seven.[7] This was true because Keynes was a pragmatist about policy, who drew his policy views from several different models. He was a student of Marshall, and he stated: "The theory of economics is a method rather than a doctrine, an apparatus of the mind, a technique of thinking which helps its possessor to draw correct conclusions" (Keynes 1921: v).

This quotation is the epitome of the Marshallian method. It tells us to use economics as an engine of analysis, not as a set of principles. If we keep that Marshallian method in mind, we will be giving our students a good foundation in understanding macroeconomics and we will be treating Keynes the way he should be treated—as an economist who carried on an important tradition in Classical economics.

Notes

1. In his first edition, Mankiw (1998) began the movement, and many other texts have followed. This paper was originally written in the late 1990s.
2. Robert Barro (1996) argues this position most strongly, but it can be found in many intermediate texts. Texts in the early 2000s have continued this tendency and reflect the arguments being made here.
3. This view can be found in almost all intermediate and introductory textbooks.

4. Mankiw (1998) starts his introductory book with a presentation of long-run growth; and most intermediate macro books have changed their presentation to emphasize the Solow growth model.

5. The term "coordination problems" comes from game theory and is based on the possibility of multiple equilibria. The economy will arrive at an equilibrium but it may not be the most desirable equilibrium. In macro what is meant is that expectational conundrums can develop that lead the economy to an equilibrium at other than the desirable output. See Colander, ed. (1996), for a further discussion.

6. For a discussion of these, and other, economists' predictions of the natural rate, see Amanda Bennett (1995).

7. As usual Keynes had a retort. When challenged for his inconsistency he replied that when he was presented with new evidence he changed his mind, and then he asked what the questioner did when faced with new evidence.

12

The Stories We Tell: A Reconsideration of AS/AD Analysis

The economics we teach undergraduates is a combination of simple models with highly limiting assumptions and storytelling that relates the simple model to the economy. The models are comparative static; the stories generally fill in the missing dynamic analysis. At the introductory economics level, where the models are highly simplified, the storytelling grows in relative importance. A good principles of economics teacher is a good storyteller.

In introductory microeconomics, the central model we teach is a variant of Marshall's partial equilibrium analysis. The dynamic disequilibrium story we tell to accompany it involves opportunity cost and substitution: if the quantity supplied exceeds the quantity demanded, suppliers find that they cannot sell all their goods and find it in their interest to lower prices, and so on. . .. It's an appealing intuitive story that the majority of economists are reasonably comfortable with. It also meets an important teaching criterion: the majority of students can relate to it and say, "Yeah, it makes sense."

In the 1950s and 1960s, introductory macroeconomics had such a simple model: the Keynesian cross. The model came with an intuitively appealing dynamic disequilibrium adjustment story—the multiplier story. If aggregate expenditures exceed aggregate production, then production increases, which causes income to increase, which causes expenditures to increase, and so on . . . This chase between expenditures and production occurs in declining amounts (since the marginal propensity to consume is less than one), which means that eventually, an aggregate expenditures/production equilibrium is reached. This dynamic adjustment story may or may not be true; in its simple form, it is believed by only a few economists. We taught it nonetheless because, given the assumptions, it is a logically consistent story, and for most students, it meets the "Yeah, it makes sense" criterion.

In the 1990s, the Keynesian cross has been supplanted by the AS/AD model. Unfortunately, that model as currently presented is seriously flawed. First, it does not fulfill the minimum requirement of a model:

logical consistency. Its component parts are derived from models that reflect different, and inconsistent, models of the economy. Second, the appropriate disequilibrium adjustment story with which it is consistent—one in which short-run aggregate adjustment occurs because of price level flexibility—is consistent neither with observed reality nor with the disequilibrium adjustment story that most macroeconomists accept.

The problems with the dynamic disequilibrium story are often not apparent, since telling this AS/AD dynamic disequilibrium story properly requires such high-level mental gymnastics that the proper story is not discussed in intro texts, and is not seriously considered in most intermediate macro texts. Instead, the background dynamic story that gives the model intuitive meaning to the student is typically glossed over, or told in a way that is inconsistent with the model. The result is a model of the worst type—a model that obscures, rather than clarifies, that invites students to make the incorrect logical jump that AS/AD analysis is similar to partial equilibrium supply demand analysis, and that discourages thinking deeply about the inner workings of the model.

These problems are not unknown to textbook authors. Their attempts to contort the AS/AD model into a coherent pedagogical tool have led to inconsistencies and confusions in the standard exposition. In this paper I try to make those inconsistencies and confusions clear, and discuss alternatives.

The Standard Exposition of the AD Curve

There are various ways of introducing the AS/AD model. Here, I will focus on the typical derivation of the AD curve from the Keynesian aggregate expenditure/aggregate production (AE/AP) model. Let us assume that the students have learned the Keynesian AE/AP model (or at least have had it presented to them) and are now being taught AS/AD analysis. Typically, the presentation goes as follows:

"Last class, I presented the Keynesian AE/AP analysis. Any questions? Good; I will assume that you all understand it. In this class I will show how we can get an AD curve from that analysis. Consider Figure 1a. What is this graph? Right; it's the Keynesian AE/AP model with equilibrium at income Y_1. We didn't discuss price in that analysis, but we can assume that the price level was at some level, say P_1. The AE curve, AE_1, is the relevant curve for price level P_1. Let's now go through a thought experiment, specifying the effect of a change in the price level on aggregate expenditures.[1] What effect will a change in the price level have on aggregate expenditures?" The typical silence from the class ensues. "Well, then, let me help you."

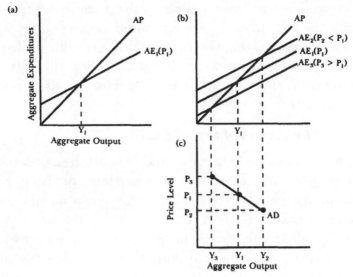

Figure 1

The professor then explains that the quantity of aggregate expenditures will increase with a fall in price level and decrease with a rise in the price: "In Figure lb I show how a fall in the price level from P_1 to P_2 shifts the AE curve up to AE_2, thereby giving a new higher AE_2 curve at lower price level, P_2. Similarly, a rise in the price level lowers aggregate expenditures, giving us a new lower AE_3 curve at higher price level P_3 ($P_3 > P_1 > P_2$). So we now have three different AE curves, each associated with a different price level."

The professor usually offers some subset of four effects as intuitive justification for these movements: the wealth or Pigou effect (a fall in the price level makes the holders of money richer, which leads them to increase expenditures), the international price level effect (a fall in the price level, given fixed exchange rates, decreases imports and increases exports), the Keynes effect (a fall in the price level increases the real money supply, lowering interest rates, increasing expenditures), and the intertemporal price level effect (a fall in the price level, expectations of future price level constant, causes people to switch from future to present consumption).

The professor then proceeds to derive an AD curve from the AE/AP model. "Notice that we have three price levels and three different levels of aggregate output. Consider Figure lc. It has price level on the vertical axis and aggregate output on the horizontal axis. So, let us now plot the price/output points from the top graph on to this bottom graph."

The professor then draws a curve in the price level/output space underneath the AE curve. It is a downward sloping curve, which is presented to the class as the AD curve. At this point, the professor may show how expansionary monetary and fiscal policy will shift the AD curve to the right, and contractionary monetary and fiscal policy will shift it to the left.

The Standard Exposition of the AS Curve

The professor now switches gears and presents the aggregate supply curve. Here, generally, there is somewhat less consistency in the presentation. In a typical presentation, both a long-run and a short-run AS curve are discussed.

The long-run AS curve is usually presented as a perfectly inelastic curve at the economy's potential output level. Its shape is generally justified by reference to the neutrality of money in the long run. Since a price level change—in which all relative prices move in tandem—makes no difference to anyone, it is reasonable to assume that aggregate output is unaffected by changes in the price level. Often, the long-run AS curve is related to the "natural rate" equilibrium of the economy, and the argument is made that if the wage rate is flexible in the long run, the economy will always be at "full employment."

The short-run aggregate supply curve is presented as upward sloping for one of two reasons: fixed nominal input prices (perhaps due to explicit or implicit contracts) or misperceptions of workers or firms. For example, the sort of heuristic presentations generally found in intro texts might hold that when faced with higher prices for their output caused by an increase in the money supply, firms incorrectly think the price level would remain constant, their relative price had increased, and they can make higher profits by increasing production. They consequently increase production only to discover that the price level (including input prices) has risen and, had they had full information, they would not have chosen to increase output. Thus, after some unspecified time period the short-run AS curve shifts back to the long-run supply curve. In more formal models it is generally the fixed nominal wage that leads to the short-run increase in output (implicitly assuming money illusion on the part of the workers), but the general reasoning is the same. The underlying dynamics of that shift are often left undiscussed; however, since, in the long run, the AS curve is assumed to be perfectly inelastic at full employment, the shift must take place.

Both the short-run and the long-run aggregate supply curve come from a fundamentally different conception of the economy than did the AD curve. Neither the long- nor the short-run supply curve fits the Keynesian model, so the above presentation of the shape of the AS curve is often supplemented in intro texts by what might be called a "pure Keynesian" case. In this pure Keynesian case, the supply curve is presented as perfectly elastic. This is generally not derived: it is simply presented as an assumption of the Keynesian model.

Often the three cases are combined together into an AS curve, which has three ranges: a Keynesian range in which the AS curve is perfectly horizontal, a classical range in which the AS curve is perfectly vertical, and an intermediate range in which the AS curve is upward-sloping. In this combination AS curve, the long-run/short-run distinction is generally dropped, and the potential instability of the intermediate range is not discussed.

Policy Analysis with the Standard AS/AD Curves

The above aggregate supply-curve is then combined with the AD curve derived from the Keynesian model to arrive at the standard textbook AS/AD model. Let me briefly specify the typical analysis presented. Expansionary fiscal and monetary policy shifts the AD curve out to the right, with the effect on real output and price level dependent on the elasticity of the AS curve. In the Keynesian range, expansionary policy affects only real output. In the classical range, it affects only the price level. In the intermediate range, the effect of monetary and fiscal policy is split between price level changes and real income changes, with the relative division being determined by the elasticity of the AS curve. A price supply shock will shift the AS curve up, causing real output to decrease and the price level to rise. A negative supply shock will shift the AS curve to the left, causing price level to rise and real output to decrease.

Most professors know this drill well, and it is to get to that policy drill that most professors put up with the AS/AD analysis. After all, the general effect of monetary and fiscal policy and of supply shocks in the standard AS/AD model are those that the majority of economists believe will occur. Moreover, significant room is left for differences of opinion about the short run, depending on what portion of the composite AS curve the economy is in.

Problems with the Standard Exposition

The above presentation seems relatively straightforward. The problems arise when the veneer of the model is scraped off, either because one is forced to scrape it off due to a question by a precocious student, because one is trying to carefully spell out the underlying logic specification of the model, or because one is carefully going through the dynamics accompanying it.

An Incorrectly Specified AD Curve

The logical specification problem concerns defining the AD curve that was derived from the Keynesian model. An appropriate definition of the AD curve derived from the Keynesian model would be as follows: The AD curve is the combination of points at which the Keynesian model is in equilibrium, given the relationship between price level and real output specified in the price-level thought experiment. The standard intro book does not give this definition; instead it gives a definition that parallels the definition of the partial equilibrium demand curve. A typical definition of an AD curve presented in an intro text is the following: Aggregate demand is a schedule, graphically represented as a curve, which shows the various amounts of goods and services that society as a whole will desire to purchase at various price levels, other things being equal. Notice that this definition parallels the definitions of the partial equilibrium demand curve, making appropriate distinctions between relative price and price level and quantity of a good and real output.

This textbook definition is a reasonable one of what the AD curve should be, although it is somewhat vague about what other things are being held constant. Typically, the explanation of what determines the slope of the AD curve, which focuses on the four effects discussed above, clarifies that everything except the direct effect of changes in the price level on output is being held constant.

The problem with this definition and delineation of what determines the slope of the AD curve is that it is not consistent with the derivation of the AD curve from the Keynesian model, because that Keynesian model-derived AD curve does not hold other things constant.[2] The Keynesian model is quite explicitly a model of expenditures and production; it does not hold other things, specifically supply, constant. Listing factors such as the Pigou effect and the Keynes effect as the determinants of the slope of the AD curve does not include the multiplier effects, which are central to the Keynesian model. Thus, the standard presentation of the AD curve misses the point that in the AD curve derived from the Keynesian model, all these effects of price level on output are multiplied by some amount before one derives an AD curve. The two approaches are equivalent only if the multiplier is zero.

To see how this inconsistency can get a professor into trouble, let's introduce a precocious student. We all know the type: the one who asks the simple but difficult questions. This student asks, "Professor, I'm trying to draw the AD curve, and I want to make sure that I have it right. Say the price level falls by 2 and the real output caused by that fall in the price level, other things constant, is 2. Does this mean that the AD curve will have a slope of -1?"

If the professor isn't paying too much attention when asked this question, he or she responds, "Yes, that sounds right."

"But professor," the student responds, "that isn't what I got when I did my derivation of the AD curve. Specifically, when I shifted up my AE curve by 2, real output increased by 6 because I had a multiplier of 3. So the slope of the AD curve I got was -3, not -1."

"Oh," the professor responds, trying to regroup as we all have a tendency to do in such cases. "The definition isn't quite the definition we meant; we also want to take into account the multiplier effect. So you are quite right, the slope of the AD curve is indeed -3 when the multiplier is 3, and the initial response of real output to price level is in a one to one ratio."

"But professor," responds the student, "now I'm even more confused. Didn't you tell me before when you were explaining the Keynesian disequilibrium process that the multiplier was an interaction of production and expenditures—that when aggregate expenditures increased, it brought about a supply response from firms who increased output? Didn't you also say that this increase in income would cause income to increase even more, which would cause firms to increase output, which would cause income to increase, which would cause expenditures to increase, and that this process continues until the iterations ground to zero? Or have I misunderstood the multiplier? But, now you're telling me that the AD curve holds other things constant, and that must mean that supply is being held constant, right? Is supply or quantity supplied being held constant in the Keynesian model? Or are they not? And if they are not being held constant, how can we derive an aggregate demand curve from the model that does not hold other things constant?"

At this point the professor, if he or she is like me, gives the "retreat and regroup" response: "You raise some very interesting issues, but they are difficult ones; let's discuss it after class."

After class, the professor tells the student something like this: "The problem here is that the AD curve derived from the Keynesian model is not really an AD curve.[3] The AD curve defined in the book would only include the initial effects, not any multiplied effects of that initial effect. As you quite rightly recognized, the Keynesian model defines equilibrium points, and thus the curve we derive from it would better be called an 'aggregate equilibrium curve,' not an AD curve. For some reason it wasn't, and the book and I are simply following standard nomenclature and definition, which are, I agree, inconsistent.

"The reason we accept this inconsistency is that in the 1990s we don't really believe that the Keynesian model defines long-run equilibrium; instead we believe that the long-run equilibrium is determined by aggregate supply considerations and that, at best, the Keynesian model describes a temporary and fleeting aggregate equilibrium. To get into these issues would totally confuse the class, so, to be honest, we fudged a bit and talked about the AD curve we defined and the aggregate equilibrium curve we derived as if they were the same curve, so as not to confuse students. This allows us to avoid some complicated dynamic issues that the profession has not fully resolved. You understand, right?"

The precocious student nods and decides to switch to another major.

In short, the logical problem here is that one cannot derive an AD curve from the Keynesian model, because the Keynesian model includes a dynamic interactive effect between supply and demand in the form of the multiplier. The Keynesian model has embodied in it what Robert Clower (1994) calls Hansen's Law—the proposition that demand creates its own supply. This analysis of supply might be totally wrong, but there is no denying that the Keynesian model has assumptions of supply responses in it. As you move along the 45-degree line, supply is changing independently of any change in the wage/price ratio.

Given that the Keynesian model includes assumptions about supply, one cannot logically add another supply analysis to the model unless that other supply analysis is consistent with the Keynesian model assumption about supply. The AS curve used in the standard AS/AD model is not; thus the model is logically inconsistent. It has two inconsistent supply analyses: one implicitly built into the slope of the AD curve, the other explicitly behind the AS curve.

AS/AD Disequilibrium Dynamics

The second problem with the AS/AD model is that the implicit dynamic adjustment story that lies behind it is not consistent with observed reality and is not a story most economists accept. To understand this problem, consider the situation where both wages and prices are perfectly flexible, so the AS curve is perfectly vertical. Say that the economy is initially in equilibrium and that it suddenly experiences a negative demand shock. What is the underlying dynamic adjustment story?

Most intro books are good at pointing out that the necessary adjustment is not a micro-style partial equilibrium story. But most do not delve into the appropriate adjustment story, which would be complicated because an autonomous shift of expenditures of say, 10, will cause a shift of the standard AD curve by $(1/1 - MPC)$ 10. Pointing this out would lead students to see what a strange type of demand curve the standard AD curve is, so the books simply don't point it out. Instead, when discussing dynamic adjustment, most books simply switch and implicitly use a more reasonable aggregate demand curve that corresponds to their definition, not their deviation.

Say that there is a negative real demand shock that causes excess supply in the goods market. (Here, to simplify the presentation, I describe only the dynamics behind the Pigou and Keynes effect; the intertemporal price level effect and the international effect have different dynamics and different problems.) The appropriate dynamic adjustment story is the following: The price level falls, increasing the real money supply. This lowers interest rates, stimulating investment- and interest-related consumption expenditures (the Keynes effect). The fall in the price level also makes the holders of real money balances richer, increasing their expenditures (the Pigou effect). The combination of these two effects moves us along the defined AD curve (including no multiplier effects since this is not the derived AD curve) until, finally, equilibrium is reached at the starting point—the natural rate of output.

The problems with the above dynamics are fourfold. First, they don't correspond to observed reality. The last time the U.S. price level fell was back in the 1930s, yet the economy has experienced many adjustments to negative demand shocks. Second, these effects are simply too weak to be the driving forces in the aggregate adjustment process. Pigou, when he first presented the wealth effect, agreed that it was only a debating point, unimportant on the checkerboard of real life. Similarly, falls in the price level of a magnitude large enough for the

Keynes effect to be significant simply are not observed. And, as Keynes pointed out in *The General Theory*, if this were a sensible adjustment mechanism to follow, increasing the nominal money supply would achieve the same end.

Mechanism of the Falling Price Level

A third problem is that if the above two effects are the entire dynamic story, then the story assumes that a falling price level will affect the goods market only indirectly through its effect on the money supply. But if you ask any business economist to predict the effect of an unexpected 10 percent fall in the price level, you are likely to hear that it would tear the economy apart through its effect on financial obligations specified in nominal terms. Such an unexpected fall in the price level would transfer significant wealth from debtors to creditors, and since many entrepreneurs are debtors, it would significantly disrupt the economy, reducing both aggregate supply and aggregate demand.

Waiting for Equilibrium

A fourth problem is that the dynamics assume that as all this indirect dynamic adjustment is taking place, the participants in the goods market are assumed to be making no adjustments of their own. Firms and individuals facing excess supply are sitting around, waiting for equilibrium to be brought about by the falling price level's effect on the money supply, even though firms cannot sell all their goods. Any student who looks at the real economy knows that isn't what happens. It is intuitively much more plausible to assume (as Keynes did) that faced with excess supply, firms will, to some degree, decrease real output supplied. As they do that, they will decrease aggregate income. Put simply: in the aggregate economy it is almost inconceivable that supply and demand are not interdependent in some way. Any dynamic adjustment story that does not take account of that interconnection, or at least explain why such an intuitively obvious interconnection is not present, is simply nonbelievable.

I suspect that it was to capture that interdependency that most books chose to focus on the aggregate demand curve (really an aggregate equilibrium curve) derived from the Keynesian model rather than on the appropriately defined AD curve. But they can't have it both ways. If that goods market adjustment eliminates some portion of the goods market disequilibrium, the effects of the money market dynamics on the goods market will be changed. If interdependent shifting of aggregate supply and aggregate demand brings the goods market closer to equilibrium, as the Keynesian model assumes it does, what is the dynamic adjustment mechanism that leads the economy back to the original supply curve? It isn't to be found in the texts. It simply is assumed to happen.

The above dynamic disequilibrium problem is central to macroeconomics. If aggregate supply and demand are interdependent, the standard disequilibrium dynamics do not lead to a unique equilibrium with anything less than instantaneous price level adjustment. That story is vacuous; it works only if there is never disequilibrium. This was the essence of the Keynesian revolution spelled out by Keynes in his one paragraph Chapter I of *The General Theory*. The standard AS/AD analysis emasculates both Keynes and common sense.[4]

I think most economists would agree that the underlying disequilibrium adjustment story that appropriately accompanies the AS/AD model is not descriptive of the real world, but is simply a defensive story to maintain the logic of the AS/AD model of the economy. If we honestly told students that these are the underlying stories behind the analysis, most of them would ask, "Why are you teaching us this? This is not the way the economy works."

Proposed Solutions

There are three alternative ways of dealing with the problems with AS/AD described above: the "pedagogy is dirty" solution; the "banishment" solution; and the "coordination augmented production function" solution. Although I am biased toward the third of these, I will try to give a fair presentation of all.

The "Pedagogy is Dirty" Solution

The first solution is practical. It is implicitly the solution we are currently using. It views the AS/AD model as a rough and dirty policy model and holds that what we should be doing in the principles course is simplifying the essence of the macro policy problem to something that is understandable. The standard AS/AD analysis does that. It captures certain tendencies in the economy—for aggregate demand to affect both real output and the price level in the short run and for the economy to be limited by a supply constraint in the long run. If we can get intro students to understand that, we're lucky; and all this other stuff is theoretically nice but pedagogically quite irrelevant.

After all, the reality is that most students retain only a small amount of what we teach them. If, in our teaching, we focus on analytic distinctions that only macro specialists understand or care about, students will get all involved in these distinctions and will not learn the important policy lessons of the model.

Many professors must find this viewpoint reasonable. If they didn't, the inconsistencies and sloppiness currently found in the standard presentation of AS/AD analysis would have been removed long ago. But while I understand the reasoning behind this view, I am not convinced by it, and I find it pedagogically troubling. Even "dirty pedagogy" should be internally consistent. It can be exceedingly vague, but it should not be logically wrong as the standard AS/AD model is. Teaching the standard inconsistent model discourages students from questioning the workings of the model. That may not bother those students who are interested in getting their grade and getting out of the course. But it decidedly turns off the good students, the ones we all want to encourage.

If one wants a quick and dirty analysis, why not present to students a quick and dirty analysis, with no pretensions of it being anything else? We could simply tell students that in the short run when expenditures increase, generally output increases, often by a bit more than the initial increase, but that in the longer run, that increase often results in an increase in the price level. Similar descriptions of the other normal effects of policy could easily be given—without any formal AS/AD model that seems to give the analysis rigor when actually none exists. Why use a logically inconsistent model to explain what can be far more simply explained?

The Banishment Solution

The second solution is what might be called the banishment solution. In it one would simply do away with aggregate supply and demand analysis. New classicals who advocate this approach argue for a focus of principles courses on micro issues, leaving macro issues for later courses. Old-time Keynesians who support the banishment solution often recommend teaching the Keynesian model as most descriptive of the real-world adjustment process; in other words, return to the way macro was taught before AS/AD analysis became popular. Thus, we have the wonderful irony of a coalition between new classicals and old-time Keynesians arguing for banishment of AS/AD analysis, although their alternatives are polar opposites.

In the "micro only" view, we would explain to students that aggregate disequilibrium analysis is complicated, and quite likely chaotic, and that economists have little to say explicitly about such complicated dynamics, especially at the introductory level. This alternative is a return to pre-Keynesian days when macro issues were not part of the principles course.

Given the chaotic state of macro theorizing today, this solution is logical enough. But it has problems. Students want to know what economists have to say about the aggregate economy, and if an interest is there, it seems a pity not to meet it. In the 1930s, it was precisely that lack of discussion of the issues that made the younger students ripe for joining the Keynesian revolution. Moreover, this solution would eliminate one-half of the intro courses, although probably a third to a half of that half could be saved by expanding what we teach in micro. But intro courses are the bread-and-butter courses of most departments, which would consequently recoil at a solution that so reduced the demand for economists.

The alternative banishment solution—going back to teaching the Keynesian model—is essentially a "return to the '60s"solution. The problem here is even if the simple Keynesian model ever was a reasonably good description of the determination of aggregate income, it certainly wasn't in the 1990s, and isn't today. Few macroeconomists today believe that fine-tuning will work; that expansionary fiscal policy is called for in such cases as Western Europe in the 1990s where the unemployment exceeds 10 percent; or that we can talk about macro policy without directly incorporating inflation, or at least a changing price level, into the analysis. The policy debates in the 1990s were not about fiscal policy—which the AE/AP model was designed to highlight. They were about monetary policy that can fit into the AE/AP model, but that doesn't fit directly into it, or about policies that directly affect supply. The movement away from the Keynesian model occurred precisely because it often didn't fit observed reality and because we needed a model that did not assume the price level constant.

A final argument against the banishment solution is that it would lead to a bifurcation of the teaching of macro. In the principles course, Keynesians would teach Keynesian macroeconomics, and classical economists would simply ignore macro issues. Intermediate courses could no longer assume a common base. Neither of the polar solutions would prepare students to deal with the views of modern macro theorists who approach macro from a dynamic perspective that is neither pure Keynesian nor pure classical. The reality is that few macro theorists accept a simplistic, mechanistic Keynesian view. Similarly, fewer and fewer modern classical economists are telling strong, efficient market stories of the aggregate economy where partial equilibrium micro explains all macro issues. Instead, they are considering the dynamic issues, and telling stories of potential "sunspot" and "bootstrap" equilibria in which expectations can influence the final equilibrium—stories with path dependencies and no unique equilibrium. In short, in abstract theory the Keynesian/classical theoretical distinction is breaking down, as both camps more carefully investigate complex dynamic adjustment models of how the economy might respond to real shocks and monetary shocks.

The Coordination Augmented Production Function Solution

I call the third solution the "coordination augmented production function" solution. This solution continues to use the AS/AD model, but offers a different specification of the AS and AD curves, and thus an alternative interpretation of the model—one that is consistent with modern debates.

In this approach, the definition of the AD curve would be changed so that the AD curve would no longer be derived from the Keynesian AE/AP model. The shape of the AD curve would reflect only the direct effect of any combination of the Pigou effect, the Keynes effect, the international effect, and the intertemporal price level effect that one believes makes logical sense. It would not include the multiplied effects of those initial effects. If none of the multiplied effects is very large, the AD curve would be nearly vertical.[5] What this redefinition buys is logical consistency. Since Keynesian dynamics involving the multiplier effect and assumed interactions of aggregate supply and demand are not incorporated into the shape of the AD curve, the AD curve can logically be incorporated with alternative AS curves.[6]

Having specified the AD curve so that it fits the definition of an AD curve, one must then make explicit that for this AD curve, aggregate supply is being held constant and that if a change in aggregate supply has an effect on aggregate demand, it must be explicitly accounted for. As output changes for any reason other than the direct effects of a change in the price level on the quantity of aggregate demand, the AD curve shifts.

On the aggregate supply side, this solution involves a respecification of the AS curve to accommodate the dynamics implicit in the Keynesian model, and more complicated dynamics as well. At a root level, this change involves modifying the specification of the underlying aggregate production function. One way to incorporate complicated dynamics into the production function that is consistent with recent developments in macro theory is to separate out the coordination function needed in the economy from the production process and to specify it directly in the production function. Aggregate output depends on production technology, inputs, and "coordination technology"—the institutions that coordinate individuals' actions. Thus the aggregate production function would be $X = f(K, L, C(K_c, L_c))$. Coordination shocks or changes in coordination technology (such as a change in policy regimes) could cause shifts in the production function. This specification allows for the possibility of the economy moving from one aggregate equilibrium to another even if the wage price ratio is constant. If people suddenly have a wave of pessimism, so that expectations of output fall, and firms decrease supply, output does fall. The pessimism is a self-fulfilling coordination shock, and the economy falls to an alternative equilibrium.

Using such a production function, aggregate supply is no longer a simple function of capital and labor used in production, but also depends on the coordination function—how well current institutions in the economy coordinate individuals' actions. One portion of the macro course would involve teaching about how markets coordinate, or fail to coordinate, in the aggregate. It would deal with topics such as interdependent expectations, the role of real-world institutions in the coordination, the public good aspect of coordination, and the difficulty of any coordination solution that involves political processes.

This change looks small, but it is not. It opens up the analysis to new, complicated transmission mechanisms through which policies could affect the economy. Specifically, policies could work through this coordination factor without affecting relative prices. In such a specification there would be no general presumption that policies work, as there is in the Keynesian model, or do not work, as there is in the current classical model. Such discussions would be institutionally specific and open to discussion.

Let me give an example of how this expanded production function could avoid the current problems with AS/AD analysis. Since the Keynesian model assumes aggregate supply depends on aggregate demand, or at least on expected demand, the revised production function behind the AS curve must have expected demand as a component. The Keynesian model becomes a supply model in which aggregate demand, or more specifically expectations of aggregate demand, influences aggregate supply. In this Keynesian model expected demand must be coordinated since there is no market in expectations to keep those expectations optimal. The micro foundation for Keynesian stabilization policy is the missing market in expectations; it has nothing to do with fixed nominal wages.

The Keynesian multiplier model shows one way in which expectations can go wrong and be self-fulfilling, leading the economy to an undesirable equilibrium. In my view, the simple Keynesian model is far too simple; our economy has many institutions and standard operating features that tend to stabilize and coordinate expectations, and thus, there is a stability of expectations given to the system by institutions. Are the institutions ideal? That's debatable, and that is precisely where the high-level debate is.

An economy with this coordination augmented aggregate production function is far more complicated than those presented in the standard textbook models. Aggregate results cannot necessarily be deduced from individual maximization analysis. The self-equilibrating tendency of the aggregate economy cannot be asserted in a classroom setting without explanation. If one believes the economy arrives at the desirable aggregate equilibrium despite no market in expectations, the explanation of how it does so will be part of the story about the determinants of coordination variable. Nor is there a presumption that any type of intervention into the economy will improve it, as there is in the standard Keynesian models. Those positions must be argued on their merits; they are no longer implicitly built into the specification of aggregate supply.

The coordination augmented production function is general; it is simply a framework within which various alternative explanations of how the economy works can be given algebraic and graphical presentations. It allows the telling of complex dynamic stories about aggregate adjustment.

In this chapter I am not arguing for the "coordination solution" as a theoretical advance, although I believe addressing macro problems within this framework would be far more fruitful than our current approaches.[7] My focus here is on pedagogy, and I am arguing for this approach as the solution to a sticky pedagogical problem. It is quite true that the coordination variable is simply a fudge factor that allows us to express our lack of knowledge of aggregate dynamics. It would be nice if such a fudge factor were not necessary, but given the state of macro dynamic theorizing today, it is necessary to tell a reasonable story. At the textbook level, there is nothing wrong with that.

The coordination solution allows a fundamentally different interpretation of the Keynesian/classical debate than is currently presented in most standard textbooks. The debate will shift from comparative statics to dynamics and the implications of path dependency of dynamic adjustment on aggregate equilibrium.

To illustrate this point, let me describe the analysis of expansionary aggregate fiscal policy from both a simple Keynesian and a simple classical perspective. To keep the analysis simple, let us assume in both cases that the AS curve is perfectly vertical. One can be so cavalier about the shape of the supply curve in the Keynesian exposition since in this explanation of the Keynesian model, adjustment does not occur through movements along the supply curve, but instead through interdependent shifts of the supply and demand curves.

A Keynesian dynamic adjustment process holds the price level fixed, and a boost in aggregate demand triggers the multiplier: aggregate supply depends on aggregate demand, and aggregate demand depends on aggregate supply, and so on. This interdependency makes it almost impossible for the individuals to coordinate their production and spending decisions and leads one to expect significant fluctuations in aggregate output—sometimes it would be too high; sometimes it would be too low. If aggregate output is too low, government can use expansionary fiscal policy to shift the AD curve to the right. Given the Keynesian coordination assumptions, that shift in aggregate demand causes the AS curve to shift out by an equal amount. However, this shift in AS increases income and thus induces a further outward shift in AD by an amount determined by the marginal propensity to consume. The multiplier interaction continues until a new equilibrium is arrived at, at a constant price level. Notice that this answer is totally consistent with the Keynesian AE/AP model, since it uses the same goods market dynamic adjustment explanation. Notice also that the shape of the AS curve is of secondary importance, since the economy is not adjusting through price level fluctuations.

In the simplest classical model, disequilibrium is impossible since the price level is perfectly flexible. Thus, the expansionary fiscal policy in the previous example would shift out the AD curve. But as it did so the price level would instantaneously adjust before any other dynamic adjustment process could occur. The result is a rise in the price level, real output remaining constant.

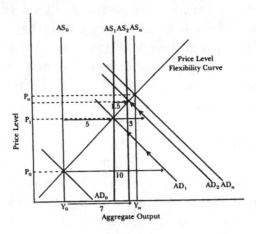

Figure 2

In this explanation, the key difference between Keynesian and classical models does not focus on the real wage or the issue of nominal wage rigidity. Instead, it focuses on the self adjusting properties of the aggregate equilibrium. The classical model assumes the long-run equilibrium is unaffected by dynamic adjustment. That assumption leads to the natural rate equilibrium result. The standard Keynesian model assumes the dynamic adjustment process can affect the long-run equilibrium; it incorporates short-run path dependency, multiple equilibria, and no natural rate.

These simplistic Keynesian and classical views can also be combined into a more realistic story that parallels what is currently being told in the textbooks. In this case, one must specify the relative degree of price level and output sensitivity, as well as the shapes of the AS and AD curves. Figure 2 shows an example. AS is vertical. AD has a slope of -1. The new ingredient is a "price level flexibility curve"—a curve that reflects the institutionally imposed degree of price level flexibility on individuals and firms. A flat curve would illustrate inflexible prices, while a vertical curve would show perfect flexibility. As drawn in the figure, the price flexibility curve describes an economy that has a 50-50 split between price level and real output flexibility.

In this case, expansionary fiscal policy first shifts the AD curve out to the right. Aggregate supply starts responding (the Keynesian view) but so does the price level (the classical view). If the original outward shift in aggregate demand is 10, the 50-50 price level flexibility curve means that aggregate supply initially increases by only 5. With a marginal propensity to consume of, say, .6, this leads to a second shift in aggregate demand of 3, half of which is reflected in a boost to aggregate supply, and so on. Given these illustrative numbers, the original increase of 10 in aggregate demand leads to an increase in real output of 7. This may seem small (assuming less flexibility in the price level would make it larger); but it should be pointed out that in this model any increase is permanent, not temporary, at least in regard to the adjustment mechanisms specified. If the economy is to return to a natural equilibrium, some additional adjustment mechanisms must be identified that drive it there.

This combination model in which the price level is partially flexible looks very similar to the standard approach. It differs, however, in three fundamental ways. First, as discussed above, changes are permanent, not temporary; this composite model is a multiple equilibria, not a unique equilibrium, model. The second is that the AD curve used in this model is the AD curve without a multiplier effect included in its slope; the Keynesian iterative shifts must be shown. The third is that the slope of the supply curve did not really enter into the above discussion, because the AS curve is replaced by a curve reflecting the hypothesized level of price level flexibility in the economy. This price level flexibility curve is a dynamic phenomenon; at the introductory level it will most easily be presented as an empirically observed phenomenon (like the size of the marginal propensity to consume) rather than a deductively derived curve. It is a locus of shifting AS/AD equilibrium points.[8]

I show the above combination simplistic view not because I think it is descriptive of real- world adjustment processes, but simply to show how, using this model, the Keynesian and classical analyses can be combined along standard ways, arriving at almost identical results as the standard AS/AD model while avoiding the logical inconsistencies found in the standard model. It is, however, an integration of views that, I believe, is unfair to both Keynesian and classical views. The reality is that when one gets into dynamics, so many things can be changing that any simplistic explanation of the dynamic adjustment processes will necessarily be unfair. The policy effects of monetary and fiscal policy that sophisticated Keynesians and classicals believe occur are much more complicated and subtle than is allowed for in the above combination model. That's what's nice about the coordination variable in the production function approach. With it one can tell an almost infinite number of stories, including ones that fit far more sophisticated interpretations than the above graphical model allowed.

The dynamic story I find reasonably convincing is one in which policy affects expectations, expectations affect coordination, and coordination affects real output in a multitude of ways. In this story, existing institutions play an important role in determining which of the multitude of possibilities will actually occur. (Somehow, I've always believed that one cannot discuss the real-world economy without discussing the real-world institutions that shape it.) This dynamic story gives a reasonable (to me) presentation of the views of both sophisticated Keynesians and sophisticated classicals.

The sophisticated classical view accepts the possibility of muted multiplier effects and hence fluctuations in real output in the economy that are not reflective of individuals' decisions. However, it denies that, practically, there is anything the government can do about it. Thus, for practical purposes, it holds that business cycles can be considered real business cycles. As a practical matter, the economy will be best left alone. This is not, however, a theoretically deduced view; it is an argument based on political economy. One reason is that differences between aggregate supply and demand will be minimal since the financial markets will operate relatively efficiently, eliminating the need for price level fluctuations. In addition, this view generally sees the workings of government as too slow and too politically influenced to warrant policy action.

The sophisticated Keynesian view accepts that the actual adjustment process is far more complicated than the simple Keynesian multiplier allows. It also accepts that, as a practical matter, government policy, whether fiscal or monetary, is far from a perfect coordinating factor and that often one is better off leaving the economy to fend for itself, rather than trying to adjust a dynamic system that is so complex that actions and consequences cannot be easily connected. However, as a judgment call, it sees some relevance for government policy action in specific circumstances. That government action need not only be monetary and fiscal policy. It is any government action that will help coordinate aggregate supply and demand decisions in a cost-effective way.

In these sophisticated stories, often the real policy action is not in the policy itself, but is in the expectations of policy, and in the expectations of expectations of policy. In a world where expectations influence real variables, policy is not, and cannot be, mechanical; it is an art to be studied in a game-theoretic setting. Thus, macroeconomics becomes a study of the aggregate coordination problem in a realistic setting. The coordination approach automatically leads to a discussion of policy that reflects the real-world policy discussions that occur, not the simplistic mechanistic effects of policy that follow from the standard models.

In this interpretation, there is little theoretical difference between sophisticated classicals and Keynesians. Their differences lie in judgments about politics and about interconnections in the economy that are beyond empirical verification, and hence they are differences that reasonable people can have.

Conclusion

The problem of the AS/AD presentation of macro to students reflects larger problems in macro. It is not just a pedagogical problem; it is a problem of the way economists think about the macro economy and the way we treat textbook models.

There is, and there must be, a fundamental difference between textbook models we present students and the models we develop to extend theory. When there is such a difference, textbook models should not be taught as definitive models of the economy; because of the limitations on exposition, they must necessarily be far too simple for that. Textbooks models are exercises of the mind that give one a sense of how economic variables may interact. Such exercises are absolutely necessary if one is to deal with the far more complicated real-world interactions. These exercises are a tool for helping one understand some of the interconnections in the economy and can be useful only in conjunction with a broader knowledge of the institutions in the economy. As Keynes argued, "The theory of economics ...is a method rather than a doctrine, an apparatus of the mind, a technique of thinking which helps its possessor to draw correct conclusions." To put it another way, textbook models illustrate a way of thinking; they are not a replacement for thinking.

All too often, economists try to draw logical links between textbook models and the broad theoretical models that seek to describe how the economy actually works. Unless the standard textbook models are broad enough to incorporate reasonable dynamics in the accompanying dynamic adjustment story, making that link between textbook models and the real world hurts both theoretical work and teaching. In theoretical work, such links limit the development and extension of new insights, as people's imaginations are limited by their textbook conception of issues. In teaching, such links force us into the inconsistencies and gerrymandered dynamics illustrated by the standard AS/AD exposition. By broadening the textbook model to allow for dynamics to affect statics, as is done in the coordination approach, we can use textbook models to sharpen students' analytic skills. Then, through the stories we tell to accompany those models, we can convey to students the complexity of the economy and the insightfulness of economists' thinking about that economy.

Notes

1. The same derivation can be done from an IS/LM model in an intermediate macro course.
2. In this article I concentrate on what might be called the Keynesian aggregate demand curve—so-called because it is derived from a Keynesian IS/LM or AE/AP model or is developed using reasoning (such as the Pigou or Keynes effect) that developed after the Keynesian revolution. I do not discuss what might be called a classical aggregate demand curve, which is derived from the quantity theory and which assumes velocity constant. This rectangular hyperbola aggregate demand curve follows from the assumptions of the quantity theory and is not derived from any other analysis. As such, it avoids the criticism of being logically inconsistent; it is, simply, arbitrary and, given the real world fluctuations in short-run velocity, hardly supportable as an empirically relevant curve. What is not pedagogically defensible is to present the classical AD curve in one part of the book and, without discussion, present a Keynesian AD curve in another part of the book.
3. Variations of this criticism of the AD curve have been made by a variety of economists. Besides myself, they include Robert Clower (1994), Robert Barro (1994), Fields and Hart (1990, 1994), and, I'm sure, many others. But nonetheless the presentations described here are standard in many texts.
4. I am not arguing here that Keynes was right that the economy has multiple equilibria. I am only arguing that the standard disequilibrium stories are insufficient to justify assuming a unique equilibrium.
5. If one assumes falling price levels disrupt production, it is even possible to have an AD. curve that looks like an AS curve.
6. If the multiplier is zero—that is, the marginal propensity to consume is zero—because expenditures and income are unrelated, then the two demand curves become one, but for the Keynesian AE/AP model, that would imply a horizontal aggregate expenditures curve. This would deny the essence of the Keynesian model, that autonomous expenditures have induced effects on other expenditures.
7. It can accommodate support and bootstrap equilibria models whereas the standard production function cannot. For an early presentation of this, see Colander (1996); and for a discussion of how this fits modern theories and a stronger argument concerning the theoretical issues, see Bryant (1994) and Colander (1994).
8. One can add differential wage price flexibility to the model and hence have an upward sloping AS curve. Doing so can increase the degree of fluctuation in the economy rather than decrease it. In this model there is no presumption of any relationship between the real wage and output without a full specification of the dynamics.

13

Telling Better Stories in Introductory Macro

Teaching first-year economics involves telling stories. These stories are simplifications of far richer stories that we economists tell, test, and study. In first-year macro the stories we tell include multiplier stories, natural rate stories, and growth stories. We embody those stories in simple models, such as the AE/AP model, the AS/AD model, and a production function based growth model. These models structure our story and give professors something solid to hang exam questions on. Using the growth story we teach as a case in point, this paper argues that structuring introductory macro stories around formal models makes the stories we tell unnecessarily boring to students.

Why Does Economics Seem Boring When it Isn't?

It is sometimes said that an economist is an accountant without a sense of humor. When introductory students hear that description, you can see them nodding in agreement; the reality is that most introductory students consider economics and the economists who teach it boring. We economists know that they are wrong; we are dynamic, exciting individuals, and the story we have to tell is fascinating, rich with all the ingredients of a great story: exciting story lines, plot, passion, and intrigue.

When I listen to top economists discuss their research, I'm infused with their passion and excitement. Unfortunately, something happens in the translation of that high-level story down to the first-year student: The exciting becomes the boring. An important reason why is the way in which we combine the telling of the story with the teaching of simple models.

The Problem with Combining Introductory Stories with Formal Models

The problem with tying our stories to formal models is that a large portion of our audience doesn't know the language of models, mathematics. Textbook authors and intro professors know that, and to make the models somewhat understandable to these students we water down the research models into "teaching models." Thus the stories we

165

tell go through a multiple translation process—from a researcher's general understanding (1) to a research model, (2) to an easier intermediate pedagogical model, (3) to an even easier principles model, and finally (4) to a student's general understanding. At each stage of this multiple translation process some of the excitement of the economic story is lost. Our stories would be far less boring if we eliminated the multiple translation process and went directly from a researcher's general understanding to a student's general understanding.

It is only for the principles level that I am making this suggestion. I am fully aware that while we lose something whenever we translate ideas into models, we also gain something. In research we are willing to accept the loss because of the precision and possibility of empirical testing that a formal model allows. Similarly, intermediate modeling can possibly be justified because the modeling provides students who intend to go on in economics with a needed introduction into how economists go about economic analysis.[1]

It is at the principles level that the costs of the multiple translation far exceed the benefits. Ninety-nine percent of principles students are not going on to become economists. We require stories to follow from formal models. In making the formal models accessible to a broad range of students we have so simplified the models that they are vague shadows of the research models economists use to consider the questions. Allowable introductory models can involve nothing beyond tenth-grade algebra, geometry, and logic. This causes three problems.

First, to mathematically sophisticated students, the introductory models look naive and simplistic; these students are discouraged from going into economics because it is too simple. Second, by tying the models to stories we limit the stories we tell. Dynamics, stochastic processes, path dependencies, non-linear processes—areas where the excitement in economics research is—are all ruled out, or tend to be ignored or downplayed. Third, we generally do not succeed in teaching students the value of formal modeling, or even in teaching them remedial algebra and geometry. The problems are too deep-seated; the mathematical deficiencies built in through years of schooling are not going to be corrected in one course where the primary goal is to teach about the economy. The reality is that these students end up spending most of their time struggling with the math of the models rather than with ideas of the story.

To say that we shouldn't teach introductory students elementary formal models is far too radical a suggestion to have any hope of being considered. Thus, in this paper, I am proposing a less radical solution—that we separate the two: If we want to teach models, we do so as a type of calisthenics of the mind. We do not tie our central story line to that formal model, as we currently do.

Separating the teaching of models from the teaching of the ideas frees us to teach the story of economics within an historical, case study, *+simulation* structure. This alternative structure will let us better relate to students the exciting conundrums with which the top researchers are struggling. It allows us to demonstrate the challenges economists have faced as they have struggled with the problems, and to present the many ideas they have developed to deal with those challenges. Separating the stories we tell from the models we teach will be enormously enabling. It allows us to tell about informal ideas, that cannot be modeled formally, but that excite the imagination.

I will demonstrate the argument in terms of our introductory presentation of growth.

The Current Intro Growth Story

Currently we tell the growth story centered around the Solow growth model. In introductory macro we don't teach the Solow growth model explicitly; that would be much too hard for principles students, and, to be honest, is pushing the limits of most intermediate students. But the Solow growth model determines the structure of the way we present growth in introductory courses. It focuses the presentation on the production function, and focuses on the role of savings and investment and diminishing marginal returns. Technological change enters into the story as a supporting idea, which can temporarily overcome the unrelenting pressure of diminishing marginal returns.

If one were interested in telling an exciting story, and, in my view, a more insightful story of growth, the order would be reversed. The dynamic aspects of growth involve technology, and thus technology is the natural center of the introductory story. Similarly, increasing returns, and the many other elements of the economy that can lower costs over time—path dependencies, dynamic feedbacks, and network externalities—replace diminishing marginal returns as the central guiding elements of the story. Investment and saving become supporting ideas. The story line focuses on the tendency of a market economy toward explosive growth, which somehow is held in check by political, physical, and social constraints. We don't tell that story to introductory students because the formal models that incorporate such stories are too complicated.

An Historical Introduction to Growth

I propose that we replace the current model-centered story with a historical-centered story that introduces students to growth through a consideration of the broad historical developments and facts about growth. A natural introduction to the historical approach to growth is the work of Douglass North (1973) or Rosenberg and Birdzell, Jr. (1986). That work shows how growth rates are correlated with the development of markets, and that those growth rates have accelerated over time. Angus Maddison (1995) sums up the historical evidence on growth with a single graph that shows the growth rate from 1000 to the present. In the graph it is clear that (1) before markets were the main organizing structure of society, growth was minimal; and (2) growth rates have increased over time.

The historical approach centers the growth story around the explanations of these two empirical phenomena. It presents students with the question: Why have markets and growth proceeded together? In answering this question students are directed toward stories involving the division of labor, increasing returns flowing from that division of labor, technological development, and the "extent of the market." Markets allow specialization; specialization allows people to focus on what they have a comparative advantage in, and to develop comparative advantages through learning by doing.

The Role of Case Studies in the Historical Approach

Case studies in the historical approach have a different purpose than case studies in a modeling approach. In a modeling approach case studies are examples of principles that students learn from models. In the historical approach case studies are the raw material from which students derive the principles. In the historical approach one builds up from examples to principles, rather than builds down from principles, developed in models, to cases. Possible cases include the development of the Swiss watch industry, the Industrial Revolution in Britain, and recent developments in computer technology in Silicon Valley.

One can extrapolate from these cases to central issues in growth such as network externalities, technological change, and decreasing costs. One can show examples of where one technology overtakes another, and emphasize the point that growth often involves new goods replacing old goods, not producing more of the same good. All these issues are hard to fit into the current production function framework.

Building up (with guidance) from case studies is an exciting way to teach that allows students to develop their own principles and insights. Because they have developed the principles themselves, those principles will fit into their mindset, which is the world they are currently experiencing, better than principles developed from abstract models that have no meaning to them.

One does not have to generalize from this case study to a theory; in fact, Nathan Rosenberg (1994) whose work serves as a model of the historical approach to growth, argues specifically against doing so, since each case is particular. But a case study can be suggestive of certain principles. At our current level of understanding of the growth process, anything other than suggestive propositions would be too much.

Some Differences in Emphases

The historical approach leads to some different emphases than does the current model-based approach. One difference in emphasis is that saving and investment play supporting roles, not the central role given to them by the Solow growth model. In the historical approach, the growth process is a cumulative process; growth creates wealth, which creates the saving, and investment, which fuels the growth. An economy can end up in either a vicious circle or a virtuous circle. There is no foregone conclusion that growth will return to any predetermined growth rate.

A second difference in emphasis is that the roles of increasing and decreasing returns are reversed—the main thrust of the historical story is increasing returns, and the self-propelling nature of growth. Diminishing returns is de-emphasized. Increasing returns and other factors that lead to lower costs through time dominate the discussion because historically they have done so. In the Solow growth model approach we have to develop the concept of diminishing returns, and then explain why, empirically, diminishing returns have not led to decreased growth rates. We force students to learn technical ideas and then modify them. As they do, they get lost in the models. In the historical approach, we can get right to the elements that have won out in the past.

A third difference concerns efficiency. The historical approach to growth gives far less emphasis to the static concept of efficiency and focuses instead on dynamic efficiency—the role of markets in bringing about innovation and technological change.

A fourth change in emphasis concerns the long run/short run division. The model-driven approach emphasizes the separation of the long run and short run. In high-level research, we know that separation is problematic; the two must be tied together, and many of the interesting developments in macro involve the assumption that expectations of what happens in the long run will influence what happens in the short run. In the historical approach an increase in demand could stimulate the economy, and induce innovation that could lead to a continual change in the growth rate. In the Solow growth model, that could not occur.

Historical Precedent for the Historical Approach

The historical approach to growth is not new. It was the connection between markets and growth that led Adam Smith to write his *Wealth of Nations*. Adam Smith emphasized the division of labor, and the general advantages of markets. Markets, by allowing trade, create an environment of growth. In Smith's story the division of labor is mixed with increasing returns to scale, capital accumulation, and learning by doing into a story in which markets lead individuals to create the wealth of nations. Smith's story is one in which the extent of the market, increasing returns, and dynamic feedbacks play central roles.

A Simulation Approach to Growth

History and case studies get us only so far. I fully agree that to show complex relationships we need to get into formal models. While I do not believe that we can tie the growth story line onto formal models that the introductory students develop from scratch, I do think that we can usefully tie growth stories to "pre-digested" models, which is essentially what computer simulations are. While simulation involves a lot of math, the math is hidden; all intro students need do is use the computer, which is a skill that students are more likely to have than the math skill necessary to understand a standard model. Roughgarden's (1996) text on ecology provides an example of how the growth story could be presented with simulation models.[2] Simulations allow one to demonstrate open rather than closed models, and let one talk about certain periods of explosive growth.

One simulation that I use in teaching introductory growth is John Conway's "Game of Life", which, starting from some simple rules, shows a dynamic process can multiply and develop. It provides a foundation for stories with increasing returns and complicated dynamic processes.

The story that these computer simulations, and, in research, agent-based models, emphasize is a different story than the Solow growth model emphasizes. In that Solow model, the economy always returns to the underlying growth rate, as if that rate were somehow a God-given constant. In these computer models fundamental indeterminacy is emphasized. The implied story line is that markets lead to growth because markets allow individuals the possibility to experiment. Experimentation and freedom to try out new things are the driving force of growth. We don't know what causes growth, but what we do know is the institutional environment that is conducive to growth.

Conclusion

There are many ways to teach a subject, and it is natural for economists to structure their teaching around formal models. But at the introductory level, that approach makes economics boring to students because they don't know the language of models. By presenting economic ideas in a language with which they are more comfortable, we make introductory economics more exciting for them, and more satisfying for us to teach.

Notes

1. I qualify this because in liberal arts programs without business schools, most majors are not planning to go into economics; they are planing to go into business.
2. Roughgarden's presentation is at a higher level than I am suggesting here, but it has some excellent, creative approaches of tying simulations with learning about growth.

14

The Strange Persistence of the IS/LM Model

Why has the IS/LM model persisted? In this paper I consider that question, along with the related, and in some ways more interesting, question of how the use of the IS/LM model has changed over time. I begin by discussing some general issues about the persistence of IS/LM and how its treatment has changed, presenting some bibliometric evidence about the appearance of IS/LM in the literature over the last 40 or 50 years. Then I look specifically at how the treatment of IS/LM has evolved from the 1960s until today, comparing a 1960s intermediate macro text with a modern intermediate text. Finally, I relate that discussion to some thoughts about the future of the IS/LM model.

Some General Comments on the Persistence of IS/LM

IS/LM analysis is a creature of pedagogy, and to understand its persistence one must understand the nature of economic pedagogy in the intermediate macro course, where the IS/LM model predominates. Since just about every economics student takes intermediate macro, just about every economist has taken intermediate macro, so as long as IS/LM continues to be used in that intermediate macro course, IS/LM will retain its central role in rough and ready discussions of macro policy. IS/LM provides a common framework (the "trained intuition") that economists can use to discuss macro policy, as suggested by Tobin (1980), Solow (1984), and others.

To say that the IS/LM model has persisted is not to say that its use has remained the same, or that it currently plays a central role in advanced discussions of macroeconomic policy and theory. In the 1960s it did play a significant role in both theoretical and empirical discussions of macro, but that is no longer true, which means that the way in which the model is used has changed considerably over the last 40 or 50 years. Today IS/LM has a very limited range of applicability. For example, it does not appear in the principles texts, whereas back in the 1960s it could be found in some high-level principles texts and in appendices to others. Even the AE/AP building block of the IS/LM model is disappearing from the intro texts and is being replaced with the AS/AD model.[1]

Another example of its limited range is that modern theoretical debates in top journals make little reference to the IS/LM model. For example, in the two-volume Handbook of Macroeconomics (1999) the term IS/LM is hardly mentioned and no discussion of policy or theoretical issues is centered on it. Similarly, other than sometimes being referenced in a review of intermediate macro, graduate courses in macro at top schools seldom mention this model.[2]

There are attempts to translate modern work into the IS/LM framework, such as we see in the work of McCallum and Nelson (1999), Yun (1996), or Clarida, Gali, and Gertler (1999). But the foundation of their models is in dynamic general equilibrium theory, and the translation into IS/LM is not central to their analysis. The translation is done simply to give policy-oriented economists a way of relating their conclusions to an IS/LM framework. It is the underlying dynamic general equilibrium model, and not the translation of that debate into the IS/LM model, that is central to modern theoretical debates[3]

The current situation is in marked contrast to the 1960s when both policy debates and theoretical debates were centered on the IS/LM model. In the 1960s what one learned in intermediate macro provided a foundation for what one learned in upper level and graduate courses. IS/LM was the end of the line—providing a synthesis of the Keynesian and Classical models, which were central to the policy debates and higher theoretical work in economics. Since one learned IS/LM in the intermediate course there was no quantum jump between intermediate and advanced work in macro. For example, in 1965 Duncan Foley, based on a senior seminar in macro he took at Swarthmore, exempted out of the graduate macro course at Yale. (Foley 2005)

As late as the mid-1970s IS/LM remained the foundation of the graduate course. For example, in my first graduate course in macro in 1971, we had a new Stanford graduate as a professor under whom we studied matrix IS/LM models where significant disaggregation was allowed, but the IS/LM structure was maintained. So IS/LM was still the core structure being taught. Today that has changed; the discussion of the multi-market goods and money market equilibria gets far less emphasis, and instead IS/LM is used for little else than a handy framework for discussing policy. So IS/LM has persisted, but its role has changed substantially.

In the 1960s, the IS/LM model not only was a stepping stone to theoretical macro, it was also a stepping stone to empirical macro and the large econometric models that were then the center of advanced macroeconomic forecasting and policy analysis. When students learned IS/LM in the 1960s they were learning a very simple example of the much larger econometric models, which had thousands, rather than tens, of equations, but otherwise had the same structure. Lawrence Klein (2000) nicely presents this pedagogical use of IS/LM and shows how IS/LM would be presented and given empirical content, if it still played that role. He suggests that "systems that are carefully fitted to observed data and capable of generating realistic values are far better for teaching purposes." (p. 158) This is, of course, true, but that is not the way IS/LM is generally taught today, in part because the profession is far more suspicious of large-scale econometric models and the information that can be drawn from them. So IS/LM is still taught but it is not taught as a theoretical or empirical stepping stone as it was in the 1960s and early 1970s.

Bibliometric Evidence

To shed light on the question of how much IS/LM has persisted I had a student and a research assistant do a bibliometric study of the appearance of IS/LM in the EconLit database.[4] Specifically, they asked how often the term IS/LM appears in articles from 1969 through 2000.[5] My expectation was that the evidence would show that the relative, and perhaps even the absolute, appearance of articles discussing IS/LM would be falling. The results, as you can see from the graph below, are

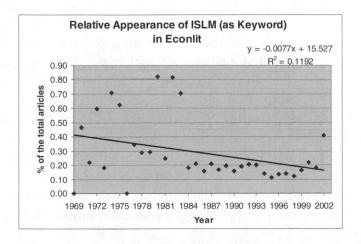

consistent with the expectation that the relative appearance of the term has been decreasing over time.[6]

The bibliometric evidence also tells us something about the changing nature of research on IS/LM. The most articles cited appeared in the *Journal of Macroeconomics*, *The Journal of Economic Education*, and *Economica Internazionale*. Most others appeared in lower-ranked journals. Only four of the journals ranked top-ten today had IS/LM articles over the entire period, and none of these were recent. This suggests that while IS/LM may remain a research topic, it is not part of the modern core, high-level, research.

Looking further at the nature of research on IS/LM, I went through the list of articles and made an informal classification of the articles into four categories: theoretical, empirical, pedagogical, and historical, to see if a trend was readily apparent. The results are presented in Table 1.

Table 1
Percentage of Articles Fitting Various Approaches

Year	Historical	Pedagogical	Theoretical	Empirical	Total
1970-1980	0	15%	85%	0	100%
1980-2002	16%	19%	44%	21%	100%

As you can see from the table, from 1970 to 1980 I classified 85% of IS/LM articles as theoretical and 15% as pedagogical. In the post-1981 period the percentage I classified as theoretical declined to 44%, while more articles fell into the historical, pedagogical, and empirical classifications. Also, a significant number of books (not captured in the data base) on the history and pedagogy of IS/LM (for example: Young 1987, Young and Zilberfarb 2000) have been published in the recent period. So it seems that two groups that have played a role in the persistence of IS/LM in the literature are teachers of economics and historians of economic thought.

One surprising finding, shown in the table, is the number of empirical articles on IS/LM in the later period and the lack of empirical articles in the earlier period. Looking specifically at the titles and occurrences of those empirical articles I found that the large majority of them are in foreign journals that were not included in the earlier-year data base. Almost no IS/LM article classified as empirical appeared in U.S. journals.

My interpretation of this evidence is that core macro theory and empirical work in economics has moved away from the use of IS/LM analysis, but that IS/LM analysis remains a research interest in the history of economic thought, in pedagogy, and in discussions of macro policy issues outside the theoretical core of the profession. So while IS/LM is still around, its role today is fundamentally different than its role 40 years ago. The central theoretical debates have moved away from the IS/LM model, but IS/LM's pedagogical role as an organizing structure for nonspecialists to think about macro policy has remained.

The Importance of the Intermediate Macro Course

The question of the persistence of the IS/LM model is in part a question of why, even as both the lower level and upper level consideration of macro issues change, IS/LM analysis remains in the intermediate macro course and in similar courses at graduate level public policy courses and business school courses.

To answer that question it is necessary to consider what the intermediate macro course is, and is not, designed to do. My first observation is that today the course is not designed to prepare economics majors to go on to graduate study. The reasons are simple. Few majors go on to do graduate work in economics, and many students who take this course are not majors. For example, at Middlebury College, approximately 150-175 students take the course each year and about one of those 175 goes on to graduate work in economics each year. Since only about 60% of the students who take the course are majors, and none of the non-majors go on, that means that about .3% of the students taking the course will go on in graduate work in economics.[7] So the course is not structured for students going into graduate work in economics, but rather for a set of students who are primarily interested in macro policy.[8] The course provides these students with insights into some of the workings of the macro economy, as well as an introduction to the debates about growth policies, monetary and fiscal policy, and the problems of balancing long-run and short-run policy.

The nature of the student body is important because these students are not learning a macro model as a stepping-stone to theoretical or empirical work. They are using IS/LM as a framework—and care little about the problems with it, or its substantial limitations. They want some basic information about policy and institutions, such as what will likely happen to interest rates and income if monetary policy is expansionary. Despite its many problems, the IS/LM model works for these students. It also works for older (over 50) teachers such as me, who were taught macro centered around the IS/LM model. This dual support goes a long way toward explaining the persistence of the model in the course.

The Push to Eliminate and Keep IS/LM

If there is a push to eliminate IS/LM from the intermediate course it comes from new professors fresh out of graduate school who are no longer taught the IS/LM model in graduate school. As graduate students become the teachers, they naturally like to teach what they have learned. Thus, there is pressure from younger professors to dump IS/LM analysis and to teach a simplified version of what they have learned in graduate school. As I will discuss below, this pressure has changed the way in which IS/LM is presented in the texts, but has not eliminated it. The reason, in my view, is that the graduate school models students learn are mathematically too sophisticated to present at the intermediate level, and their connection to policy too removed. They require a mathematical sophistication and interest in theory beyond that of most intermediate students.[9] No easy simplification method exists at the moment, and without one, the material can only be presented heuristically.

This is not to say that modern issues do not show up in the modern texts. Textbooks like to look modern, and textbook authors are always on the lookout for recent developments, new ideas, and discussions to include that make their book look more up-to-date than the competition. Open any intermediate text and you will see discussions of credibility, time inconsistency, rational expectations, real business cycles, and inflation targeting. But these discussions are primarily verbal presentations and have not replaced the core IS/LM structure for presentations of monetary and fiscal policy.

Why not structure an economics text with verbal, rather than geometric, presentations? Economists are not trained in verbal analysis, and exams are much easier to structure relative to a specific model that the students can handle. Questions about geometric models have the advantage of being right or wrong, and thus easily tested. Since grading is an important aspect of the course, anything that can reduce conflict and make the grading process easier creates pressure to keep it.

As older professors retire and are replaced by younger and differently trained professors, the pressure to eliminate IS/LM will intensify. But I suspect IS/LM will remain. One reason is inertia. A pedagogical model can only be replaced by another pedagogical model. For the intermediate level student IS/LM is a nice pedagogical model; the level of math is about right, so that it challenges students—but not too much. It gives students something to learn that seems to have applications to policy and has, at least in the model, right or wrong answers.

A second pressure to maintain the IS/LM model derives from the fact that it looks similar to a supply and demand model: it has an upward sloping curve and a downward sloping curve. For some reason this gives students comfort. A third reason is that it provides a nice graphic representation of crowding out, monetary policy, and fiscal policy. A fourth reason is its testability; it provides a wealth of "right or wrong" test questions. A final reason is that its elegance hides much of the underlying reasoning, allowing use of the model without a deep understanding of what does lie beneath. It can be used to talk about policy even if the students do not fully understand the underlying story of interactions of multiple markets being pushed toward equilibrium.

The pressure from younger professors who have not studied IS/LM in graduate school has, however, made a difference in the way IS/LM is presented. Because younger professors are often not familiar with the technical foundations of the curves, the technical presentation of the model has become cursory. Intricacies of dynamics, slopes of curves, or connections of IS/LM issues to earlier debates are no longer presented in the texts, since the younger professors are not trained in them. What this means is that, often, the problems with IS/LM do not become part of what is taught. For example, the fact that the IS curve refers to real interest rates and the LM curve refers to nominal interest rates is seldom discussed. Similarly, the instability of the curves as expectations change, or the problem of interpreting interest rates as differential interest rates of short-term and long-term financial assets, get little discussion. Instead, IS/LM is now presented in an almost mechanistic way; it is a model that shows the effects of monetary and fiscal policy on interest rates and real output.

A Comparison of Two Texts

One way to see how the presentation of IS/LM analysis has changed is to compare the presentation in the texts back in the 1960s with the presentation in a modern book. In this section I do that, comparing the treatment of the IS/LM model in Ackley's 1961 book with the treatment in Mankiw's 2003 book.

The Ackley Text

In the 1960s Gardner Ackley's *Macroeconomic Theory* was the leading book of its day.[10] The book was 596 pages long, and was seen as accompanying Keynes's *General Theory*. Ackley writes in the preface that he has his students purchase *The General Theory*, and that he assigns seven chapters from it. He also states that significant readings from the "vast post-Keynesian literature [are] also assigned." (1968: iii) This is consistent with my recollection of the situation in the 1960s; I remember receiving a multiple-page reading list of articles to accompany the text. The list included numerous, fairly recent, articles developing topics that the text discussed. This connection of the text to the literature conveyed the sense, which I believe was the reality at the time, that the text was providing the student an entrée into modern theoretical and policy debates.

The Ackley text is divided into four parts. Part I, Concepts and Measurement, consists of four chapters covering basic concepts, price indices, and national income accounting, the later covered in much more depth than it is covered today. The first three chapters in Part II cover Classical macroeconomics, Say's Law, the Quantity theory, full employment equilibrium, the effect of rigid wages, and the savings investment approach to the determination of the rate of interest. The fourth chapter in Part II is a summary that combines the issues discussed in the previous chapters into a model of seven equations, a production function ($y = y(N)$), the profit maximization condition ($dy/dN = W/P$), the supply of labor ($N = N(W/P)$) and the quantity theory ($M = lPy$), the savings function ($s = s(r)$), the investment function ($I = I(r)$), and equilibrium in the capital market ($s = i$) (ibid.: 157). These are the key equations in the model, and Ackley states that "a set of equations either identical with or closely resembling these has frequently been used to represent the 'Classical' in contrast to the 'Keynesian' system." In this chapter he points out that the first four equations are separable from the last three saving/investment equations. He then expands the quantity theory to include the loanable funds theory, which ties the two sets of equations together, at least in the short run. He concludes that chapter with a discussion of how, in "modern macro," fiscal policy is central.

Part III presents Keynesian Macroeconomics. It consists of seven chapters, although the seventh is actually a summary chapter comparing the Classical and Keynesian models. This part begins with a discussion of liquidity preference and how there can be an inconsistency between saving and investment. These issues are presented as qualifications to the Classical model that were first suggested by J.M. Keynes. Finally it discusses wage and price inflexibility, which is presented as part of Classical thought. The next four chapters discuss the consumption function model and the multiplier, which are presented as relevant when there is some constraint preventing the achievement of full employment. The short run, long run, and lags are discussed in these chapters, and there is a fair amount of discussion of empirical evidence. Ackley concludes that the basic Keynesian thesis that consumption is a stable function of income is tentatively accepted. (Ibid.: 308)

Chapter 13 is a discussion of multipliers, and an algebraic multiplier model with government is developed. Chapter 14 summarizes the Keynesian model, and is the first and last time the IS/LM model is used. (He calls it the Hicks-Hansen diagram.) In this chapter the IS and LM curves are developed in two ways: by adding a consumption function and speculative demand for money to the Classical model and from the simple Keynesian model, adding the necessary relationships involving wages and prices, labor, money, and the interest rate. A total of three complete IS/LM diagrams appear in the entire book.

Soon after presenting the IS/LM model Ackley gives an alternative to IS/LM—a four-quadrant diagram, which is similar to diagrams he had used in the presentation of the Classical model. He justifies this alternative model as follows:

> The Hicks-Hansen diagram has elegant simplicity that appeals to many. It has the disadvantage, however, that most of the "works" are out of sight. This means that we need to use another diagram (or an extra mental calculation) to determine the effect of a displacement of the equilibrium on the other variables of our system. Likewise, it means that if we wish to consider the effect of a change in some one of the functions which lie behind the IS or LM curve, we need another diagram (or mental process) to determine how the assumed shift will affect the IS or LM curve. Other less elegant apparatus is possible, which exposes more of the relationships to view. (Ibid.: 372)

Chapter 15 is the central chapter of the book. It consists of a comparison and evaluation of the Classical and Keynesian models, which are both reduced to a set of equations. (ibid.: 403) The differences between the models are that the Keynesian model has a speculative demand for money, rigid wages, and saving determined by income, whereas savings is determined by the interest rate in the Classical model. Later in the chapter he blends the two models together, specifying money as a function of both income and interest rates and saving as a function of both interest rates and income. This leaves the rigid nominal wages in the Keynesian model as the only difference between the Keynesian and Classical models. Chapter 15 is the end of the core presentation, and the remainder of the book, Part IV, covers selected topics such as inflation, investment growth, and the relationship between micro and macro.

The Mankiw Text

In the early 2000s Greg Mankiw's *Macroeconomics* is the leading book in the field. The book is 514 pages long, and is divided into six parts. In the preface he states that his four objectives include (1) to balance short-run and long-run issues; (2) to integrate Keynesian and Classical theories; (3) to present macro using a variety of simple models; and (4) to emphasize that macroeconomics is an empirical discipline. These are both similar to, and different than, Ackley's goals. One major difference in the books is that the Keynesian supplement that Ackley mentioned in his preface is not in Mankiw's book, and in many ways, for Mankiw, Keynes is simply a diversion. He writes: "Although Keynes's General Theory provides the foundation for much of our current understanding of economic fluctuations, it is important to remember that Classical economics provides the right answers to many fundamental questions." (ibid.: xxiii)

A second difference is that Mankiw focuses on multiple models that are not combined together into a complete model, whereas Ackley focuses on the development of a complete model. The various parts of Ackley's book are meant to lead to the synthesis that is presented in his Chapter 15. Mankiw's book has no grand synthesis. In the introductory chapter he writes, "The field of macroeconomics is like a Swiss army knife—a set of complementary but distinct tools that can be applied in different ways in different circumstances." (Ibid.: 11) For Ackley macro was more a single bladed knife, and the chapters are all developing the components of that knife.

Part I in Mankiw consists of only two chapters, and has far less discussion of the broader issues or national income accounting than were found in Ackley. Part II, "Classical Theory: The Economy in the Long Run," is a discussion in which Mankiw states that the economy in the long run involves a time horizon of at least several years. The discussion consists of a chapter presenting a production function, the components of demand, and the general accounting relationships inherent in a general equilibrium model with flexible prices. While the chapter presents a consumption function and a marginal propensity to consume, it makes no use of them in the determination of equilibrium. The discussion of aggregate equilibrium instead consists of specifying accounting identities that essentially state that if output remains constant government purchases must crowd out private expenditures. Thus, fiscal policy is presented as altering the allocation of output among alternative uses, not as the central policy tool of macro, as it was in the Ackley book.

Chapter 4 presents the quantity theory and a discussion of inflation. Chapter 5 discusses the open economy issues, such as trade and exchange rates, and their relation to the real economy. Chapter 6 discusses unemployment, focusing primarily on steady state rather than cyclical unemployment. Part III consists of two chapters that present economic growth, starting with the neoclassical growth model, and then progressing up through new growth theory.

Part IV in Mankiw provides the first introduction to the subject that the large majority of Ackley's book focuses on—short-run stabilization. It consists of five chapters (Chapters 9-13): Introduction to Economic Fluctuations, Aggregate Demand I, Aggregate Demand II, Aggregate Demand in the Open Economy, and Aggregate Supply. He begins with a presentation of aggregate supply and demand, with aggregate demand determined from the quantity theory with fixed velocity. Aggregate supply is presented as vertical in the long run and horizontal in the short run due to price stickiness. Short-run supply is not related to a production function.

Chapter 10, Aggregate Demand I, presents the foundations of much of what Ackley's book was about. First, the multiplier model is developed in seven pages and then related to the IS curve. The LM curve is then quickly developed from the supply and demand for money. These two curves are then put together as the model that determines the aggregate demand curve (which is a quite different aggregate demand curve than was presented in the previous chapter). This new aggregate demand curve, combined with an aggregate supply curve analysis, which he develops in Chapter 13, gives Mankiw a model of aggregate supply and demand, which is his core model for explaining short-run economic fluctuations.

Chapter 11, Aggregate Demand II, uses the IS/LM model to talk about policy, discussing fiscal and monetary policy. The algebra of IS/LM is briefly presented in an appendix. Chapter 12 discusses open economy issues in reference to the IS/LM model for the case of a small open economy where interest rates are set by international markets. Chapter 13 develops three alternative models of aggregate supply. Mankiw does not use any of these models to formally close the system as Ackley did, but instead puts them together informally with an aggregate supply curve to provide a close of the system.

Parts V and VI are devoted to tying up loose ends. Part V discusses macroeconomic policy debates. Chapter 14 raises issues that are being discussed in the current theoretical literature: credibility, time inconsistency, inflation targeting, and rules and discretion. Chapter 15 discusses government debt. Part VI discusses microeconomic foundations to macroeconomics, raising issues in consumption, investment, money supply and demand, and advances in business cycle theory.

Differing Treatments of the IS/LM Model

As should be clear from the above discussion, Ackley and Mankiw use the IS/LM model in substantially different ways. In Ackley IS/LM is an elegant summary of what he has presented before. While IS/LM is used as the model, much of the presentation is about the development and thinking behind that model. It is the ideas behind IS/LM, not the model itself, that Ackley is interested in. He even states that a problem with the IS/LM model is that it hides important elements of the reasoning. Ackley did not give IS/LM very much focus because, in its elegance, the model tended to hide the ideas that he considers to be most important. Consistent with this use of IS/LM, there is no entry in the index for IS/LM or its components, and there are only three complete IS/LM diagrams in the entire book. IS/LM appears in only one chapter of the book even though the majority of the book is about the short run, and there it is supplemented by an alternative geometric exposition that "exposes more of the relationships to view." (ibid.: 372)

For Mankiw, IS/LM serves a fundamentally different role. It is not meant to synthesize the ideas he has presented earlier, but instead is a subsidiary model of the AS/AD model that is useful for handling discussions of monetary and fiscal policy with a fixed price level. But, ironically, in this new role IS/LM gains prominence. Instead of being relegated to one chapter, as it is in Ackley, it shows up significantly in three chapters. The IS curve, the LM curve, and the IS/LM model all have significant entries in the index, and there are 28 complete IS/LM diagrams compared to the three in Ackley. This is the case even though Mankiw gives much less focus to short-run stabilization issues than did Ackley.

Summarizing: In Ackley IS/LM is simply a minor expositional tool used as one means of conveying multimarket equilibrium and the components that built it up are discussed at length. The ideas behind the model, not the model, are what is important. For Mankiw, and for modern texts generally, far less discussion goes to the components of IS/LM. Instead, the IS/LM model becomes primarily a tool for discussing policy.

This change in the use of IS/LM reflects the change in the goal of the intermediate course discussed above. Ackley's text was designed for a much more consciously theoretical course in which learning the model connected the reader to the modern theoretical literature. Hence its title: *Macroeconomic Theory*. That is not the case with Mankiw's text. Since the upper level macro theory is far less unified, he presents multiple models, and does not tie them together in a grand synthesis model. Hence his text (and most other modern intermediate macro texts) is no longer called Macroeconomic Theory, but is simply called Macroeconomics. In modern books, the IS/LM model is not used to connect to the theoretical literature, but is instead used as a convenient focus for the discussion of short-run policy. Because the modern course focuses heavily on policy, ironically, that means that the IS/LM model is given more, not less, emphasis in Mankiw.

Recognizing this difference suggests that we must be clear about what aspect of IS/LM analysis is persisting. The theoretical focus on the analysis of the goods and the money (and the hidden bond market) that underlies the individual curves has not persisted. That discussion, while still there, has been significantly reduced. What has persisted is the particular graphical technique of looking at multi-market equilibrium in equilibrium space, and using the curves in that model to discuss monetary and fiscal policy. Today, one does not see the four-quadrant diagram in any major intermediate macro text, but one sees the IS/LM diagram in every one of them.

The way in which the IS/LM model is used today suggests that one of the reasons that the particular IS/LM graphical technique is so persistent is that its elegance allows it to be used in a rough and ready fashion, in which the underlying model is less important than whether some underlying model exists that gives one the upward and downward sloping curves one needs to close the model and determine equilibrium. If correct, this suggests that IS/LM has remained central to the teaching of macroeconomics because of its chameleon nature which has allowed it to evolve from a simplified description of the model economists thought described the economy—a simplified econometric model—to a pedagogical crutch that is not descriptive of theory—but is instead a convenient totem on which to hang discussions of monetary policy, fiscal policy, and their interactions.

Its elegance allows a clouding over of the theoretical issues and underpinnings of the model. I suspect that it is for that same reason that the AS/AD model has gained such wide acceptance at the introductory level. With IS/LM you've got an upward sloping curve, and downward sloping curve, and you can do exercises involving shifts in both curves and the effects of various monetary and fiscal policies.

IS/LM in the Future

The future of IS/LM is very much tied to the future of macro. Because of its chameleon-like nature and ambiguous elegance, it can continue to exist in a variety of alternative scenarios, but not in all. Perhaps the most fertile environment for IS/LM is the one I believe most likely in the near term—an environment in which economists generally accept that IS/LM is loosely consistent with a dynamic general equilibrium model, and that, given appropriate nominal rigidities, an inverse relationship between short-run goods market equilibrium and real interest rates is possible. Add to that an assumption that monetary authorities can choose a real interest rate in the short run, and one has a foundation for an IS/LM type model. Within that environment the future of IS/LM as a pedagogical device for rough and ready discussions of stabilization policy seems assured, not because of its strength, but because of the lack of an alternative.

In the more distant future I see macro coalescing as a field whose foundation is in the study of complex systems. By that I mean that macro variables will be seen as following from interrelationships that include nonlinear dynamic relationships. These complex relationships make noncontextual micro foundations for the curves impossible to derive. The reason is that these microeconomic foundations have such complex interrelationships that they are analytically intractable. If this change takes place, it will bring with it a significant change in the way macro problems and policy are thought about. Instead of macro theory being the study of infinitely bright individuals operating in an information-rich environment as it is now, it will become the study of reasonably bright and adaptable individuals operating in information-poor environments.

This change in focus significantly affects the way we see macro phenomena relating to theory. In large part the study of macro relationships will turn to the study of sophisticated statistical techniques that will search for possibly exploitable, temporary patterns in the data, and to agent-based simulations that will relate the patterns to broad general deductive laws—such as the law of one price—that loosely underlie our general analytic understanding of the economy. This alternative approach will eliminate the standard analytic foundation for the IS/LM model, as well as the new dynamic general equilibrium approach with nominal rigidities foundation. However, as I have suggested in Colander (2000c), it will not necessarily eliminate the IS/LM model, since, even in this framework, it is still possible to view the IS/LM model as capturing temporary patterns. The difference is that IS/LM will become an historical model expressing first order changes in variables that are centered on the existing institutional base; it will not be an independent model of the entire economy outside of an institutional context. The equilibrium it determines is only in reference to an historically determined starting point.

While it is possible for IS/LM to remain in this "complex system future" for macroeconomics, it is, in my view unlikely. As the work in macro becomes more dependent on data extraction and agent-based simulation, the pedagogy of macro will change. It will focus more and more on standard simulations and statistical techniques that pull information from data. As it does so, the teaching of macro will move from the printed page to the computer where dynamic models and simulations will be the standard techniques. Within this computer environment the two-dimensional elegance of IS/LM will no longer be a virtue, and IS/LM will fade away, along with the intermediate macro texts that gave it its lifeblood.

Notes

1. An interesting aspect of this development is that, technically, the AS/AD model is derivative of the IS/LM model. Earlier, the AE/AP multiplier model, a building block for IS/LM, dominated the principles texts, and thus the IS/LM intermediate macro model was an extension of the model learned in principles. Today, the multiplier model is absent from many principles books, and AS/AD analysis has become a self-standing analysis.

2. At Princeton, for instance, it does not appear in recent graduate macro syllabi. At Harvard, the professor who provided the overview told me he lectured on it briefly, but otherwise it went unmentioned. Informal discussion with professors at other schools suggests that this is the rule at top schools.

3. In their work they show that in these dynamic general equilibrium models, given assumptions of nominal rigidities, it is possible to derive a temporary negative relationship between output and interest rates that can be called an "IS" curve. They close the model not with a traditional LM curve, but instead with a specification of nominal interest rates, but that distinction is, in my view, a minor one and can be related to the standard IS/LM model by defining an effective LM curve that incorporates a monetary feedback rule. See Colander and Gamber (2002).

4. The paper was done by Fred Wyshak (2002) for my history of economic thought class at Middlebury College. My research assistant was Iqbal Sheikh.

5. The database began in full only in 1969. It contains 332,000 articles and over 400 publications. The number has been growing substantially over time, which is why relative frequency is used. In absolute terms the number of articles on IS/LM has been increasing.

6. The search was of the term IS/LM or variations of it found in the title or abstract of one of the included journals. The occurrences were then divided by the total number of articles for the year, giving the relative occurrence. I suspect that the result is an underestimate of the evidence because of a technical aspect of the database. The database represents titles and abstracts of articles. More journals now require abstracts and key words, and thus in the relevant period there is likely a bias toward finding the searched-for words in the period's later years than in its earlier years. Care should be taken in drawing inferences from this evidence since the results are highly dependent on the specification of the search. In an original search that did not include some specifications of IS/LM, my student found a slight increase in the percentage of articles on IS/LM; when the additional specifications of IS/LM was added, that increase was eliminated, and a decrease was found. My student did other searches, such as a search of titles in JStor, and these showed a stronger downward trend.

7. The course is a required course for the international politics and economics major, and a recommended course for a number of other majors. Many of these students will go on to graduate work—some in public policy, others in business or law. But they do not tend to go on to Ph.D. programs in economics.

8. It was only a slightly higher percentage of students who were planning to go on to do graduate work in the 1960s but at that time there was not such a gap between the undergraduate and graduate course, and it was possible to expect good undergraduates to understand the articles being read in graduate school. Today, because the technical level of the papers has increased so much, that is generally not the case.

9. Intermediate books such as Barro (1999), which have tried to present a general equilibrium approach more consistent with that taught in graduate school, have not done well in the market. Barro's book was initially published by a textbook publisher, but it was taken over by MIT Press because sales were below the minimum cutoff of commercial college textbook publishers.

10. I base this discussion on the 3rd printing in 1968 of the 1961 Collier-Macmillan Student Edition. The fact that an edition could exist for 7 years without a major revision is telling both in the way in which the course was stabilized in presentation and the lack of a developed second-hand book market.

Part 4: Some Thoughts on Reform

15

Reform of Undergraduate Economics Education

As I was finishing graduate school and beginning to think about a job, I was told by an advisor that if I would focus on the right type of research I had a good chance of making it (that is, getting tenure) at a good graduate school (that is, one of the twenty in the top ten). I chose a different path; I chose to teach at a good undergraduate school. In the eyes of many of my graduate instructors, I failed. I was not going to "succeed" as an economist.

I thought then, and I think now, that my advisors were wrong. Being an economist at a liberal arts college is not failing as an economist; in fact, it comes closer to succeeding than does teaching at a graduate school. It gives one an opportunity to consider substantive economic, as opposed to technical mathematical, issues.

Having the opportunity does not mean that most economists at liberal arts schools take advantage of that opportunity. Unfortunately, undergraduate economics education is closely tied to graduate education: it is subject to the same pressures on teaching and research as is graduate economics education and fewer and fewer liberal arts professors are taking advantage of the opportunities that their work provides them.

As graduate students are taught more and more about technical issues and less and less about general ideas, economic literature, and economic institutions, they naturally teach more about technical issues once they themselves begin teaching. If graduate schools do not teach ideas to graduate students, when those students become teachers they do not teach ideas to undergraduate students. Similarly with their research; if, in graduate school, the research one has done has concerned highly technical issues, the research one does as one moves on to teaching concerns those same issues. That is what is happening. More undergraduate economics professors are researching technical areas that have little or nothing to do with their teaching. The result is that they either lose interest in research, in teaching, or in both. Undergraduate programs are filled with professors who have moved out of economic research and teach their courses as if they are on automatic pilot. Their passion for economic ideas has been killed.

The interaction between graduate and undergraduate education means that what happens in graduate education plays a determining role in what happens in undergraduate education. Indeed, one of the central reasons I support serious reform of graduate economic education is that graduate schools are not teaching their students the skills I believe undergraduate teachers should have, which, in turn, makes it impossible for undergraduate teachers to teach undergraduates the skills I believe they should have. In my view, the skills and information needed by undergraduates should govern what is taught to those graduate students who will be undergraduate teachers.

That is not the way the system currently works. Currently, the focus of economics is the mind games of a small number of top theoretical economists.[1] In the big scheme of things, the fact that our society allows five or six hundred very bright people to play mind games and think about abstract relationships is not of much concern to society, even if it were an absolute waste, and I am in no way convinced that it is a waste. I believe that society is better off because Gerard Debreu, Frank Hahn, and other economists are freed from mundane tasks and are allowed to contemplate grand issues. This group of pure economic researchers should not be required to know institutional facts, nor should they be concerned with whether students of economics are, or are not, being appropriately trained.

My concern is with what happens when we make the most recent musings of these people the center of what we teach in graduate economics, which then becomes the basis of what we teach undergraduates. My concern is what happens when we lose the broader and less formal insights about economics embodied in the economic legacy of the historical literature. That loss is a crime and that crime is the primary reason graduate education needs to be reformed.

The economic lessons we convey to the million students a year in principles courses, the economic lessons we convey to the hundreds of thousands of students in intermediate courses, and the economics lessons we teach to the thirty thousand or so economics majors are important in the big scheme of things. These lessons play a significant role in determining the economic policies our country will follow and in our economy's competitiveness in the world economy. The reason society gives the economics profession the resources it does is primarily for the profession to do a job for society—teaching economic insights to undergraduate students. Their needs, and the decisions about what we should teach them, should be considered first; only after considering what we should teach undergraduates should we determine what should be taught in the graduate schools that prepare people to teach undergraduates. The teaching needs of undergraduates should come first. In reality, that is not what happens. The process is paradoxically reversed; undergraduate schools have seen themselves as feeders for graduate schools, and graduate schools' needs have determined what undergraduate schools teach.

That process is wrong. Such a small proportion of economics majors go on to graduate school that to structure undergraduate economics training for them is for the tail to wag the dog. Those individuals planning to do research work in graduate economics as it is structured today should take a joint undergraduate major in mathematics and physics, perhaps with a minor in economics.

Instead of preparing students for graduate work in economics, I see the primary goal of undergraduate economics education as helping students to understand economic events and to prepare them to evaluate current and future economic and public policy debates. Economics education is part of a broader liberal arts education, and economics should be taught partly for its own sake and partly as an example of the broader intellectual inquiry of social science.

A straightforward application of those principles to undergraduate education would require a major reorganization of most of undergraduate education, because the situation in economics is not unique. I am not going to propose such a reorganization. I am enough of a realist to recognize that a major reorganization is not about to take place, given the structure of higher education. Instead, I focus on reforms that can take place within a department and within the courses that individuals offer.

One could make an argument that one should discuss the ideal system of teaching undergraduates, leaving others to figure out how to get there. I will not do that for two reasons. First, it is unclear to me that anyone could come close to determining abstractly how an "ideal" system would realistically function and, thus, whether it is possible to discuss an ideal system meaningfully. Second, I believe that reform is seriously needed, and that the only reforms that have even a slight chance of being implemented are those that are designed for, and can operate in, the institutional context where they will be implemented.

The Politics of Undergraduate Reform

Even when one limits the scope of reform to economics departments—and it is economics departments that ultimately must adopt the reforms—the political difficulties of reform are enormous. In fact, serious undergraduate reform is even less likely than graduate reform for a number of reasons.

First, the situation in undergraduate schools is very close to a stable equilibrium. Undergraduate education in economics is a combination of lowbrow theory, institutional knowledge, and economic insights. Textbooks pretty much determine the content of core courses and maintain a consistency of what is taught. Those textbooks provide an enormous inertia that keeps the same subject matter being taught. Anyone who has written a textbook knows that you deviate from standard content at your own risk.

Second, competition from other fields is far less likely to force change in undergraduate schools than it is in graduate schools. Graduate schools are ultimately designed to teach useful skills; eventually they will face a market test. Liberal arts schools are not meant to teach skills; they are meant to create "educated students" and there is enormous debate about what should be taught to accomplish that end. The competition for undergraduate economics education is from English, political science, Greek, and history. Compared to these, even highly technical economics is relevant.

The only serious competition to undergraduate economics on the horizon is a recent development in top liberal arts schools. These schools are introducing a public policy major that offers a component of economics. That major has a potential to significantly reduce the economics major. It is already well documented (Siegfried et al. 1991) that the competition changes when schools have an undergraduate business major. And so, too, does the success of the economics major. It shrinks enormously. The introduction of a public policy major will further erode the economics major.

Both business and public policy majors use heavy components of economics, so these developments do not eliminate the demand for economics teachers, but they do change the composition of demand. Economics is becoming more and more a service department to other majors.

A third reason undergraduate reform is less likely than graduate reform is that the demanders are less likely to be able to articulate and effectively express their views. Students do not choose an undergraduate school because it has a good economics department. They choose a school because it is ranked highly and because it is known to them. What goes on in economics is only a small component of that decision. The same holds for demanders of undergraduate economics majors. Firms hire undergraduates for their entire education, not for their economics skill. Schools and majors play a role, but it is to a large degree a signaling role. Employers know that the brightest students go to top schools; bright students know that the graduates of these schools get the best jobs, so they go there. And so the process continues, almost independent of what is taught or learned. In such a situation there is little competitive pressure for reform at the department level.

Fourth, the professors at undergraduate schools are trained at graduate schools. Much of their human capital is based in technical models and major reforms will undermine that human capital.

Despite these pressures against reform, some reform is still possible. It is my belief that liberal arts teachers become liberal arts teachers because they are interested in teaching. I suspect that most of them were not highly successful at the abstract research game and thus are less committed to it than are graduate professors. Research pulls them in one direction; teaching pulls them in another. Many undergraduate departments are struggling with this problem and may be open to suggestions for a better way.

Doing Less Better

A common thread in the reforms I suggest is to try to do less, but to do less, better. This is the opposite of most previous "progressive" reforms, which have been designed to do more, better. Such reforms are the result of a tendency in U.S. education and, perhaps, in the U.S. psyche, to rush through everything. High schools want to teach college-level material. Colleges want to teach graduate-level material. Graduate schools want to teach postgraduate material. No level is satisfied with doing its job well; instead, everyone wants to do the next level's job, too. Often, the result is that nothing is done well.

In total, the sum of past progressive reforms has put U.S. education in its current state. High schools do not teach students to read or write; colleges do not teach students to think; and graduate schools present students with imaginary hurdles, teach the students to jump them, and then debate the contextual relevance of imaginary hurdle jumping.

These graduate students then become teachers, whereupon they introduce more progressive reforms.

We arrived at the state of economics education in which we now find ourselves as the result of a sequence of progressive (in both senses) reforms, each designed to improve the current situation. We tried to teach theory a little better; we tried to teach a little more formal theory; we tried to teach more sophisticated statistical techniques; we tried to teach more field specializations.

Economics education is not alone in its attempt to do more, better; high schools have similarly broadened their curricula to include a wide range of college courses, including economics. Each of these progressive reforms, if they had had no cost, would be valuable, but each reform does have a cost. They redirect effort and energy away from the original goals. High schools are now concerned about getting students to think critically; and undergraduate English departments teach students deep structural analysis of literature. I have seen the results and I am not impressed. Any time I hear the term progressive reform, my gut response is to oppose it.

Given that record, I will put forward no progressive reforms. Instead, I propose what might be called regressive reforms that are designed to slow down the educational process — to reduce, not increase, what we try to do at each level of education. I propose that we try to do less, and that might make us able to do what we do, better.

The list of reforms that I present is meant to improve the preparation of economics students so that they can use the economics they learn in college in dealing with the problems they will face in the real world. Since 99 percent of those taking economics courses are not planning to continue their economics education at the graduate level, the proposals are not designed to better prepare economists for what is currently taught in graduate schools, although the reforms would better prepare students for what I believe should be taught in graduate school.

Reform 1. Economists should oppose the Advanced Placement exam in economics.

This reform is directed at high schools, not colleges, but, because it directly affects the college economics curriculum, I think it is appropriate to begin with the teaching of Advanced Placement economics courses in high schools. This is a perfect example of where more is less.

As I stated above, more and more, high schools want to be colleges; they often rate themselves by the number of college-level courses they offer. The result is that they rush students through the high school curriculum so that the instructors can teach college-level courses.

Students know where MC = MR, but they do not know how to write, where Mexico is, or what the institutional structure of the United States is. Even good high schools are not preparing students acceptably in reading, writing, and arithmetic. Until they do so, good high schools should concentrate on teaching those skills better than other high schools do; they should not try to do what colleges do.

The problem with teaching economics at the high school level is not only a matter of opportunity costs. Because of staffing problems, high school economics courses are often taught by someone without even an undergraduate major in economics. The result is often a very technique-oriented course, designed so the students do well on the Advanced Placement exam, but not designed to convey the limitations of the models the students learn and the context within which the models might be relevant. When untrained teachers discuss policy, the discussions often mix normative and positive arguments even more than when trained teachers discuss policy.

It is not the fault of the high school teachers; often the best high school teachers volunteer to teach economics, but with only a two- or three-week background course, the difficulties they face are enormous. The insights that economics can offer are hidden in the models, and unless students are taught where to look, they end up learning models uncritically. This adds a selection bias to who goes on in economics. Students who like learning models go on to take economics in college; those who want something deeper go on to become religion or philosophy majors.

The goal of increasing the economics content of high school education is laudable, especially given the fact that if the students do not do an Advanced Placement course in economics they will do one in math or chemistry or perhaps psychology. I am not against teaching about the economy in high school. But in my view, a high school economics course should focus not on theory and models, but on economic institutions and economic history. After all, the students are not going to get those subjects in college.

Reform 2. Reduce the technical and theoretical content in the introductory course and increase the institutional and historical content.

Not only should high schools teach more about economic institutions and economic history, so, too, should colleges. Approximately one million students take the introductory course. What they learn is a mishmash of lowbrow theory, institutional knowledge, and insights. What they are tested on is primarily the lowbrow theory and some logical exercises that use those theories.

If students could somehow learn less "theory" and more economic sensibility, we would also be better serving our intended purpose. If we spent more time teaching students the limitations of theory and the way in which a small amount of theory can add insight into events, we would also be better serving our intended purpose.

Let me give a couple of simple examples. We teach students cost analysis based upon the assumption of a fixed capital input and a variable labor input, knowing that, in reality, inputs are neither fixed nor variable, but change with the decision at hand. There is no discussion of overhead costs and direct costs nor of cost accounting that applies microeconomic insights to business decisions.

A second example is in macro, where, to include the price level in the analysis, we use an aggregate supply/demand analysis that can only be appropriately derived from the IS/LM analysis and is only relevant for equilibrium conditions. Yet we do not teach our students how limited these models are.

There is nothing wrong with teaching some technical models; they are good logical exercises as long as one doesn't apply the models to reality when they do not fit. But something is seriously wrong when the teaching of models replaces the teaching of the economic ideas they are meant to convey.

Principles of Economics could be taught with three or four graphs. If it were, it would probably teach more ideas to students than our current approach accomplishes.

Reform 3. Teach less theory in the intermediate courses.

Make the intermediate sequence more applied, so that there is less hurdle jumping and more direct application of economic principles to problems. By "applied" I mean the teaching of the art of economics—showing how principles of public policy can be reasonably and objectively drawn from simple economic models. I do not mean what is often treated as "applied" in the textbooks, showing how a LaGrangian can be interpreted as a shadow price. To teach the art of economics, one must show how economic forces interact with social and political ones and how one can try to put those together to draw reasonable inferences about policy. The result will be an ambiguity of policy conclusions, a significant downplaying of efficiency, and an increase in distributional and ethical issues as a focal point of economic policy.

Most economic policy issues have no explicit answer, yet the structure of our problem sets and texts make it look as if there are such answers. A principle of teaching should be to teach information as honestly as possible. If the models do not work well, admit it. If the models are primarily logical exercises, present them as such. One should also teach the students when information is relevant and when it is not. For example, most good students, when asked what would happen to the average cost of producing cars if demand increased, would say that average costs would rise because of diminishing marginal returns. Most business people would take innovations and economies of scale into account and say that costs would fall. Why the difference? Because neither innovations nor economies of scale fit into the economic model of the firm. They are either ignored or relegated to the long run, which is seldom explicitly studied. Somehow the realities that do not fit our mathematical requirements for models are not taught, even at the intermediate or advanced levels.

Reform 4. Teach simpler methods of analyzing data.

Make the statistics/econometrics sequence less concerned with classical statistical methods and more concerned with reasonably interpreting and drawing inferences from the data. Most students graduating from high school do not know effective means of presenting or interpreting data. Most students graduating with an undergraduate economics degree do not know the difference between a linear and a log-linear scale. Most do not know where to find data, how to extrapolate it meaningfully, or how to collect it by their own empirical observation. If one asked them how to use direct empirical observation to gather data on the economy, they would have no idea what to do. They are unfamiliar with surveys, library source material, and governmental archival material.

Before we teach students how to test for statistical inference, we need to teach them to find data, how to recognize their limitations, and what the biases inherent in data are. We need to teach them how to draw inferences from observation and data. We need to teach them data sensibility and the limitations of formal statistical analysis before, or at least at the same time as, we teach them how to do that formal statistical analysis. Often, a simple plotting of data conveys far more information than does a formal analysis. Yet a formal analysis organized by computer and presented in such an unambiguous way is enticing—it lets students think they are saying far more than they are. Students like to think they are saying more than they actually are, and thus they must be continually reminded of the limitations of formal statistical analysis.

Reform 5. Reduce the amount of formal theory in upper level courses.

Make the upper level courses less theoretically oriented and more oriented toward interpreting and applying economic concepts and toward placing economic thinking in a broader intellectual perspective. Modeling will remain a central technique of what we teach in these courses, but learning the model should be only a small part of the course content. A much more important component of the course content should be how to put the analysis into perspective.

To do that, the courses should spend much more time exploring and extending the assumptions of the model. As that is done, a much broader range of literature would become relevant and knowledge of that literature would become an integral part of the course.

Reform 6. Change the research criteria for tenure and promotion to research criteria that reflect the skills we believe undergraduate students should have.

This is my most substantive reform and one that I hope undergraduate economics departments will take seriously. Why do undergraduate schools use promotion criteria that are so separate from the skills they need their faculty to have? The reason is again a chicken-and-egg reason: few students with these skills make it through graduate school. Once they begin teaching in an undergraduate college, they initially rely on their graduate school capital, trying to publish the type of research they learned in graduate school. Those who succeed initially receive tenure, but they soon feel a continual pull between teaching and research. Eventually one, the other, or both give way. But, in the meantime, they are in control of the department decisions and they see the only way to keep up on the research front is to reduce their teaching load either directly, through special arrangements with deans, or indirectly, by simply teaching pro forma courses.

The group that either takes teaching seriously, or questions the appropriate skills, is seen as lacking in research; they do not advance but, rather, move down to a lower level. The lesson is clear for new professors. Good, bright professors with the skills that are needed at the undergraduate level are driven to play the graduate research game. Most do not manage to publish sufficient articles based on dissertation and graduate school capital. They desperately struggle to meet the research standards along with the teaching standards and, in the end, feel as if they have been drawn and quartered. Sometimes sympathetic senior faculty at such teaching institutions recognize the struggle and lower the standards. At such undergraduate schools, research simply disappears.

Ironically, the group that does best in undergraduate research is heterodox economists. Not bound by mainstream conventions and often with access to their own journals and publishers, they publish research that they can also teach. Thus, a disproportionate number of undergraduate teachers are heterodox. These teachers, in turn, channel students to those few heterodox programs that exist. What is sometimes lost in the process is any advocacy of tolerance and diversity of view. Heterodox economists circle the wagons to protect their views.

If economics education is to be designed to provide the skills the students need, research and promotion criteria must change. The criteria best matching the skills that I believe that we should be teaching our students include the following:

a. Superb writing skills: Demonstration of that ability: Op-ed articles, popularly oriented books, textbooks, economic journalism.
b. Interpretative skills: Demonstration of that ability: textbooks, articles such as those published in the *Journal of Economic Perspectives*, summary and interpretative articles such as those published in the *Journal of Economic Literature*.
c. Research skills: Demonstration of that ability: case study article, creative articles that are convincing without complicated economic testing, articles based on data developed on one's own.
d. Policy skills: Demonstration of that ability: develop policy proposal and work with candidate in implementing that proposal, article in policy-oriented journal, consult for business.
e. Communicative skills: Demonstration of that ability: Interpretive work for local news media, consult for lawyers or local government.

I am not suggesting that undergraduate schools lower their tenure and promotion criteria: they can, and should, be demanding. But be demanding of research that is relevant for the candidate's teaching. Irrelevant research criteria for undergraduate teachers would include the following.

1. Highly technical theoretical publications in research journals;
2. Research requiring highly sophisticated econometric manipulation of data; and
3. Articles that could not be reasonably taught at the undergraduate level.

To keep undergraduate professors active in both research and teaching, the two activities must complement each other. Currently, many undergraduate departments derive their tenure criteria from graduate schools; it should be the other way around.

Conclusion

Even if one believes that these reforms are the correct ones, it is difficult to see how they can come about without a fundamental change in graduate education. For such reforms to be put in place requires undergraduate teachers trained in a quite different fashion than graduate students are currently trained. That is why I believe that undergraduate and graduate education must be simultaneously reformed.

Notes

1. I am pleased to say that the focus of graduate economics education has become much more empirical. But the issues of empirical relevance are still given far less importance than I believe they should be given, and the undergraduate texts continue to focus on deductive models.

16

Reform of Graduate Economics Education

Reforms do not just happen. They occur because a coalition of individuals decide, or are forced to decide, to undertake reforms. Why will someone in power adopt a reform? That is a complicated question that involves the decision makers, their self-interest, their benevolence, and their belief that the reforms will actually bring about an improvement. Timing and institutional structure also play roles; they are the elements that determine which views and whose views will be heard. Considering all these elements, there is no foregone conclusion about what reforms will or will not be adopted.

In considering reform of graduate economics education, the decision makers are the graduate professors—the set of professors who have succeeded in the present institutional structure—and the institutions within which reforms will be made are graduate economics departments. To determine whether any reform will be undertaken, one must consider those reforms from the perspective of professors in graduate economics departments. The COGEE Report (COGEE 1990), written primarily by graduate professors sympathetic to reform, strongly criticizes what goes on in graduate schools, agreeing with the critics that classes tend to be idiosyncratic, that they focus on technique rather than ideas, and that they fail to provide students with a background in economics. Its authors are unwilling to take the next step—to say that there are serious problems in what the profession does, which is why there are problems with what it teaches. The commission's discussion of the problem is followed by a set of general reforms.

For most critics, and certainly for me, the reforms proposed by the commission do not go far enough. They are too general and too accepting of the status quo in economics. My view is that the reforms must go deeper, and be much more specific, to have any effect. They must embody a change in the purpose of graduate economics education. Currently, graduate schools see their purpose as teaching theory and turning out economists who are theorists. I believe that most graduate schools should be teaching the art of economics, which, according to J. N. Keynes, who first developed the tripartite division of economics into positive economics, normative economics, and the art of economics ([1891] 1955), is the study of how to apply positive economics to achieve ends that are determined in normative economics. The positive and normative divisions of economics are well known, but the art of economics has been lost, both as a division of economics and as a skill that economists possess.

As J. N. Keynes saw it, the art of economics involved an integration of economic insights with political, social, institutional, and historical knowledge to lead to reasoned judgments about appropriate policy. It was applied economics, and was, of necessity, nontechnical in nature. Thus, teaching the art of economics is what graduate schools should do because the art of economics is what most of their graduates will go on to use.

Most of the people desiring serious reform are quite pessimistic about the possibility of such reform. That pessimism is based upon a recognition that any reform will most likely work against the self-interest of the people who must decide on reforms. I understand this general pessimism, but I see three provisos to that pessimism.

The first is that there is some benevolence in the most neoclassical of economists; to the degree that reforms don't totally threaten their self-interest they will institute reforms that they believe are in the students' interest. Also, when one says "department," it is not clear how the decision-making process weights the views of various members of the department. Self-interested professors avoid committees discussing educational reform and departmental committee work. Thus, in specific instances, a reform-minded professor could institute reforms that would be in the students', rather than the department's, interest. Her personal cost of doing so, however, would likely be high.

The second proviso is that departments are not the sole decision makers. In theory, administrators control education practices, and, to some degree, in reality, administrators actually affect educational practices. Administrators can put pressure on departments to change. What mitigates the arguments against administration-led reform is that administrators' information, and the time administrators have to devote to one department, is highly limited, and thus they usually rubber-stamp departmental decisions about educational practices. In specific instances, however, an administrator might play a role implementing reform.

The third proviso is that even self-interested departments maximize their benefits subject to constraints, and those constraints include attracting sufficient students to their programs, and thereby getting sufficient resources to pay their faculty. Many graduate economics programs have pushed this constraint close to its limit. I seldom talk to a graduate economics professor at any other than the top ten or so schools without hearing serious complaints about the quality of their students.

These three provisos offset the self-interest motive, and lead me to believe that, given the right configuration of the stars (and a blue moon), reform is possible. (I am a realistic optimist.)

Reform is most likely at the intermediate-tier schools. The top schools can get acceptable applicants, so the third proviso is not strong. Lower-tier schools are primarily concerned with keeping their programs going. For them, the resources for reform are unlikely to exist, and self-interest in preservation of the status quo will likely be strong. At the intermediate tiers, the combination of the three provisos will likely be strongest, and so it is in such schools that proposals for reform should be focused. These schools cannot compete with the top schools in pure theory, but, given the focus of top schools on esoteric study, the intermediate-tier schools can successfully compete by re-defining the dimension upon which they compete.

Specifically, as I will discuss in detail, by focusing their research and teaching on the type of skills needed by most employers, and not on those skills needed by a few abstract theoretical departments, intermediate-tier schools could leapfrog the so-called top-tier schools.

Economic Reforms and Economics

Institutions exist because they have devised methods to see that sufficient money flows into them so they can pay the members of that institution sufficient money to keep them working at that institution. The per student cost of educating graduate economics students is high. For example, let us consider hypothetical school X, which has a faculty of 22, half of whose time is allocated to graduate education and half to undergraduate education. Assuming this 50-50 split, faculty lines are allocated to graduate economics teaching so that the direct, per year instruction costs of the graduate program are eleven times the average pay, including fringe benefits, which, for the early 1990s, might very conservatively be estimated to be about $60,000 (or $660,000 total). Let us say that school X graduates an average of five Ph.D.'s per year and ten M.A.'s per year. Assuming an M.A. requires half the instructional input of the Ph.D., the direct instructional costs of a Ph.D. are $66,000 per Ph.D. (In the past ten years, these costs have probably close to doubled so that in 2005, the direct instructional costs of a Ph.D. are more like $130,000.)

Direct instructional costs are only part of the costs of educating a graduate economist. There are other direct costs, such as classrooms, office space, and support staff, as well as indirect, nonattributable costs. Instructional expenses are often less than a third or a fourth of a school's budget, so very conservatively estimating other per student direct costs as 75 percent of direct instructional costs, one arrives at a cost of educating a Ph.D. economist of $115,500, or $38,500 per year of instruction. Were one to allocate all overall costs fully, the per year cost per Ph.D. student would likely rise to somewhere between $70,000 or $80,000 per year in the early 1990s, and well over $200,000 in 2005.

If students had to pay even the full direct cost of graduate economics programs, most graduate programs would have reformed themselves long ago, but a variety of alternative funding methods have made it possible for that not to be the case. One alternative is outside grants. Outside grants make it possible for professors' compensation to be unrelated to the revenue generated by teaching.

But outside research grants are not what reduces the cost of the graduate education of economists, nor what keeps graduate economics departments going. What keeps most graduate economics departments going is undergraduate education. Graduate students, as part of their training, teach the undergraduate courses at many universities. In return, the students are given teaching assistantships that give them free tuition and a small stipend to live on.

These teaching assistantships provide sufficient surplus to allow the system to work. Say each undergraduate brings in an average of $10,000 in tuition and state aid per year. On average, they take eight courses, so revenue per student per undergraduate course is $1250. If a teaching assistant teaches two courses (one course a semester) and there are 40 students per course, the total revenue per year per graduate student is $100,000. Subtracting the tuition and grant the graduate student receive, that leaves $80,000 per year, which more than covers the direct cost of the graduate program and some of the overhead. In short, teaching undergraduate courses indirectly by having a graduate program often works out cheaper than teaching an undergraduate program directly and not having a graduate program. That is why the United States has about 100 Ph.D. programs in economics to train about 900 Ph.D.'s per year. (In 2005 these figures are likely to have increased proportionately with the costs suggested above.)

What makes reform possible at intermediate-tier schools is that, even with tuition grants and fellowships, the demand for graduate education at such institutions is low, especially among U.S. students.

The lack of demand by U.S. students for graduate economics education has created enormous pressure at many schools because mathematically oriented foreign students often are ill-equipped to teach U.S. undergraduates. These foreign graduate students are often very bright and technically competent. Since they do not have institutional knowledge of the U.S. economy, they teach the same technical economics they learn in their graduate courses. The result is loud complaints from undergraduate students and an ensuing impetus for reform.

This impetus is strong in a number of intermediate-tier graduate schools and it is why I believe that, if reform comes about, it will come about at intermediate-tier schools.

A List of Reforms

I now turn to a discussion of some specific reforms that I believe will lead to improvements in graduate economics education.

Reform 1. Increase the amount of information about what actually goes on in graduate programs.

The AEA or some other formal group should ask that all graduate schools make their preliminary exams, with their answers, available to all students. The appropriate institution to do this probably would be the Boulder Institute or the Joint Council of Economic Education. These could be provided on a website, giving students a much better sense of what they will learn in graduate school. For schools that do not comply, perhaps a blank page could be left on the website after a statement that some schools have chosen not to comply. Students at undergraduate schools should be thoroughly informed about:

a. the employment picture of recent graduates of a department;
b. what skills the department believes the student will learn in the program and how the program will teach them those skills; and
c. the nature of the qualifying exams; past exams with answers should be provided.

The argument for this informational proposal is my belief that much of what goes on in graduate schools is not the result of conscious decision making; it is, rather, the result of neglect. Courses are assigned on the basis of professors', not students', needs, and the choice of topics taught, often even in core courses, reflects the teacher's research needs, not any reasoned consideration of what information would be most helpful to students.

I have met few economists who will defend the current practices of many graduate schools; most agree they are almost unconscionable from a teaching point of view. They accept those practices nonetheless, believing that, with an incentive structure weighted toward publication, asking untenured professors to prepare a serious course with an appropriate review of the literature would be the equivalent of asking that professor to commit academic suicide. They justify the lack of a coherent core program as a cost of research.

To change the situation, something in the department must change. I believe if information about what goes on in graduate schools were generally known, far fewer U.S. students would choose to pursue graduate economics training. The resulting decline in numbers of students would make departments change more than would any other reform I can think of.

Reform 2. Demanders should organize and make their needs known.

Graduate economics schools are not providing the education that is wanted by most employers of graduates of economics schools. Discussions at the conference where this paper was originally presented (Colander ed. 1992, Woolf 1992, Woos 1992, and Zevin 1992) give one a good idea of how graduate schools were failing then and are still failing. Other than voting with their feet (hiring from public policy schools rather than from economics programs), employers have done nothing to change the situation. If they want to make a difference, groups of employers should get together and provide statements of the skills and knowledge they believe are important. Sample questions that get at those skills should be distributed to members of the group and they should be encouraged to ask those questions in interviews.

Employers should make it clear to students the skills they want, and broaden their search process to reward schools that provide the skills. All too often, the hiring process becomes a self-fulfilling process. Employers hire graduate students from the elite graduate schools, not because of the training they receive there, but because the employers believe the brightest students go to those schools. Knowing that, the brightest students go to the elite schools, fulfilling expectations and completing the circle. What the students have learned while studying at the elite schools becomes irrelevant, and eventually the demanders are themselves composed of people trained by those graduate schools. When that happens, the circle is not only complete, it becomes self-defining; the demanders honestly believe that what is done at graduate schools is what they need. As this happens, the demand for economists by the market-constrained organizations, such as private business, will dry up, and most of the demand will be by non-market-constrained organizations, such as the IMF, central banks, and universities.

Intermediate-tier graduate schools try to emulate the top-tier graduate schools. They generally do not succeed. But in trying they reinforce the process and, ironically, provide a prime outlet for the top-tier schools' students. Their students can teach their research to others-which makes even irrelevant research relevant. In short, the intermediate-tier schools provide a demand for the top-tier schools' products, together with a cheering section to be impressed by the notoriety of the top tier's elites.

The problem of demand for the products of these intermediate-tier graduate schools is much more difficult, but the excess demand is picked up by foreign students who either want to emigrate to the United States or who want a U.S. degree to increase their marketability and prestige in their home country.

The better information about skills acquired through these questions about the training graduate students receive in many programs will reduce the signaling aspect of the school one attends and increase concern about the content of what one learns.

Reform 3. Encourage competition among graduate programs and reward those schools that instruct students in what one considers desirable skills.

In principle, there should be three or four types of elite graduate schools. For example, one department might specialize in the training of liberal arts and undergraduate professors; another might specialize in the training of government economists; another in the training of research economists. In reality, little explicit specialization takes place, although some informal specialization does take place. Instead, the specialization that takes place occurs in areas of research specialties. Binghamton specializes in econometrics; the University of Washington specializes in resource economics. But within that research specialty, these schools compete on the same dimension as the elite graduate schools. The school that ranks the highest is the school that has the theorist in that area.

The reason, I suspect, that there is a one-dimensional ranking of schools is that there is a one-dimensional promotion and tenure procedure. In just about every graduate school and a number of undergraduate schools, promotion and tenure depend upon publication in the top journals, and publication in the top journals is made easier by a theoretical research focus.

An intermediate-tier school could become a first-tier school on a different dimension by changing its promotion and tenure criteria. Specifically, let me offer this proposition. Any graduate school that hopes to compete for a specific branch of the market can more likely succeed by using the same standards for promotion as does that market. For example, say a graduate school decided to specialize in teaching undergraduate teaching. They would use as research criteria the list of criteria that I provided in the previous essay, since they are teaching the people who will be teaching that work. There will, of course, be other skills that would be required for other areas. Research, for example, would focus much more on technical empirical skills. But the overall mix of skills taught would focus much less on pure theory and much more on empirical work, and on interpretive skills.

Unfortunately, as I stated above, even many undergraduate programs do not use these reasonable criteria, so it is rather hard to suggest that a graduate school attempt to institute them. But that is exactly what I am suggesting. The graduate schools should introduce these changed tenure criteria with great fanfare. They should work directly with undergraduate schools that emphasize those criteria to determine how those graduate schools can best fill the needs of the undergraduate schools. They should develop an alternative ranking criterion that ranks schools according to the skills that they find appropriate and they should strive to be the best at teaching their students the skills the students will need.

What I am suggesting is that an intermediate-tier graduate program redefine its tenure and promotion criteria to emphasize the skills needed by liberal arts schools. I am not suggesting a lowering of the requirements for tenure. The research expectations for tenure at such a school should be substantial. An alternative, comparative ranking of research output should be developed that demonstrates the desired skills. Only those who place at the top of this ranking system should be eligible for tenure. That alternative, comparative ranking system would define the new dimension of competition.

This discussion focuses on liberal arts economics professors. A different list of skills could be made for other demanders: government, consultants, and businesses. I do not know exactly what those skills will be, but it is my strong suspicion that they will be similar to the ones I have listed and that they will differ enormously from the skills currently taught.

By organizing together and specifically matching the skills they want with the research expertise they look for, a group of intermediate-tier graduate programs could totally change the nature of graduate education. They could become the top training ground for government and for top undergraduate colleges which, in response, could also change their criteria for tenure. The result of the multidimensional competition would be better teaching, more meaningful research, and a stronger voice for economists in policy.

To many, this proposed reform will seem to be radical. That a proposal to teach the students the skills they will use in their work could seem radical demonstrates how far removed graduate economics education is from the demander's needs.

Reform 4. Schools that decide to focus on training formalistic researchers should increase the mathematics requirements for entrance and increase the length of training.[1]

My argument against too much formal work taught in graduate school and reflected in much of the research of economists is not that it is irrelevant or a waste because it is formal. It only becomes irrelevant if researchers do not keep it in proper perspective. One of the reasons that happens is that the people who are doing the research are not fully trained in the conceptual aspects of the tools and in economics. To do creative work in a language, you need to know that language backward and forward. Then you can focus your mind on ideas, not language.

Most graduate economics students I talk to are not highly trained mathematicians or statisticians. They have a working knowledge of the tools, but most do not have a deep enough knowledge to use the tools with sensibility and perspective. Requiring much more rigorous training in mathematics and statistics for anyone studying formal abstract theory, so that those people who are doing abstract research have both the background and the perspective, would make that research more relevant.

Most natural science degrees require seven years to complete the technical training, because the training begins in undergraduate school.

I challenge those graduate schools that believe that economics is a formal, technical discipline to make their entrance requirements reflect their beliefs. At such schools, an M.A. or Ph.D. degree in both mathematics and statistics as a minimum entrance requirement would seem appropriate for what is currently asked of economists.

Reform 5. Undergraduate professors, government economists, and consultants should be considered when openings become available on editorial boards controlled by the AEA, starting with the AER, JEL, and JEP. Ideally, they should be represented in rough proportion to their membership in the AEA.

An army travels on its stomach; professors travel on their journal articles. Theoretical research economists have controlled the journals and, thereby, have controlled who gets promoted.

If one looks at the editorial boards of *AER, JEL,* and *JEP,* how many undergraduate professors, government economists, or consultants does one find? There are a few, but most of those few have previously been associated with graduate programs or have been recently appointed to reflect the noise made by such practitioners about the state of the profession.

I doubt whether this change will make much difference in practice; I am not claiming that non-graduate school economists are blossoming with ideas that will forever change economics. But I do believe they will bring a different perspective, and they might add a bit more relevance to economic theory.

Conclusion

Economics is many things; and schools should be ranked on multiple dimensions. For some reason they are not, and I am not sure why. In friendly conversation I have challenged some of my fellow critics who teach in such departments and whose departments seem most likely to fit the bill for change. I ask them why they acquiesce in the maintenance of the status quo. The answer I get is that it is easier not to rock the boat. Change requires the expenditure of enormous political capital and effort. I understand this view, and I make no pretense that implementing reform will be easy. But then, meaningful change seldom is.

Notes

1. This has happened; at top programs students come in with excellent mathematical backgrounds, so the technical work is far less of a problem today for them than it was for students twenty years ago, even though that technical work is far more technical today than it was then.

Bibliography

Ackley, G. [1961] 1968. *Macroeconomic Theory*. New York: Macmillan Company.

Anderson, P. W., K. J. Arrow, and D. Pines, eds. 1988. *The Economy as an Evolving Complex System*. Redwood City, CA: Addison Wesley.

Arthur, W. B., S. N. Durlauf, and D. A. Lane, eds. 1997. *The Economy as an Evolving Complex System II*. Redwood City, CA: Addison-Wesley.

Auyang, S. 2000. *Foundations of Complex-system Theories in Economics,* Evolutionary Biology and Statistical Physics. Cambridge, UK: Cambridge University Press.

Axelrod, R. 1997. *The Complexity of Cooperation, Agent Based Models of Competition and Collaboration*. Princeton, NJ: Princeton University Press.

Axtell, R., and J. Epstein. 1996. *Growing Artificial Societies from the Bottom Up*. Cambridge, MA: MIT Press.

Barro, R. 1998. *Macroeconomics*. 5th ed. Boston, MA: MIT Press.

——. 1996. *Getting it Right*. Cambridge, MA: MIT Press.

——. 1994. "The Aggregate-Supply/Aggregate-Demand Model." *Eastern Economic Journal* 20.

Basmann, R. L. 1990. "The Professional Responsibility of the Econometrician for Truthfulness in the Teaching of Economics." In: *Educating Economists*. Edited by D. Colander and R. Brenner. Ann Arbor, MI: University of Michigan Press.

Baumol, W. 1982. "Book Review of *What Price Incentives? Economists and the Environment*." *Journal of Economic Literature* 20.

Bennett, A. 1996. "Economists + Meeting = A Zillion Causes and Effects." In: *Case Studies in Macroeconomics*. Edited by D. Colander and J. Gamber. Burr Ridge, IL: Irwin-McGraw Hill.

Bertrand, M., and S. Mullainathan. 2004. "Are Emily and Greg More Employable than Latisha and Jamal? A Field Experiment on Labor Market Discrimination." *American Economic Review* 94(4).

——, 2005. "Complexity, Pedagogy, and the Economics of Muddling Through." In: *The Economics of Complexity*. Edited by M. Salizar. Aldershot, UK: Edward Elgar.

——. 2000. "Complexity and Policy." In: *The Complexity Vision and the Teaching of Economics*. Edited by D. Colander. Aldershot, UK: Edward Elgar.

Bryant, J. 1994. "Coordination Theory, the Stag Hunt and Macroeconomics." In: *Problems of Coordination of Economic Activity*. Edited by J W. Friedman. Boston: Kluwer Academic Publishers.

Clarida, J. G., and M. Gertler. 1999. "The Science of Monetary Policy: A New Keynesian Perspective." *Journal of Economic Literature* 37(4).

Clower, R. 1994. "The Effective Demand Fraud." *Eastern Economic Journal* 20.

COGEE (Commission on Graduate Education in Economics). 1990. "COGEE Report." Paper Presented at the Annual Meeting of the American Economic Association, Washington, DC.

Coase, R. 1994. *Essays on Economics and Economists*. Chicago, IL: University of Chicago Press.

Colander, D. 2006. [1993] *Economics*. New York: McGraw-Hill Irwin Publishers.

——. 2005a. "Muddling Through and Policy Analysis." *New Zealand Economic Papers*. Wellington, New Zealand: New Zealand Association of Economists (Inc.)

——. 2005b. "The Making of an Economist, Redux." *Journal of Economic Perspectives*.

——. 2001. *The Lost Art of Economics*. Aldershot, UK: Edward Elgar.

——. 2000a, ed. *Complexity and the History of Economic Thought*. New York: Routledge Publishers.

——. 2000b. "New Millennium Economics: How Did It Get This Way and What Way Is It?" *Journal of Economic Perspectives* 14(1).

——. 2000c. "Post Walrasian Macroeconomics and IS/LM Analysis." In: Young, W., and B. Z. Zilberfarb. *IS-LM and Modern Macroeconomics*. Boston and London: Kluwer Academic Publishers.

——. 2000d, ed. The Complexity Vision and the Teaching of Economics. Northampton, MA: Aldershot, UK: Edward Elgar.

——. 1996, ed. *Beyond Micro Foundations: Post Walrasian Macroeconomics*. Cambridge, UK: Cambridge University Press.

——. 1993. "The Macro Foundations of Microeconomics." *Eastern Economic Journal* 19.

——. 1992, ed. *Educating Economists*, ed. D. Colander and R. Brenner. Ann Arbor, MI: University of Michigan Press.

——. 1991. *Why Aren't Economists as Important as Garbagemen? Essays on the State of Economics.* Armonk, NY.: M.E. Sharpe.

——. 1990. *The Making of an Economist* (with Arjo Klamer). Boulder, CO: Westview Press.

——. 1986. *Macroeconomic Theory and Policy*. Glenview, IL: Scott Foresman and Co.

——. 1984. "Was Keynes a Keynesian or a Lernerian?" *Journal of Economic Literature* 22.

Colander, D., and E. Gamber. 2002. *Macroeconomics*. Upper Saddle River, NJ: Prentice Hall.

Colander, D., and H. Landreth, eds. 1996. *The Coming of Keynesianism to America*. Aldershot, UK: Edward Elgar.

Colander, D., and P. Sephton. 1998. "Acceptable and Unacceptable Dirty Pedagogy: The Case of AS/AD." In *Aggregate Supply and Demand: A Critique of Orthodox Modeling*, in B. Rao, ed. London: Macmillan.

Colander, D., R. Holt, and B. Rosser. 2004. *The Changing Face of Economics*. Ann Arbor, MI: University of Michigan Press.

Conway, J. Game of life. http://encyclopedia.thefreedictionary.com/Conway's%20Game %20of%20Life.

Davidson, P. *Money and the Real World*. London: Macmillan.

Donohue, J. J., and S. D. Levitt. 2001. "The Impact of Legalized Abortion on Crime." *Quarterly Journal of Economics* 116(2).

Fields, T. W., and W. Hart. 1994. "Inconsistencies in the Conventional Model Aggregate Demand and Aggregate Supply." Working Paper. Harrisonburg, VA: James Madison University.

——. 1990. "Some Pitfalls in the Conventional Treatment of Aggregate Demand." *Southern Economic Journal* 56.

Foley, D. 2005. "Interview." In: Colander, D., B. Rosser, and R. Holt. *The Changing Face of Economics: Interviews with Cutting Edge Economists*. Ann Arbor, MI: University of Michigan Press.

——. 2000. "Complexity and Economic Education." In: *The Complexity Vision and the Teaching of Economics*. Edited by D. Colander. Northampton, MA: Edward Elgar.

——. 1994. "A Statistical Equilibrium Theory of Markets." *Journal of Economic Theory* 62(2).

Frank, R. 2000. "Does Growing Inequality Harm the Middle Class?" *Eastern Economic Journal* 26(3).

Gabaix, X. 1999. "Zipf's Law For Cities: An Explanation." *Quarterly Journal of Economics* 114(3).

Georgescu-Roegen, N. 1971. *The Entropy Law and the Economic Process*. Cambridge, MA: Harvard University Press.

Goeller, H., and A. Weinberg. 1976. "The Age of Substitutability." *Science* 191.

Hall, R., and J. Taylor. 1997. *Macroeconomics*. New York: Norton.

Hayek, F. A. 1952. *The Counter-revolution of Science, Studies on the Abuse of Reason.* London: George Allen and Unwin Ltd.

——. 1945. "Use of Knowledge in Society." *American Economic Review* 35(4).

Heilbroner, R. [1953] 1999. *The Worldly Philosophers*. New York: Simon and Schuster.

Hirschman, A. 1997. *The Passion and the Interests: Political Arguments for Capitalism before Its Triumph*. Princeton, NJ: Princeton University Press.

——. 1970. *Exit and Voice*. Cambridge, MA: Harvard University Press.

Hunt, E., and D. Colander. 2005. *Social Science*, 12th ed. NJ: Allyn and Bacon Publishing Co.

Hutt, W. H. 1979. "The Keynesian Episode: A Reassessment." Indianapolis, IN: Liberty Press.

Jonsson, P. O. 1995. "On the Economics of Say and Keynes' Interpretation of Say's Law." *Eastern Economic Journal* 21.

Keynes, J. M. 1936. *The General Theory of Employment, Interest and Money.* London: Macmillan.

——. ed. 1921. "Introduction to Cambridge Economic Handbooks." In: Robertson, D. H.. *Money.* London and Cambridge: Cambridge Economic Handbooks.

Keynes, J. N. [1891] 1955. *The Scope and Method of Political Economy.* 4th ed. New York: Kelley and Millman.

Kirman, A. 1992. "Whom or What Does the Representative Agent Represent?" *Journal of Economic Perspectives* 6(2).

Klein, L. 2000. "The IS-LM Model: Its Role in Macroeconomics." In: Young, W., and B. Z. Zilberfarb. *IS-LM and Modern Macroeconomics.* Boston and London: Kluwer Academic Publishers.

Kreps, D. 1997. "Economics—The Current Position." *Daedalus* 126(1).

Landsburg, S. 1993. *The Armchair Economist: Economics and Everyday Life.* New York: Free Press

Leamer, E. E. 1988. "The Interplay of Theory and Data in the Study of International Trade." Mimeo. University of California at Los Angeles.

——. 1983. "Let's Take the Con out of Econometrics." *American Economic Review* 73(1).

LeBaron, B. http://people.brandeis.edu/~blebaron/acf/index.htm

Lerner, A. 1944. *The Economics of Control.* London: Macmillan Publishers.

Lowman, J. 1984. "What Constitutes Masterful Teaching?" In: *Mastering the Techniques of Teaching.* Hoboken, NJ: Jossey-Bass Publishers, Inc. (Division of Wiley Publishers).

Maddison A. 1995. Monitoring the World Economy, 1820-1992. Washington DC: Organization for Economic Cooperation and Development.

Mankiw, N. G. 2003. *Macroeconomics.* New York: Worth Publishers.

——. 1998. *Economics.* San Diego, CA: Dryden Press.

Mayer, T. 1993. *Truth vs. Precision in Economics.* Aldershot, UK: Edward Elgar.

Marshall, A. 1890. (1997). *Principles of Economics.* New York: Prometheus Books.

McCallum, B., and E. Nelson. 1999. "An Optimizing IS-LM Specification for Monetary Policy and Business Cycle Analysis." *Journal of Money, Credit and Banking* 31(1).

McCloskey, D. 1994. *Knowledge and Persuasion in Economics.* Cambridge, UK: Cambridge University Press.

——. 1985. *The Rhetoric of Economics.* Madison, WI: University of Wisconsin Press.

McCloskey, D. and S. Ziliak. 1996. "The Standard Error of Regression." *Journal of Economic Literature* 34.

McConnell, C., and S. Brue. 1999. *Economics.* New York: McGraw Hill.

Medema, S., and W. Samuels. 1996. *A Guide to How to Do Economics.* Aldershott, UK: Edward Elgar.

Nagel, R. 1995. "Unraveling in Guessing Games: An Experimental Study." *American Economic Review* 85(5).

North, D., and P. Thomas. 1973. *The Rise of the Western World.* Cambridge, UK: Cambridge University Press.

Robbins, L. 1981. "Economics and Political Economy." *American Economic Review* 71(2).

——. 1953. *The Theory of Economic Policy in English Classical Political Economy.* London: Macmillan and Co.

Roughgarden, J. 1996. *Primer of Ecological Theory.* Upper Saddle River, NJ: Prentice Hall.

Rosenberg, N. 1994. *Exploring the Black Box: Technology, Economics and History.* Cambridge: Cambridge University Press. Cambridge UK.

Rosenberg, N., and L.E. Birdzell, Jr. 1986. *How the West Grew Rich: The Economic Transformation of the Western World.* New York: Basic Books.

Samueson, P. 1948. *Economics.* New York: McGraw Hill.

Say, J.B. [1803] 1971. *Treatise on Political Economy.* New York: Augustus M. Kelley.

Schelling, T. 1999. "Rationally Coping With Lapses From Rationality." In: *Getting Hooked: Rationality and Addiction.* Edited by J. Elster and S. Ole-Jorgen. New York: Cambridge University Press.

Schumpeter, J. 1954. *History of Economic Analysis.* New York: Oxford University Press.

Scott, J. 1998. *Seeing Like a State.* New Haven, CT: Yale University Press.

Sen, A. 1999. *Development as Freedom*. New York: Random House.

——. 1970. "The Impossibility of a Paratian Liberal." *Journal of Political Economy* 78(1).

Shackle, G. L. S. 1972. *Epistemics and Economics*, Cambridge, UK: Cambridge University Press.

Siegfried, J. J., R. L. Bartlett, W. L. Hansen, A. C. Kelley, D. N. McCloskey, and T. H. Tietenberg. 1991. "The Status and Prospects of the Economics Major." *Journal of Economic Education* 22.

Smith, A. [1776] 1937. *An Inquiry into the Nature and Causes of the Wealth of Nations*. New York: Modern Library Edition.

——. 1759. *The Theory of Moral Sentiments*. Library of Economics and Liberty. On-line Edition. http://www.econlib.org/library/Smith/smMS.html.

Smith, K., and A. Waller. 1997. "Afterword: New Paradigms of College Teaching." In: *New Paradigms for College Teaching*. Edited by W. Campbell and K. Smith. Edina, Minnesota: Interaction Book Company.

Solow, R. 1984. "Mr. Hicks and the Classics." *Oxford Economic Papers* 36S, Oxford, UK: Oxford University Press.

——. 1964. *Capital Theory and the Rate of Return*. Amsterdam, North Holland: Rand McNally.

Stigler, G. 1982. *The Economist as Preacher*. Chicago, IL: University of Chicago Press.

Sunstein, C., and R. Thaler. 2003. "Libertarian Paternalism." *American Economic Review* 93(2).

Szenberg, M., ed. 1998. *Passion and Craft: Economists at Work*. Ann Arbor, MI: University of Michigan Press.

Taylor, J,. and M. Woodford. 1999. *Handbook of Macroeconomics*. Amsterdam, North Holland.

Tesfatsion, L. http://www.econ.iastate.edu/tesfatsi/ace.htm

Thaler, R. 1994. *Quasi Rational Economics*. New York: Russell Sage Foundation Publications.

Tobin, J. 1980. *Asset Accumulation and Economic Activity*. Oxford, UK: Basil Blackwell.

Veblen, T. [1899] 1994. *The Theory of the Leisure Class*. New York: Penguin Classics.

Waldfogel, J. 1993. "The Deadweight Loss of Christmas." *American Economic Review* 83.

Waldrop, M. M. 1993. *Complexity: The Emerging Science at the Edge of Order and Chaos*. Riverside, NJ: Simon & Schuster.

Wang, X. H., and B. Z. Yang. 2001. "Fixed and Sunk Costs Revisited." *Journal of Economic Education* 32(2).

Weiner, S. E. 1995. "Challenges to the Natural Rate Framework." *Federal Reserve Bank of Kansas City Economic Review* (2nd Quarter).

——. 1994. "The Natural Rate and Inflationary Pressures." *Federal Reserve Bank of Kansas City Economic Review* (3rd Quarter).

——. 1993. "New Estimates of the Natural Rate of Unemployment." *Federal Reserve Bank of Kansas City Economic Review* (4th Quarter).

Woolf, A. G. 1992. "The Skills Economists Need in Government.". In: *Educating Economists*. Edited by D. Colander and R. Brenner. Ann Arbor, MI: Michigan University Press.

Woos, J.W. 1992. "From Graduate Student to Liberal Arts Professor." In *Educating Economists*. Edited by D. Colander and R. Brenner. Ann Arbor, MI: Michigan University Press.

Wyshak, F. 2002. "IS-LM in the Economics Literature." Paper. Middlebury College, Middlebury, VT.

Young, W. 1987. *Interpreting Mr. Keynes: The IS-LM Enigma*. Cambridge UK: Polity Press.

Young, W. and B. Z. Zilberfarb. 2000. *IS-LM and Modern Macroeconomics*. Boston and London: Kluwer Academic Publishers.

——. 1987. *Interpreting Mr. Keynes: The IS-LM Enigma*. Cambridge, UK: Polity Press.

Yun, T. 1996. "Nominal Price Rigidity, Money Supply Endogeneity, and Business Cycles." *Journal of Monetary Economics* 37.

Zevin, R. B. 1992. "Economists, Judgment and Business." In: *Educating Economists*. Edited by D. Colander and R. Brenner. Ann Arbor, MI: Michigan University Press.

Index

M

macro economy
   and its complication, 140
   and its stability, 139
macro theory, and IS/LM, 175
macroeconomic perspective
   and Paul Davidson, 81
   and G.L.S. Shackle, 81
macroeconomics
   and its content, 11-13
   and dynamic disequilibrium, 152-153
   and Allen Kirman, 81
   and its modern dynamic approach, 155-156
   and pedagogy, 133-134, 140
   and undergraduate courses, 143
Maddison, Angus, and growth rate graph, 168
mainstream, in textbooks, 33-42
Malthus (Thomas), and complexity, 107
Mandeville (Bernard), and complexity, 107
Mankiw, Greg
   and Keynesian economics, 140(fn1)
   a recent IS/LM text presentation, 13, 182-186
marginality, and efficiency, 103
market failure framework, and micro principles textbooks, 85-93, 88-95
market outcomes failure, textbook treatment, 23, 26-27, 39-41
market place, and economics textbooks, 23
market, how it works, 133
markets
   and complexity, 110
   and economic solutions, 135-136
   and their joint progress with growth, 168
   and Adam Smith, 170
Marshall, Alfred
   and his key textbook, 99
   and John Maynard Keynes, 140
   and nature of economics, 54
Marxist economists, and moral issues in policy, 87

mathematical logic, and economic reasoning, 5
mathematics
   and changes in economics, 117
   and economics education, 10
   and the efficiency story, 101
   and graduate work in economics, 18
   as language of models, 165-166
   and learning economics, 106
   and models, 166
   and nonlinear organization, 109
   and a role in reform of graduate education, 211-212
Mayer, Tom, and econometrics, 81
McCallum, B., and IS/LM, 174
McCloskey, Deirdre
   and the Chicago school, 80
   and econometrics, 81
   and teaching economics, 55
McConnell, C., and Keynesian economics, 131
mechanics, and efficiency, 102
Medema, Steven, 82
micro principles course
   and its approach to policy, 85-93
   and real-world policy debates, 85
micro principles courses, their structure, 88
micro principles policy, and dual framework, 85-93
micro principles textbooks, and market failure framework, 85-93
microeconomics, and its content, 10-11
Mill, John Stuart
   and classical economics, 108
   and complexity, 105
model
   Keynesian, 66
   of supply and demand, 66
model-centered story, vs. historical-centered story, 168, 169-171
modeling
   agent-based, 29
   after "big think" reading, 81
models, AE/AP and AS/AD treatment, 39, 159